GENDER, CITIZENSHIPS AND SUBJECTIVITIES

Gender, Citizenships and Subjectivities

EDITED BY

Kathleen Canning and Sonya O. Rose

A *Gender and History* special issue

Blackwell
Publishing

© 2002 by Blackwell Publishing Ltd

First published as a special issue of *Gender and History*, 2001

Editorial Offices:
108 Cowley Road, Oxford OX4 1JF, UK
    Tel: +44 (0)1865 791100
Osney Mead, Oxford OX2 0EL, UK
    Tel: +44 (0)1865 206206
350 Main Street, Malden, Massachusetts 02148-5018, USA
    Tel: +1 781 388 8250
Iowa State University Press, a Blackwell Publishing company, 2121 S. State Avenue,
    Ames, Iowa 50014-8300, USA
    Tel: +1 515 292 0140
Blackwell Munksgaard, Nørre Søgade 35, PO Box 2148, Copenhagen, DK-1016,
    Denmark
    Tel: +45 77 33 33 33
Blackwell Publishing Asia, 54 University Street, Carlton, Victoria 3053, Australia
    Tel: +61 (0)3 347 0300
Blackwell Verlag, Kurfürstendamm 57, 10707 Berlin, Germany
    Tel: +49 (0)30 32 79 060
Blackwell Publishing, 10, rue Casimir Delavigne, 75006 Paris, France
    Tel: +331 5310 3310

First published 2002 by Blackwell Publishing Ltd

Library of Congress Cataloging-in-Publication Data has been applied for

ISBN: 1-4051-0026-5

A catalogue record for this title is available from the British Library.

Set by Advance Typesetting Ltd

For further information on
Blackwell Publishing, visit our website:
www.blackwellpublishing.com

Contents

1 **Introduction**
  Gender, Citizenship and Subjectivity: Some Historical and
  Theoretical Considerations
  KATHLEEN CANNING AND SONYA O. ROSE   1

2 Citizens and Scientists: Toward a Gendered History
  of Scientific Practice in Post-revolutionary France
  CAROL E. HARRISON   18

3 The Rhetorics of Slavery and Citizenship: Suffragist
  Discourse and Canonical Texts in Britain, 1880–1914
  LAURA E. NYM MAYHALL   55

4 Imagining Female Citizenship in the 'New Spain':
  Gendering the Democratic Transition, 1975–1978
  PAMELA BETH RADCLIFF   72

5 The Trial of the New Woman: Citizens-in-Training in the
  New Soviet Republic
  ELIZABETH A. WOOD   98

6 Enfranchised Selves: Women, Culture and Rights in
  Nineteenth-Century Bengal
  TANIKA SARKAR   120

7 Citizenship as Non-Discrimination: Acceptance or
  Assimilationism? Political Logic and Emotional Investment
  in Campaigns for Aboriginal Rights in Australia,
  1940 to 1970
  MARILYN LAKE   140

8 Producing Citizens, Reproducing the 'French Race':
Immigration, Demography, and Pronatalism in Early
Twentieth-Century France
ELISA CAMISCIOLI   167

9 Citizenship as Contingent National Belonging: Married
Women and Foreigners in Twentieth-Century Switzerland
BRIGITTE STUDER (translated by KATE STURGE)   196

Notes on Contributors   229

Index   231

Gender, Citizenship and Subjectivity: Some Historical and Theoretical Considerations

Kathleen Canning and Sonya O. Rose

Just a few years ago the concept of class, and its inflections by race, ethnicity, and gender, formed the focal point of debate across the humanities and social science disciplines. Since the mid 1990s, citizenship has gained a new salience, propelled in part by the political transformations of relations within and between those zones once termed the first, second and third world. Feminist scholars have taken a particular interest in the historical inception as well as current practices of citizenship across the globe. One of the most porous concepts in contemporary academic parlance, citizenship can be understood as a political status assigned to individuals by states, as a relation of belonging to specific communities, or as a set of social practices that define the relationships between peoples and states and among peoples within communities. Citizenship, according to sociologist Margaret Somers, is an 'instituted process' by which the social practices of peoples in particular historical settings engender citizenship rights through their 'interactions with institutions, ideals and rules of legal power'.[2] In recent years citizenship has also signified either one or all of the trio of rights T. H. Marshall identified: civil, political, and social rights. In most accounts these stages represent progressive, linear stages of citizenship, encompassing the period between the 'age of democratic revolutions' and the rise of twentieth-century welfare states, as paradigms of western history.[3] Marshall's implicitly teleological model has been the frequent target of feminist critiques that point to the impossibility of mapping the struggles of minorities, women or colonised peoples for citizenship onto Marshall's model of progressive stages.[4]

Understood as both status and practice, citizenship spans local, regional, and national spaces and involves distinct rights, claims and rhetorics in these disparate contexts. Citizenship sometimes seems virtually inextricable from nationality, in the sense of membership in national communities 'that privilege origin and culture'.[5] In other cases citizenship delineates, in the name of the state, territories that encompass a range of nationalities and ethnic groups, facilitating a common position of these disparate groups in relationship to the state. More recently, the spatial location of citizenship has also been a topic of debate, as citizenship is increasingly conceived in terms of global or international human rights that transcend the nation-state.[6] The temporal location of citizenship in 'modernity' is another topic of debate. Although the importance of citizenship for the ancient polis or early modern city-states is not in dispute, citizenship acquired new meanings in the period known as 'modernity', in which it defined new boundaries – both of nation-states and emergent public spheres.

The implication of citizenship in linear models of change and progress has also been challenged by scholars who take citizenship not primarily as a fixed juridical or legal status, but rather as a lens for analysing the changing and shifting boundaries within societies and communities. Evelyn Nakano Glenn underscores the importance of race and gender as continuous 'organizing principles of American citizenship' and as 'primary axes for contesting boundaries and rights'.[7] Yet she makes powerfully clear that the boundaries inflected by race and gender changed and shifted over time, leading not to the progressive expansion of citizenship rights for free blacks, Chinese, Japanese or Mexican immigrants, or women, but instead rendering citizenship a sustained field of contest for these groups.

These distinct meanings and scholarly usages of the term citizenship, shaped in part by different political and disciplinary traditions, have produced both fruitful debate and important new ways of thinking about the meanings of citizenship in contemporary political life. Feminist scholars have launched a critical examination of the politics of inclusion and exclusion inherent in both liberal and republican traditions of citizenship. Carole Pateman's landmark essays, widely read in the mid and late 1980s and still influential, were crucially important in stimulating interest in the relationship between gender and citizenship.[8] While some feminists regarded Pateman's work as essentialist, her analysis of the gendered contradictions of liberal citizenship and of liberal democracy's dependence on a notion of the abstract individual was groundbreaking for feminist scholarship.[9] Pateman pointed to the fashioning of the 'civil body politic' after the image of the male individual, exposing both the fraternal bonds underpinning civil society and the 'bodily removal' of women from civil society and their relegation to the realm of nature.[10] The essays in this volume attest to the continuing, even expanding, significance of Pateman's analysis.

Other critiques of the universality of modern liberal citizenship point to the discrepancy between the promise of equality and inclusivity on the one hand, and, on the other, the legal and substantive inequalities and social, political and economic incapacities that historically have generated waves of identity politics. Scholars have debated whether or not these exclusionary propensities are an intrinsic aspect of liberalism, or whether they are relatively independent of liberal political principles. Carole Pateman and Uday Mehta have argued, in different veins, that the exclusions stem from how the capacities imagined in Liberal theory to mark the universal political subject were understood and produced. Mehta has claimed, for example, that Locke's liberalism included 'mediating strategies' through which 'universalistic doctrines issued in exclusionary practices'.[11] In particular, Mehta contended that Locke detailed a set of conditions of upbringing and culture that were necessary for the 'natural individual', equipped with universal capacities, to be politically competent, an inheritance which, in Mehta's view, has probably resulted in the exclusionary political practices integral to liberal citizenship. Of course, the distinctions between those who are and those who are not full citizens are recurrent matters of contestation. Not only those who have been excluded, constrained or marginalised, or who have engaged in contestation, but also those in control of maintaining the boundaries of belonging, entitlement and participation have been politically engaged around these issues. What philosopher Charles Taylor has termed a 'politics of recognition' has been used both by those in power, to draw boundaries of inclusion and exclusion, and by those who have been marginalised, to contest those boundaries.[12]

The recent work of political scientist Rogers Smith is helpful in thinking about citizenship and exclusion. In his book, *Civic Ideals: Conflicting Visions of Citizenship in U.S. History*, Smith seeks to understand why the politics of American citizenship laws are 'likely to generate sets of rules filled with anomalies, even contradiction', and why issues of citizenship have been so intensely contested. According to Smith:

> Citizenship laws ... are among the most fundamental of political creations. They distribute power, assign status and define political purposes. They create the most recognized political identity of the individuals they embrace, one displayed on passports scrutinized at every contested border. They also assign negative identities to the 'aliens' they fence out ... Citizenship laws also literally constitute – they create with legal words – a collective civic identity. They proclaim the existence of a political 'people' and designate who those persons are as a people, in ways that often become integral to individuals' senses of personal identity as well.[13]

At issue here is the designation of 'the people', the 'we', that master category of group identity that we have understood in the modern era as 'the nation', '*our* nation'. The practices of inclusion and exclusion, which stem from what Smith calls 'ascriptive civic myths', were crucial to the project of forming and maintaining a sense of common political identity. Thus, citizenship, as Rogers Brubaker has argued, is a powerful instrument of 'social closure'.[14]

Having uncovered the ideologies and exclusions of gender at the heart of civil society and liberal democracy, feminist scholars have more recently sought to render citizenship a useful category of social analysis. They have embraced the dualities, contingencies and contradictions encompassed in the concept of citizenship, which render it 'a site of intense struggle', both theoretical and political.[15] As Ruth Lister has shown, conceiving of citizenship as *both* (rather than *either*) status and practice provides a useful framework for examining the gender differences that are intrinsic to citizenship. Lister argues that women who have the status of citizen may not always be able to 'fulfill the full potential of that status' by practising or acting as citizens. Her point is to underscore that women whose political participation as citizens is constrained by domestic or caring responsibilities be counted as citizens politically and historically. The approach taken by Pnina Werbner and Nira Yuval-Davis, who understand citizenship as a relationship 'inflected by identity, social positioning, cultural assumptions, institutional practices and a sense of belonging', adds considerably to the usefulness of the concept and resonates with the historical studies of gender and citizenship collected in this volume.[16]

One of the purposes of this volume is to explore the implications of these critical conceptions of citizenship for the historical study of gender and citizenship across a range of regions, nations, and historical settings. In addition to historicising the politics of gender, race, and location in the studies collected here, this volume also probes the notion of citizenship as subjectivity. Citizenship can clearly be understood in both discursive and experiential dimensions. As a multi-dimensional discursive framework, citizenship provides the languages, rhetorics, and even the formal categories for claims-making, sometimes in the name of national belonging or on behalf of specific rights, duties, or protections, or visions of political participation. Invocations of citizenship can serve at times to buttress the integrative practices of states, while in other instances they might enunciate visions or claims of those formally excluded from citizenship. Citizenship was experienced by subjects, that is both by historical actors and by those subjected to various instances of power. In highlighting the ways in which citizenship serves as a basis for claims-making, we mean to link the experiential and discursive dimensions of citizenship. We also would like to suggest first that the juridical and legal inscriptions, as well as the unwritten traditions, of citizenship, create subject positions that have meanings for those governing and those inhabiting citizenships, as well as those excluded from citizenship. Second, actors in different historical situations appropriate these subject positions in order to challenge, redefine, or honour the boundaries of citizenship. Those who were excluded from all or some citizenship rights on the basis of gender, race, or ethnicity frequently took up the discourses and rhetorics of citizenship to make claims upon nation, state or local communities, which is why claims-making is of crucial interest to us in this volume.

In proposing an understanding of citizenship as subjectivity rather than confining its meanings to the social identities and practices anchored in law, we do not mean to eschew the importance of the realms of law or the policies of states in designating the margins of inclusion and exclusion for specific communities or in defining the formal rights and obligations of their citizens/members. The legal, philosophical, and administrative framings of citizenships are already well understood in most cases. Our main interest is the process by which historical actors assigned meanings to the prescriptions and delineations of citizenship and hence became subjects in their encounters with citizenship laws, rhetorics, and practices. Our analysis of this process does not presume resistance or subversion but is most interested in the subject positions of those on the margins or formally excluded from full citizenship, for whom citizenship was nonetheless meaningful.

The word 'subject', according to Cultural Studies scholar Nick Mansfield, suggests that 'the self is not a separate and isolated entity'.[17] 'Subjectivity', Mansfield contends, 'defies our separation into distinct selves' and 'encourages us to imagine that … our interior lives … involve other people, either as objects of need, desire or interest or as necessary sharers of common experience'. Subjectivity is central then for citizenship because it fundamentally involves the positioning of a subject in relation to 'something outside of it – an idea or principle, or the society of other subjects'.[18] In her study of autobiographical texts, Reginia Gagnier understands a subject as being (1) a subject to herself, (2) a subject to and of others, and (3) a subject of knowledges.[19] The work of Michel Foucault, and of the scholars he has inspired, has provided us with considerable insight into the manifold ways that social actors in the modern era became subject to webs of social institutions and their increasingly specialised disciplinary knowledges. The essays in this volume by Carol Harrison, Brigitte Studer and Elisa Camiscioli suggest the importance of thinking about how these forms of knowledge often infused politics, helping to delineate civil rights, realms of political participation and social entitlements.

Finally, subjectivity captures the complexities of citizenship as both highly individualised and, at the same time, a collectively invoked social identity and subject position. American historian Nancy Cott suggests that citizenship confers 'an identity that may have deep personal and psychological dimensions at the same time that it expresses belonging'.[20] Furthermore, a subject can also be understood, as Gagnier points out, 'as a body that is separate (except in the case of pregnant women) from other human bodies', even if it is, like other bodies, closely dependent on its physical environment. Gagnier's location of the subject in the body also prompts reflections on the ways in which discourses about citizenship have collectively embodied citizens by race, gender, and age.[21] At the same time, the personal and psychological dimensions of citizenship are experienced in individual bodies, which often, in turn, inform citizenship claims. The complex ways in which citizenship as a subjectivity is simultaneously both individual and collective are integral to Aihwa Ong's notion of 'cultural citizenship', defined as a process of self-making and of being made within webs of power linked to the nation-state and civil society.[22] In a similar vein literary critic Lauren Berlant suggests that 'practices of citizenship involve both public-sphere narratives and concrete experiences of quotidian life that do not cohere or harmonize'. Citizenship, in her view, provides 'important definitional frames for the ways people see themselves as *public, when they do'*.[23]

The essays in this volume analyse the ways in which discourses of citizenship worked to enact hierarchies, to institute registers of difference along lines of gender and race, ethnicity, or marital status. Transformations were most acute at moments when national boundaries or identities were contested internally through revolutions or civil strife, or externally by wars, formations or dissolutions of state, or changes in imperial rule. At the centre of each article is an analysis of the ways in which gender shaped claims-making activity in the name of citizenship; and in most of the cases examined here, women, often aligned with immigrants or minorities, had a leading role in staking these claims. Yet their claims upon and visions of citizenship vary markedly, ranging from the right to vote and represent oneself politically (Mayhall, Radcliff, Lake), to the right to marry a foreign citizen (Studer, Camiscioli), to the immunity from intellectual, physical or sexual death (Sarkar). In nearly every case, citizenship for women remained partial, improvised, or contingent. Wherever women sought formal equality, from revolutionary France to prewar Britain, Spain after Franco, Bolshevik Russia or within the campaigns for Aboriginal rights in Australia, they remained citizens under the tutelage of male citizens, comrades, or state authorities. In still other cases, such as in interwar France, women became citizens in the sense of national duties but not in terms of civil or political rights; here women, conjoined with desirable immigrants, were entrusted with saving the nation from population decline (Camiscioli).

The essays collected here take different approaches to the question of citizenship as subjectivity. In Tanika Sarkar's study of nineteenth-century Bengal, women became subjects or attained 'selfhood' through 'self-narrativising against the grain of ancestral culture', which took place in the form of women's novels and autobiographies. Carol Harrison offers insight into the subjectivities of bourgeois men in nineteenth-century France during a prolonged period after the abolition of the Old Regime when constitutional definitions of male citizenship remained fluid and contested. She argues that science had a crucial role in identifying masculine capacity for citizenship: as both a language and practice of citizenship, science also shaped subject positions for those whom it disqualified from civic capacity. Marilyn Lake's interest is similarly the different subjectivities that emerged in various mobilisations around Aboriginal rights in Australia. The participation of each of the three women activists at the centre of her study was constituted by 'structures of feeling', by 'different kinds of wounded attachments to the past which spoke to different but not mutually exclusive histories of pain'. Laura Mayhall's view of politics as chiefly a 'realm of speech' underpins her emphasis on citizens as 'speaking beings'. Her essay explores two of the major sources that informed British suffragists' subjectivities and which influenced the theories and strategies of their movement: John Stuart Mill's *The Subjection of Women* and Giuseppe Mazzini's *The Duties of Man*. The studies by Camiscioli and Studer attend mainly to the discourses of state, jurists and social reformers, which redefined the boundaries of nationality and citizenship, in one case rendering women 'stateless' and in the other, racialising the ways in which French women and their foreign husbands should belong to the nation. Elizabeth Wood and Pamela Radcliff's examinations of moments of political trans-formation – the transition to socialism in Russia and to democracy in Spain – also highlight the power of past symbols, images and ideologies of gender in the politics of transformation, shaping and at the same time marginalising the new subject positions of feminism.

Several of the essays in this volume probe the question of women's activism and their public/political participation. Marilyn Lake's essay examines the fate of a coalition of feminist and Aboriginal groups when their claims for the inclusion of Aboriginal people as citizens gave way to an indigenous people's movement for self-determination and group-specific rights. Mayhall maintains that the two widely studied texts by Mill and Mazzini, read dialogically, provided suffragists with new ways of thinking about women's relationship to the political. In particular, she proposes that the concepts of slavery and tyranny functioned by analogy in these texts to enlarge and delimit the arena in which women could act. Mayhall's essay thus complements other recent studies of the British feminist movement that have examined the larger cultural and political contexts informing debates about the suffrage, such as those by Antoinette Burton and by Jane Rendall.[24]

Women's relationship to the political arena is also the focus of Pamela Radcliff's essay on gender and the transition in Spain from Francoist authoritarian rule to the 'new democracy' between 1975 and 1978. She examines the tensions and contradictions in the construction of the female citizen of the 'New Spain', articulated within a supposedly gender-neutral discourse. While women and the family continued to be linked in representations of the nation in the post-Franco years, Radcliff argues that the new regime fostered a 'communitarian passive' form of citizenship, meaning that democratic rights were bestowed upon the people by the elites. Her essay analyses how feminist activism in public around the issue of equal citizenship 'collided with expectations of communitarian passivity' and was perceived as threatening to divide Spain at a crucial point of national consensus-building. Elizabeth Wood examines agitation trials in Bolshevik Russia, in which women's activism was displayed and encouraged in the course of the transition to socialism during the early 1920s. The Communist Party and the Soviet state undertook the project of socialist 'enlightenment', including the instruction of women in public political participation. Wood's analysis of mock trials designed for political education makes clear that the status of woman as equal citizens was in no sense assured, for women remained 'citizens-in-training', still subordinate to party comrades, the only full citizens of Soviet Russia.

Not only does citizenship call up diverse sets of rights, duties, visions, and immunities in the cases examined here, but those excluded from citizenship also adopted a range of subject positions in articulating their claims. Citizenship was alternatively confrontational or performative (Wood, Radcliff, Mayhall, Harrison); argued within the confines of courts, ministries and police (Studer); brought into public debate through women's written or spoken representation of self (Sarkar, Lake); or gendered by the relegation of women to realms of nature, family, domesticity or leisure that were ostensibly far removed from the terrain of politics (Camiscioli, Harrison, Sarkar).

Furthermore, these articles also each contend with the meanings of public and private for gendered citizenships. Social theorists generally assign citizenship to the public domain (state, civil society or public sphere), but feminists have refused this dichotomy by emphasising that women's subordination in the realm of the family, or the elevation of women 'as reproducers of the nation', has served to undermine the formal rights they may have gained in the public domain.[25]

While many of the essays in this volume probe the changing meanings of private and public over time, they also offer powerful evidence of the impossibility of establishing a meaningful boundary between the two. In this sense our notion of citizenship as subjectivity seeks to link collective or public prescriptions and invocations of citizenship, to the interior, individualised meanings and experiences of citizenship.

Pnina Werbner and Nira Yuval-Davis have also analysed citizenship in terms of subjectivity, emphasising the 'aspirational politics' of citizenship, which 'raises its eyes towards the future, to common destinies', thus forming a 'politics of desire' that linked rather than divided public and private concerns. Illustrative is Laura Mayhall's contention in her essay that both John Stuart Mill and Giuseppe Mazzini analysed the 'private realm of family life' as 'embedded in the heart of public life'. Mayhall stresses how reading Mill and Mazzini in dialogue provided suffragists with a vision of active resistance against their exclusion from the political arena, and enabled them to connect family to the realm of the political. She asserts that both Mill and Mazzini deployed the analogy of slavery to insist that women's oppression 'should not remain a relationship embedded within the private realm, but should be a matter of concern within the public'.

Two decades of feminist scholarship have made clear that western representations generally equated women and domesticity and under-stood femininity as characterised by partiality and emotion.[26] Hence women's issues, raised in the French Revolution, the democratic transition in Spain, or amidst the reform of empires, were generally defined as particularistic or private. Carol Harrison's study of 'Citizens and Scientists' argues for the significance of science and scientific societies in the mapping of public and private in the wake of the French Revolution. Scientific societies endowed men with the capacity for citizenship in the sense of imparting to them certain citizenly qualities, like rationality, expertise, and public spirit, performed in the public sphere of the salons, while banishing women from the domains of science and citizenship. In Harrison's view 'preserving the link between science and civic capacity' meant 'maintaining the masculinity of both. They were to remain closed to women by nature, not merely by social custom'. During the mid- and late nineteenth century, social reformers and intellectuals mobilised science to explain that women could be neither citizens nor scientists. Yet Harrison also emphasises that the 'links among science, citizenship and masculinity' were unstable and thus 'refused to stay put in the masculine camp'. By the later decades of the nineteenth century the 'serious, scientific, and virile world of bourgeois male sociability' had been undermined by the growing proximity between masculine public and amateur science, and female artistic hobbies, which women pursued at home.

Tanika Sarkar's study of women, culture and rights in nineteenth-century Bengal argues that the Indian public sphere was organised around issues that were 'highly domestic', such as the age of consent to marriage, widow immolation and remarriage. These issues were legislated and debated as the colonial state sought to gain custody over those 'domestic' realms it had previously relegated to the governance of religious communities. Women in Bengal gained 'rights-like competencies' then, not as an outcome of movements 'aspiring to produce citizenship', Sarkar argues, but in the course of struggles over the age of consent and immunity from death (sexual, physical, intellectual) in the domestic realm.

Pamela Radcliff's study argues persuasively for the new symbolic importance of the public/private divide in Spain during the transition from Francoism to democracy, when 'conquest of the public carried specific political meanings'. Because the private familial sphere, and women's particular place within it, had been sanctified by the Franco regime, many democratic reformers concluded that women would have to become 'modernised' before entering realms of public debate or becoming full citizens. Yet when Spanish feminists began to mobilise actively on behalf of women's civil, political, and reproductive citizenship rights in the 1970s, thus moving their politics 'outside of the family metaphor and the private sphere', progressives refused to view them as 'truly public' because of their pursuit of particularistic or 'selfish interests'. In an interesting parallel to the passive communitarian citizenship that emerged in Spain in the 1970s, Elizabeth Wood analyses why and how, during the transition to socialism in Soviet Russia, brutal husbands who tried to educate their wives politically were contrasted with the party authorities who 'took women delegates in hand' and taught them by example. In Wood's analysis, even heroines of the agitation trials moved 'seamlessly from the "we" of the family into the "we" of the state, extending their seemingly ineradicable maternal qualities to the "whole collective"'.

While women may have been excluded from the arena of public discourse because of their association with domesticity, the *topics* of family life, maternity, sex, and reproduction, as well as norms about women's proper behaviour and activities, were all subjects of frequent public debate and scrutiny. Tanika Sarkar shows the political centrality of the domestic, a space claimed by Indian nationalists to be outside the purview of the colonial state, that became a battleground in the struggle for women's immunities and entitlements. Marriage, intermarriage (Studer) and 'the reproductive potential of citizens' (Camiscioli) shaped discourses and legal definitions of citizenship in interwar France and Switzerland. At stake in both cases were the reciprocal duties of nation and female citizens: the loss of nationality that occurred when Swiss women married foreigners meant that the nation, or their home communities, no longer had to provide for them in times of crisis. Brigitte Studer explores the issue of the relationship between marriage rules and citizenship in twentieth-century Switzer-land, a relationship that Nancy Cott and Linda Kerber have examined for the United States.[27] Women who married non-Swiss nationals lost their Swiss citizenship, a practice legally codified in 1941 and not totally eliminated until 1992.[28] Studer's analysis of the debates among jurists from the 1930s reveals that the control of women's bodies was central to their support for the exclusion. Women, it was presumed, were only weakly attached to the nation, and would transfer their loyalties to the homelands of their non-Swiss husbands. This vision underscored the idea that there was a 'natural' gender hierarchy. Studer argues that women were 'borderline' citizens, occupying a contingent and conditional place within the nation-state. As Nancy Cott has put it, 'formal inclusion … is never as decisive and determinative as formal exclusion'.[29]

Elisa Camiscioli places race and gender at the centre of her inquiry into the changing meanings of citizenship in interwar France. In the aftermath of the First World War, she argues, French women were called upon as 'social citizens' to relinquish the purported economic and sexual independence of the postwar period in order to restore the nation. In the pronatalists' vision, immigration offered one solution for the French 'demographic crisis'. They hoped to import men who were believed to be readily assimilable to serve in the labour force and as husbands of French wives and fathers of their children. Pronatalists would not encourage immigration of men from the French African and Asian colonies, but rather those from European countries with traditionally high birth rates – Italy, Spain and Poland – men who could serve not only as workers and husbands, but as fathers who would produce white children. Race and gender therefore determined the perception of their 'assimilability'. The two essays by Studer and

Camiscioli underscore the significance of both biological and social reproduction to national belonging. In the case of France, pro-natalists were concerned about reproducing French nationhood by encouraging white European men to immigrate, while dutiful French women, as Republican mothers, would foster their assimilation. In the case of Switzerland, only those married women under the control of Swiss husbands could be trusted to reproduce the Swiss nation.

Essays by Marilyn Lake and Tanika Sarkar consider the complex interplay between the discourse of rights on the one hand and a politics of self-determination and recognition on the other. Marilyn Lake explores the struggles around the formal inclusion of Aboriginal people within the Australian nation. She proposes that a rhetoric of non-discrimination (understood in Australia as a language of inclusive citizenship) could create very different subjectivities, depending upon the circumstances and the particular activists involved. Lake analyses the battle for equal citizenship or civil rights waged by a coalition of white and black women who united around a shared anti-racist stance and a language of non-discrimination. She argues that non-discrimination had as its corollary a citizenship of inclusion. But the move toward inclusion was critiqued as a repressive politics of assimilation by Aboriginal peoples as they increasingly demanded self-determination and group-specific rights. Australian citizenship was conceived on the principle of universality. While redressing the racial exclusion of Aboriginal people, it 'worked to reinforce [indigenous people's] sense of grief as a people who had lost their country'. What began as a movement for equal citizenship was transformed into a 'politics of recognition'.[30] The contradictions produced by the discourse of equal citizenship for indigenous people in Australia echo a more global phenomenon. Concerns about human rights across the globe, especially, but not exclusively, the treatment of women, have raised difficult questions about cultural difference and autonomy on the one hand, and human rights, assimilation, and national sovereignty on the other.

In India a different dynamic than in Australia has been at play, as Tanika Sarkar's essay demonstrates. She suggests that, in the present conjuncture, the logic and rhetoric of cultural nationalism, in the context of an extreme 'Hindu right-wing' political movement, have been used to disassemble a range of rights in spite of India's formal democracy. Ironically, Sarkar suggests that in nineteenth-century Bengal, women acquired 'rights-like competencies' in the context of a budding political and cultural nationalism. While Elizabeth Wood

uses the term 'citizenship' to mean fully participating and politically
equal 'comrades' in Soviet Russia – outside the liberal democratic and
republican contexts in which citizenship as a concept emerged –
Sarkar applies the concept of 'citizenship rights' in the context of
colonial India where subject peoples' struggles were not about a
'self-conscious articulation of rights as such'. Her essay examines the
conditions within which women in nineteenth-century Bengal made
'fitful progress' towards attaining 'a legal personhood for the woman
– underpinned by state guarantees for certain immunities and entitlements'. This fitful progress was made, she argues, in the context of
and in dialogue with the long struggle for Indian independence and
nationhood, and in a period during which nearly all colonised Indians
were disenfranchised. Widow immolation, widow remarriage, and the
age of consent were the sites of struggle between liberal and conservative factions of Hindu nationalists on the one hand, and the
colonial state on the other. In nineteenth-century Bengal, women
appropriated the discourse of national self-determination to assert
their own political agency, often in opposition to family, community,
and male guardians.

When read together, the essays by Lake and Sarkar suggest the fraught
politics that seem to be inherent in the framework of citizenship.
What in the past was considered by feminists to be a central dynamic
in feminism – equality or difference – has increasingly come to be
understood as the dilemma of universal rights versus particular rights.
Some feminist scholars have come to understand the quandary of
equality/difference as a core feature of feminist politics that simply
will not disappear. It seems as though a similar conflictual politics lies
at the heart of discourses of citizenship. As Sarkar suggests in the
conclusion to her essay, the dialogical relationship among the various
participants in the public sphere around issues of self-determination
or cultural nationalism and rights may result not in democratic consensus, but rather in compromising one or the other or both.

This volume of essays, then, probes issues that continue to be central
to feminist scholars concerned with gender and citizenship. The articles
collected here examine how race, ethnicity, gender, and marital status
combine to shape the rhetorics and practices of citizenship in different time periods and locations. Collectively these studies demonstrate
the critical but ironic place of the public/private divide in the histories
of gender and citizenship. The so-called public/private dichotomy
remains significant as women, often viewed as symbiotically attached

to domesticity and outside the public realm, have a variety of competencies and immunities, thereby p estic, including biological reproduction, at the cen recurring public debates. These essays offer powerful evidence public and private, individual and collective meanings of the experiences of exclusion, and the denial of bodily and/or cultural integrity. Indeed, in many of the instances analysed here, in which women spoke, wrote, consented or refused consent, envisioned or enacted citizenship, women 'vaulted over the public/private divide' in the process of becoming subjects.[31] The notion of citizenship as a subjectivity has made clear the arbitrariness of any imagined line distinguishing public and private.

In this volume we have considered citizenship both as a prescribed (legal) status and as a set of social practices. In emphasising the specific practice of claims-making, these essays offer insights into the ways in which gendered and racialised historical subjects have taken up the discourses of citizenship to make claims about rights, belonging, participation and recognition and, in the process, have also transformed subjectivities. This volume has aimed not to detach citizenship from its juridical roots, but to complicate our understandings of its meanings beyond law, in the social movements and subjectivities of those who ambivalently inhabited this status or did not possess it at all.

Notes

The authors would like to thank editiorial assistant Meghan Hays for her creative assistance in preparing this Special Issue for publication.

1. On the dual nature of citizenship as a status and a practice, see Ruth Lister, 'Citizenship: Towards a Feminist Synthesis', in *Citizenship: Pushing the Boundaries*, ed. Pnina Werbner and Nira Yuval-Davis, special issue of *Feminist Review*, 57 (1997), pp. 29–33, and Bryan S. Turner, 'Contemporary Problems in the Theory of Citizenship', in *Citizenship and Social Theory*, ed. Bryan S. Turner (Sage Publications, London, Newbury Park and New Delhi, 1993), pp. 2–3.

2. Margaret R. Somers, 'Citizenship and the Place of the Public Sphere, Law, Community and Political Culture in the Transition to Democracy', *American Sociological Review*, 58 (1993), pp. 589, 610–11.

3. T. H. Marshall and Tom Bottomore, *Citizenship and Social Class* (Pluto Press, London and Concord, MA, 1992).

4. See, for example, Sylvia Walby, 'Is Citizenship Gendered?' *Sociology*, 28 (1994), pp. 379–95, and Linda Gordon (ed.), *Women, the State and Welfare* (University of Wisconsin Press, Madison, 1994), p. 18.

5. Pnina Werbner and Nira Yuval-Davis, 'Introduction: Women and the New Discourse of Citizenship', in *Women, Citizenship and Difference,* ed. Pnina Werbner and Nira Yuval-Davis (Zed Books, London and New York, 1999), p. 2.

6. See, for example, Jacqueline Bhabha, 'Embodied Rights: Gender Persecution, State Sovereignty and Refugees', and Jan Jindy Pettmann, 'Globalisation and the Gendered Politics of Citizenship', in Werbner and Yuval-Davis, *Women, Citizenship and Difference*, pp. 178–91, 207–20.

7. Evelyn Nakano Glenn, *Unequal Freedom: How Race and Gender Shaped American Citizenship* (Harvard University Press, Cambridge, MA, forthcoming spring 2002), ch. 2: 'Citizenship', ms. pp. 11–28.

8. Carole Pateman, *The Sexual Contract* (Stanford University Press, Stanford, CA, 1988), and Carole Pateman, *The Disorder of Women: Democracy, Feminist and Political Theory* (Polity Press, London, 1989). On Pateman's influence, see Birte Siim, *Gender and Citizenship: Politics and Agency in France, Britain and Denmark* (Cambridge University Press, Cambridge and New York, 2000), pp. 1, 31.

9. See also Zillah Eisenstein, *The Female Body and the Law* (University of California Press, Berkeley and Los Angeles, 1989); Iris Marion Young, 'Impartiality and the Civic Public', in *Feminism as Critique: Essays on the Politics of Gender in Late-Capitalist Societies*, ed. Seyla Benhabib and Drucilla Cornell (Polity, Cambridge, 1987); and Anne Phillips, *Engendering Democracy* (Polity in association with Blackwell, Cambridge UK, 1991).

10. Carole Pateman, 'The Fraternal Social Contract', in *Civil Society and the State: New European Perspectives*, ed. John Keane (Verso, London and New York, 1988), pp. 101–27.

11. Uday Mehta, *Liberalism and Empire: A Study in Nineteenth-Century British Liberal Thought* (University of Chicago Press, Chicago and London, 1999), p. 65.

12. Charles Taylor, 'The Politics of Recognition', in *Multiculturalism: Examining the 'Politics of Recognition'*, ed. Amy Gutmann (Princeton University Press, Princeton, 1994), pp. 25–74.

13. Rogers M. Smith, *Civic Ideals: Conflicting Visions of Citizenship in U.S. History* (Yale University Press, New Haven and London, 1997), pp. 30–1.

14. Rogers Brubaker, *Citizenship and Nationhood in France and Germany* (Harvard University Press, Cambridge MA and London, 1992), ch. 1, 'Citizenship as Social Closure', pp. 21–34.

15. Werbner and Yuval-Davis, 'Introduction: Women and the New Discourse of Citizenship', p. 2. See also *Citizenship*, special issue of the Austrian journal *L'Homme: Zeitschrift für Feministische Geschichtswissenschaft*, 10 (1999), ed. Erna Appelt.

16. Werbner and Yuval-Davis, 'Women and the New Discourse of Citizenship', p. 4.

17. Nick Mansfield, *Subjectivity: Theories of the Self from Freud to Haraway* (New York University Press, New York, 2000), pp. 3–4.

18. Mansfield, *Subjectivity*, pp. 3–4.

19. Regenia Gagnier, *Subjectivities. A History of Self-Representation in Britain, 1832–1920* (Oxford University Press, New York and Oxford, 1991), pp. 8–9.

20. Nancy Cott, 'Marriage and Women's Citizenship in the United States, 1830–1934', *American Historical Review*, 103 (1998), p. 1440.

21. Gagnier, *Subjectivities*, pp. 8–10.

22. Aihwa Ong, 'Cultural Citizenship as Subject Making: Immigrants Negotiate Racial and Cultural Boundaries in the United States', in *Race, Identity, and Citizenship: A Reader*, ed. Rudolfo D. Torres, et al. (Oxford University Press, Oxford and New York, 1999), p. 262. See also her *Flexible Citizenship: The Cultural Logics of Transnationality* (University of North Carolina Press, Durham NC and London, 1999).

23. Lauren Berlant, *The Queen of America Goes to Washington City: Essays on Sex and Citizenship* (University of North Carolina Press, Durham NC and London, 1997), p. 10.

24. Antoinette Burton, *The Burdens of History: British Feminists, Indian Women and Imperial Culture, 1865–1915* (University of North Carolina Press, Durham NC and London, 1995), and Jane Rendall, 'The Citizenship of Women and the Reform Act of 1867', in *Defining the Victorian Nation: Class, Race, Gender and the Reform Act of 1867*, ed. Catherine Hall, Keith McClelland and Jane Rendall (Cambridge University Press, Cambridge UK and New York, 2000), pp. 119–78.

25. Werbner and Yuval-Davis, 'Women and the New Discourse of Citizenship', p. 12. See also Tanika Sarkar's brief discussion of Nancy Fraser's views on this issue in her essay in this volume.
26. See, for example, Joan B. Landes, 'The Public and the Private Sphere: A Feminist Reconsideration' and Iris Marion Young, 'Impartiality and the Civic Public: Some Implications of Feminist Critiques of Moral and Political Theory', in *Feminism, the Public and the Private*, ed. Joan B. Landes (Oxford University Press, Oxford and New York, 1998), pp. 135–63, 421–47.
27. See Cott, 'Marriage and Women's Citizenship', and *Public Vows: A History of Marriage and the Nation* (Harvard University Press, Cambridge, MA, 2000); and Linda K. Kerber, *No Constitutional Right to Be Ladies: Women and the Obligations of Citizenship* (Hill and Wang, New York, 1998).
28. In the US this was the case until 1934; in the UK, until 1948.
29. Cott, 'Marriage and Women's Citizenship', p. 1473.
30. Charles Taylor, 'The Politics of Recognition'.
31. Both Laura Mayhall and Tanika Sarkar make this point and use the term 'vaulting' in reference to crossing the public/private divide.

Citizens and Scientists: Toward a Gendered History of Scientific Practice in Post-revolutionary France

Carol E. Harrison

In December 1879, Gustave Flaubert, at work composing his last, and ultimately unfinished novel, *Bouvard and Pécuchet*, explained the project in a letter to a friend: 'The subtitle will be *On the failure of method in the sciences*. In short, my ambition is to survey all modern ideas. Women will have little role, and love none at all.'[1] The novel is indeed a catalogue of failures; Flaubert's heroes pursue and then abandon all of the nineteenth century's fads and fashions, particularly in the world of science. *Bouvard and Pécuchet* remains unfinished and, in a sense, the novel was unfinishable because the nineteenth-century bourgeois fascination with science was inexhaustible. Embedded within the endless catalogue of scientific failure, however, the historian finds Flaubert's reflections on the uses of science, and, in particular, on its gendered nature.

This essay juxtaposes literary and satirical representations of science, such as Flaubert's, with an analysis of the social practices of Bouvard and Pécuchet's counterparts among bourgeois Frenchmen of the nineteenth century. Like Flaubert's heroes, thousands of bourgeois Frenchmen pursued scientific pastimes, but Bouvard, Pécuchet and the other amateurs of the nineteenth century do not usually find their way into accounts of the history of science. They rarely, if ever, contributed to the production and advancement of scientific knowledge. At best, these innumerable *savants* generated 'bad science' – methodologically flawed, derivative, and trivial. It is important to note, however, that these men felt little sense of failure. Bouvard and Pécuchet abandoned each of their hobbies in turn because they felt that science had failed them, not because they had failed science. Although membership rolls fluctuated, the learned societies of the nineteenth century in many cases survive to the present, again suggesting members' general satisfaction. If nineteenth-century gentlemen scientists considered themselves successful, it begs the question of what the point of science was in the first place.

I argue that the purpose of scientific activity among nineteenth-century bourgeois men was primarily the production of status, not knowledge. In particular, science contributed to the construction of an autonomous masculinity closely linked to contemporary ideas of citizenship. Social and political status in early nineteenth-century France was marked by extreme fluidity and uncertainty concerning social categories. The French Revolution effectively demolished old regime social hierarchies and gender identities. When it came to replacing the social and sexual signposts by which French men and women navigated their world, however, the revolution was far less successful. The implementation of new, widely acceptable, social and gender ideologies was the essential project of the early nineteenth century. Science, redefined for the new century, played a crucial role in identifying masculine achievement: scientific competence defined bourgeois men as deserving of citizenship. The French state concurred, offering a limited suffrage to members of particularly distinguished scientific societies. The link between science and citizenship passed necessarily through gender; in order to remain mutually supporting, both had to be protected from female encroachment. The exclusion of women from Flaubert's catalogue of 'modern ideas' was in no way accidental; rather, it served as the guarantee of the seriousness and scientific value of Bouvard and Pécuchet's hobbies.

Protecting science from feminine intrusion was not as simple as the successful exclusion of women from modern, professionalised science might suggest. As several historians of early modern science have noted, the gender of *ancien régime* science was extremely ambiguous, and exceptional women succeeded in making names for themselves in science. Professionalising science of the nineteenth century efficiently excluded women, but the process of professionalisation manipulated gender stereotypes, particularly in its definition of the amateur. Thus even in a world without women, effeminacy, in the person of the male amateur, might still taint science. For the gentlemanly *savants* for whom science was more a matter of social status than of knowledge-production, the threat of being labelled effeminate was a serious one.

The social meanings of science and the social and political implications of gender are narratives that intersect in mutually revealing ways. If we broaden our understanding of 'science' to include the hobbies of amateur *savants* and expand our notion of 'citizenship' to cover its social practices as well as its political manifestations such as voting, then science, citizenship and the gender of each become closely related tales. The practice of science in revolutionary Europe had gendered implications that derived from the legal status assigned to sex. Moreover, the rhetoric and practice of science contributed to the construction of gender as a social and political category. Before, during, and after the revolution, science remained a term to claim, an attribute that gave weight to any project to which it was attached. From the *philosophe*'s science of society to the scientific socialist, the rhetorical value of 'science' remained high. Nonetheless, the social meaning of science – and particularly its connection to gender identities – underwent a transformation from the late eighteenth to the mid-nineteenth century.

Any investigation of science's alignment with male citizenship should begin in the old regime, prior both to the definition of the citizen and to the equation of science with masculinity. As Geneviève Fraisse has argued, exceptional women enjoyed a remarkable degree of tolerance under the old regime.[2] In a political order based on privilege, the exception never threatened the rule. The admission of some widows to guilds did not suggest that all female artisans deserved guild membership any more than the reception of an outstanding woman like Elisabeth Vigée-Lebrun to the Royal Academy of Painting meant that that august body would have to admit every woman with a paintbrush.[3] Privileges enjoyed by exceptional women like Vigée-Lebrun remained just that – exceptional privileges. Being a woman neither assured nor denied particular privileges; as long as privilege governed legal status in France's absolute monarchy, gender was a category whose political implications could not be fixed.

Similar rules governed women and scientific practice in Enlightenment France. Just as the exceptional woman might enjoy guild membership, she might also produce scientific work. Recent scholarship has explored the breadth of the scientific activities available to eighteenth-century women.[4] Botany, which, in the eighteenth century, was energised by the introduction of Linnean classification, was widely understood as an appropriate field of inquiry for women. Indeed, the language of Linnaeus was saturated with metaphors of love and family that even relatively ordinary women were assumed to grasp immediately.[5] 'Botanising' was not the only scientific activity available to enlightened women. Exceptional women, acting on the Cartesian dictum that 'the mind has no sex', pursued mathematics and physics.[6] Emilie du Châtelet, the leading proponent of Newtonian thought in France, enjoyed just such an exceptional life in science.[7] Moreover, women governed the salons in which scientific research and speculation often found its first audience.[8]

As Lorraine Daston has observed, while not all eighteenth-century observers thought that the female scientist was a creature to be encouraged, none supposed her to be an impossibility.[9] The stereotypical figure of the woman engaged in scientific dialogue who appeared in many early modern scientific texts indicated that, while women's minds might be untrained, they could nonetheless be shaped to the rigours of scientific inquiry. Enlightenment commentators might not approve of Mme du Châtelet's dedication to her mathematics, but no one suggested that her publications were fraudulent. The exceptional female intellect might be perverse, but it was nonetheless real. The woman-scientist might be a curiosity – an apparent abrogation of nature's rules – but curiosity, for early modern scientists and natural history collectors, was often the site of truth about nature.[10]

The old regime ended with a lively and often vituperatively misogynist debate about the exceptional woman. Building on Rousseau's condemnation of *salonnières*, each of whom 'gather[ed] in her apartment a harem of men more womanish than she',[11] political pamphleteers of the 1780s asserted that fiscal crisis and a morally bankrupt monarchy could all be blamed on the nefarious activities of women.[12] Even revolutionary feminists like Olympe de Gouges believed that the crisis of the French state was connected to sexual politics via the 'nocturnal administration of women'.[13] Revolutionary men agreed that women whose exceptional abilities or status gave them influence over affairs of state – or merely over the private affairs of public men – threatened the good order and repose of society. Thus, when the revolutionaries set about transforming subjects into citizens, they took gender as a fundamental constituent of legal identity. Full and active citizenship belonged to men alone.[14]

In the newly democratic order of revolutionary France, exceptional women threatened to become the rule. Admitting one woman to political debating societies, to the vote, or to circles of power, suggested that any woman could exercise citizenship; their exclusion from all political activities, therefore, had to be complete.[15] The exceptional female intellect was, as Daston argues, simply written out of the realm of possibility altogether. A woman of intellect was no longer unusual, or even perverse, but simply a fraud, passing off the achievements of her husband or lover as her own. As the nineteenth century progressed, science increasingly came to explain why women could not be scientists: their experience was too limited, their brains too small, or their wombs too demanding for true scientific speculation.[16] The masculine gendering of both science and citizenship was a rule established by nature, and the expulsion of exceptional women from science necessarily coincided with the exclusion of all women from democratic citizenship.

No consensus on the meaning of citizenship emerged from the revolutionary years, however, and the identity of the citizen remained a matter of contest throughout the post-revolutionary decades. Women's exclusion from citizenship continued to generate debate from a nascent feminist movement that drew on the egalitarian principles of the revolution.[17] Even among men, however, the limits of citizenship were not clear in the early nineteenth century. Confident that citizenship excluded women, most men were nonetheless not certain that they themselves could be counted among the ranks of full citizens. Replacing the subject with the citizen as the object of law was no easy task, and it continued to preoccupy Frenchmen throughout the first half of the nineteenth century.

The limits of male citizenship remained a problem because no regime distributed political rights equally among men in early nineteenth-century France. From the 1791 Constitution's distinction between 'active' and 'passive' citizens to the limited suffrage regimes of the Restoration and the July Monarchy, *capacité* – most commonly demonstrated through property ownership – determined voting rights. The Restoration inaugurated the nineteenth century's ambiguous reaction to the revolutionary legacy of citizenship. In the 1814 Charter, Louis XVIII erased citizenship altogether: Frenchmen were 'subjects' who were nonetheless, according to article one, 'equal before the law'. The revised Charter of 1830 spoke of 'citizens' but extended the suffrage only marginally.[18] The republican experiment of 1848 was a disappointment to those who expected universal manhood suffrage to produce a stable and moderate republicanism. Its successor, Bonapartist universal manhood suffrage, was hardly a meaningful expression of the citizen's will. Throughout this period the industrialising economy introduced new economic inequalities among men as well as new socialist visions of equality, all of which complicated ideals and expressions of citizenship. Although the revolution had erased the old regime subject, it had by no means definitively established the identity of the citizen.

The fluidity of constitutional definitions of the citizen made it possible to propose alternative social and cultural criteria for citizenship. In the absence of a solid, generally accepted legal category, nineteenth-century Frenchmen set about establishing *practices* of citizenship for the post-revolutionary world. National Guard membership, for instance, or a rhetoric of productive labour association functioned in some circles as claims to a citizenship that was far broader than the electoral rolls.[19] Bourgeois Frenchmen elaborated a practice of citizenship focused on rationality and public utility that, while more inclusive than the limited suffrage, was nonetheless an exclusive category. Bourgeois citizenship rejected hierarchies of birth but stopped short of revolutionary *égalité*. It was theoretically open to all but in practice closed to most. Merit, rather than wealth or birth, was the ultimate basis for inclusion in the ranks of bourgeois citizens.[20] Science was one of the most widely accepted means of demonstrating that an individual possessed the calm rationality and the public spiritedness that merited full citizenship. The scientist, as much as the nobleman or the landowner, deserved to participate in the nation's affairs as a citizen. Indeed, science achieved the ultimate mark of distinction for a bourgeois cliché: inclusion in Gustave Flaubert's *Dictionary of Platitudes*. A 'laboratory', Flaubert tells us, is something that 'one must have in the country'.[21] As guarantors of rationality and competence, laboratories and the scientific knowledge they represented were desirable symbols of *capacité*, useful in the contested realm of citizenship.

In effect, the practice of bourgeois citizenship mirrored liberal rhetoric of *capacité*. Neither liberal politicians nor bourgeois Frenchmen were willing to accept the market as the ultimate arbiter of an individual's fitness for citizenship. Economic success demonstrated by property ownership was certainly one measure of *capacité*, but not the only one. According to François Guizot, Louis Philippe's prime minister and the leading liberal theorist of citizenship, society harboured 'natural electors', distinguished by their 'ability to act according to reason', or *capacité*.[22] Reason was a quality provided by nature; wealth, on the other hand, was the reward of what appeared to many to be a random and amoral marketplace.[23] Not only property owners, but also military officers and members of the *Institut*,[24] lawyers and other university diploma holders, mayors and members of departmental councils,[25] national guard officers, members of learned societies and chambers of commerce, judges of the peace, and retired bureaucrats[26] demonstrated the necessary *capacité* to serve the nation as electors. *Capacité*, Odilon Barrot argued, was 'the best means of making electoral law sufficiently elastic so that it expands at the same rate as the intelligence and political education of the masses'.[27] Ultimately, wealth was merely a useful indicator of the citizen's more fundamental qualifications: his rationality and competence for public affairs.

The problem with acknowledging *capacité* as 'a complex and profound fact … a certain collection of faculties, of knowledge, and of means of action that make up a man'[28] was that it was impossible to reach consensus about how to measure such a phenomenon. Thus, despite general agreement that *capacité* was not reducible to wealth, national electoral laws included few categories besides property ownership. Bourgeois Frenchmen, however, remained convinced that within their own communities they were capable of identifying *capacité* – and of distinguishing between mere economic success and suitability for citizenship. What Pierre Rosanvallon has described as *l'impossible citoyen capacitaire* – the unachievable goal of a citizenry defined by *capacité* alone[29] – appeared to bourgeois Frenchmen to be quite possible. Indeed, navigating bourgeois society was all about recognising and assessing the *capacité* of one's neighbours and associates.

Because rationality and public service were generally accepted indicators of *capacité*, science, particularly as practised by bourgeois learned societies, could mark a claim to citizenship. The bourgeois man who practised and, more importantly, promoted science among his fellows demonstrated his dedication to the public good and deserved inclusion among the ranks of citizens. The state cooperated in this bourgeois equation of science and citizenship and offered suffrage to members of some eminent learned societies, recognising that intellectual *capacité* was as relevant as property.[30] Provincial *savants* sought out the state's designation 'of public utility' for their learned societies because it enabled members to vote in municipal elections and was a probable category for inclusion in government proposals for national suffrage reform. Learned societies benefited from state recognition and patronage in other ways as well: the cash, journal subscriptions, books, experimental seeds, and artwork that societies received from various governments were an assurance that the state recognised the value of its citizen-scientists. As one *savant* observed, a gift for his society's museum from Napoleon III, France's *génie tutélaire* (guiding genius), had to be maintained as 'a souvenir of [the emperor's] good will and gratitude'; he therefore demanded that the departmental council continue to pay an annual stipend for museum maintenance to a learned society that had not met in several years.[31]

Tens of thousands of bourgeois Frenchmen hurried to join learned societies in which they could demonstrate their erudition, their devotion to the public good, and the resulting connections to the government. Learned societies were venues in which bourgeois men could demonstrate their competence in scientific matters and also display the public utility of their science.[32] These associations were even more useful for demonstrating *capacité* than the private laboratory of Flaubert's clichés because they removed science from the domestic sphere of wives and children into the world of public affairs. The pedantic pharmacist M. Homais of *Madame Bovary* was by no means the only man in nineteenth-century France to sign himself 'member of several learned societies'.[33] The highly publicised activities of these societies, in which bourgeois citizens brought the benefits of science to their towns, announced that members were men of *capacité*, the 'natural electors' to represent their communities.

Learned societies enthusiastically promoted science to the less educated public by publishing journals, opening museums, founding libraries, sponsoring prizes, and organising expositions. Civic spirit was the dominant value of bourgeois science in the early nineteenth century. The learned society that sponsored a competition to develop dyes that resisted soap, or that embarked on a major study of water quality in all of a department's communes,[34] knew that it represented the local community's best interests. An exposition that displayed all of the products of local industry was a 'solemn engagement of patriotism';[35] locals should recognise that men 'heated by the fever of progress who have tried to save our town from backwardness and to inaugurate an era of regeneration' deserved 'a hymn of gratitude and the dedication of a monument in their memory by their fellow citizens'.[36] A society that sponsored the latest in agricultural techniques could view its research as supporting the institutions of the liberal state:

having 'conquered civil equality', farmers were now 'conquering equality before science and before the state; not a bitter, socially levelling equality ... but a tutelary and beneficent equality'.[37] In the words of one provincial *savant*, admission to a learned society signified his readiness 'to bring the necessary enlightenment to the task of rendering my work useful to my *patrie*, to tie my knowledge to that of centuries to come' and, in conjunction with his new colleagues, to 'ensure the fame of our *pays* through useful discoveries'.[38] In a learned society, 'an elite of intelligence' dedicated itself to the public good and 'found the true remuneration of its efforts in the population that benefited from its works'.[39] Museum collections, industrial expositions, horticultural or zoological gardens all removed science from the home and made it accessible to the public. They demonstrated that the bourgeois man who undertook scientific study abandoned private concerns and acted in the public interest; his science was a sign of his civic *capacité*.[40]

The culture of bourgeois learned societies clearly aligned science with publicity, civic spirit, and, consequently, masculinity. The bourgeois citizen was indubitably male. The opposite of the active bourgeois citizen was not the passive male citizen (who might, with practice or through profit, attain the status of full citizen) but the domestic, intellectually limited woman. The restrictions biology had placed on the female intellect clearly denied women the autonomy necessary both to full citizenship and to scientific inquiry. The boundaries between the bourgeois citizen and other men, however, were necessarily vague: citizenship was a potentially universal category from which no man was automatically excluded. Bourgeois citizenship did not admit to recognising class as a barrier: citizenship and bourgeois status were both elastic, potentially universal categories for men.[41] The non-citizen – the never-to-be citizen – was female. Preserving the link between scientific and civic *capacité* meant maintaining the masculinity of both, ensuring that both were understood to be closed to women by nature, not merely social custom.

This opposition between the citizen-scientist and woman is typical of the pressure of gender that was a feature of early nineteenth-century French society. In the aftermath of the revolution, in the absence of the old regime's stable social categories, gender dichotomy became increasingly important as the foundation of social order.[42] Early nineteenth-century Frenchmen imposed gender dichotomy on all manner of social phenomena. Social diversity – both inherited from the revolution and invented by industrialisation – was more easily interpreted when it corresponded to gender difference. Citizenship was a more manageable concept when viewed through the simplifying lens of gender dichotomy: men were citizens or potential citizens; women best served the state as mothers. The pressure of gender similarly positioned science as masculine and effectively erased the lives of early modern women scientists: accounts of eighteenth-century women of science were replaced by explanations of women's biological incapacity for intellectual pursuits.

The link between science and *capacité* also demonstrates the instability of the pressure of gender. In principle, science and civic *capacité* were clearly manly qualities, made and measured in the public sphere of civic usefulness. In fact, however, the links between science, citizenship, masculinity, and the public good were by no means stable. Subjected to the pressure of gender, science and citizenship reacted in unexpected ways and often refused to stay put in the masculine camp. Having posited science as a particularly bourgeois qualification for citizenship – as an obstacle to all but those with education and leisure -- the bourgeois Frenchmen might be startled to discover that science was not a barrier that completely excluded women. In other words, the class boundaries of bourgeois citizenship could be permeable to gender. Busily engaged in the preparation of natural history museums, statistical tables, horticultural specimens, or technological expositions, bourgeois citizens did not always notice the overlap between their amateur science and the leisure pursuits of women.

Thus by mid century, bourgeois Frenchmen did not always find that the possession of a laboratory and membership in a learned society guaranteed their status as responsible citizen-scientists. In particular, the professionalisation of science increasingly called attention to analogies between amateur male science and the hobbies of idle women. Earnest *savants* found their scientific contributions rejected and their claims to status mocked. Just as many men faced exclusion from citizenship, so many bourgeois *savants* were threatened with dismissal from the community of science, now populated by professionals. The emergence of science professions, defining themselves in masculine terms, threatened amateurs with relegation to a feminised periphery.[43] Many bourgeois Frenchmen found that their science refused to maintain a stable association with masculinity and citizenship: the practice of bourgeois science was a perpetual struggle to keep science aligned with manliness and to ensure that women's work (and women's leisure) remained totally foreign to the scientific enterprise.

The gender instability of the bourgeois citizen-scientist becomes particularly clear if we combine three types of sources concerning scientific practice: accounts of what these men *did*, what they *said* about it, and how their detractors satirised it. The contrast between the rhetoric of bourgeois *savants* and the actual practices and artefacts of their science helps explain the humour many observers of bourgeois society, Gustave Flaubert foremost among them, found in scientific hobbies. Getting the joke is, quite centrally, about understanding the gender gap between the ambitious, manly rhetoric of bourgeois science and its more mundane, and often domestic, practice.

In their determination to align science with civic responsibility and citizenship, bourgeois *savants* of the nineteenth century increasingly excluded the arts from their learned society programmes. The fine arts had been a standard feature of eighteenth-century academies, but post-revolutionary learned societies eliminated them in favour of more useful, serious, and scientific pursuits. By the nineteenth century, one observer noted, bourgeois men had realised that they 'could not pay their debt to their country with limping madrigals'. Poetry gradually vanished from their meetings ('just as poppies disappear from well-cultivated fields to make room for grain'[44]), and male associations for instrumental music gradually declined in the middle years of the century.[45] Learned societies included paintings in their museum collections, but they displayed art in much the same spirit as herbaria or stuffed birds, and they often showed greater interest in the donor of the painting than in its style or aesthetic quality. Instead of promoting amateur production in the visual arts, the societies of the Friends of the Arts (which multiplied after 1850) offered members opportunities for the acquisition of art objects produced by others.[46] Bourgeois citizen-scientists promoted 'utility above all',[47] and they found little purpose in aesthetic pleasure.

Flaubert captured the bourgeois rejection of aesthetic production and its gender ambiguities. His *Dictionary* represented literature as anti-aesthetic: the novelist ceded creativity to the cliché and to the dictates of alphabetical order. The arts appear in the *Dictionary* – right before 'asp' – where they are defined as 'quite useless, because they can be reproduced by machines, which produce things even quicker'. Artists come off little better: they are 'all phonies' about whom one should express 'surprise that they are dressed like everyone else'. They 'earn ridiculous sums of money but fritter it away' and, in conclusion, 'a woman artist can only be a trollop'.[48] The ill-dressed, long-haired, and slightly effeminate artist was a stock character in early nineteenth-century illustration. (See Figure 1, 'Schools and Examinations' by Gavarni, from *Le Tiroir du diable* (Paris, n.d. [1845]).) Bouvard and Pécuchet, enacting the *Dictionary*'s clichés, clearly sided with the machines rather than the artists. Fervent practitioners of the nineteenth century's crazes, they became gymnasts, archaeologists and anatomists, but they never dabbled in painting; they avoided music; and their primary venture into literary matters was the production of a dictionary.

Bouvard, Pécuchet, and thousands of other bourgeois Frenchmen avoided art in an attempt to differentiate their leisure from feminine idleness. Art and leisure, like science and all other aspects of early nineteenth-century social life, were subject to the pressure of gender. This pressure was not consistent, however, and it did not produce fixed meanings. For instance, although 'work' and 'leisure' could easily be mapped onto 'male' and 'female', they could also correspond to 'bourgeois' and 'worker'. Leisure thus became a complicated imperative for the bourgeois man – necessary to distinguish him from his social inferiors but also threatening to de-differentiate him from his womenfolk. Science and learned societies functioned as a response to this leisure dilemma: accessible as a leisure pursuit only to the successful, well-educated bourgeois with ample free time, science was 'useful' and thus resembled work rather than feminine idleness.[49]

Like leisure, art was susceptible to the ambiguous pressures of gender. Historians and critics have recently investigated why aesthetic production in the nineteenth century increasingly risked contaminating association with femininity. As men donned dark suits and serious demeanours, they left beauty and display to their wives.[50] The imitative aspects of artistic production suggested female capabilities: the nineteenth century's distinction between male creation and the lesser female ability to imitate did not secure art against female competence.[51] A talented female mimic might manage to produce an object that so closely resembled art as to be taken for the real thing. Small forms and genres, in particular, were perilously vulnerable to imitation and increasingly feminised. From Chopin's Nocturnes to rococo painting, smallness and ornamental detail were intimately associated with female nature.[52] As Flaubert's definitions suggested, art belonged to the realm of the feminine, to trollops and outrageously dressed men. The (male) speaker of the *Dictionary*'s clichés aligned himself instead with science and machines.

Figure 1: Gavarni, 'Schools and Examinations', from *Le Tiroir du diable* (Paris, n.d. [1845]). The fine arts student is second from the left. Contrast the science student from Polytechnique, third from left.

The link between women and small genres referred not only to essential feminine qualities but also to contemporary female practices. A nocturne, after all, was accessible to most well-brought-up young girls.[53] The piano was a standard feminine accomplishment and small forms like the nocturne demanded intimate, often domestic spaces, rather than large (and still occasionally rowdy) concert halls.[54] Similarly, forms like watercolour lent themselves both in production and in viewing to parlours as well as studios.[55] Likewise at home in the salon was lyric poetry, and the early nineteenth century celebrated the achievements of young female poets like Delphine Gay.[56] The outrage and panic over the 'woman of ideas' that Janis Bergman-Carton documents in French art of the 1830s was at its most virulent in just such small forms – journalism, illustration, commercial art – in which women featured as both producers and consumers.[57] Finally, the aesthetic (rather than intellectual) cultivation of the self was, next to motherhood, the primary activity of the nineteenth-century *bourgeoise*.[58] Even if improving and ornamenting one's body and its surroundings were not intrinsically feminine qualities, women indisputably had more practice than men in such arts.

Men's artistic activities were by no means universally problematic in the early nineteenth century. 'Great' art maintained its association with male performance. The link between artistic excellence and male capacity derived from earlier norms that were reworked and refreshed in the revolutionary period. Thomas Crow's recent work on David's studio, for instance, explores the notion of painting as a male heritage, passed on from figurative fathers to sons in a competitive arena marked by female absence and a rejection of 'effeminate' rococo forms.[59] Other scholars have noted that the romantic distinction between the sublime and the beautiful represented gendered aesthetic categories. Mere beauty, with its ability to please and to seduce, could not ultimately compete with the sublime and its capacity to dominate and to awe.[60] The relegation of a feminised concept of beauty to secondary status within the arts suggests some of the gender anxieties creeping into aesthetic production in post-revolutionary France. Certain art forms, notably those that opted for the large, the original, and the imposing, were more manly than others.

Professionalisation was one possible response to the pressure of gender in the production of art. Indeed, the status of professional goes a long way toward explaining how 'great art' retained its masculine associations. Linking productivity to the expertise acquired through training and tested in competitions of merit both elevated the status and secured the maleness of professions such as law and medicine. As Norma Clark and Mary Jean Corbett have demonstrated in studies of Thomas Carlyle, defining artistic activity as 'professional' could allay anxieties about the potential unmanliness of sedentary, self-indulgent authorship.[61] The 'man of letters' was as productive a market player as any other. The competition associated with the achievement of professional status contributed to reinforcing the manliness of 'great' art. As in medicine and the law, entry into professional art was by examination and trial: recognition by academies, learned societies, and awards such as the *prix de Rome* literally excluded women from the ranks of professional artists and ensured that 'real' (male) artists had proven themselves in a contested arena.[62]

The Salon painters and the men of letters could thus rest assured that professional standards protected the manliness of their occupations. Amateurs, however, received no such guarantee. Art's professional boundaries against women also excluded male amateurs and, most importantly, lumped the production of the male *ami des arts* (art enthusiast) together with the artistic dabblings of women. Male amateurism, particularly when practised in accessible small-scale genres, bordered on the effete. Given that the genres most practical for male hobbyists were also those most associated with the accomplishments of their wives and daughters, it is little wonder that learned societies preferred scientific to aesthetic production.

The ultimate male aesthetic amateur was the dandy. The connection between amateurism and effeminacy originated not only from the professionalisation of the arts but also from the dandy's example of male aesthetic self-cultivation. Taste was the defining characteristic of the dandy – he was a man of good aesthetic judgement that he applied to all elements of his life, from the furnishing of his rooms to his choice of horses. Most disturbing, the dandy, like a woman, adopted his own body as an object for ornamentation: clothing, mannerisms, and style of life combined to make the person of the dandy into a work of art. The dandy cultivated beauty for purely selfish and unmarketable purposes. Anne Martin-Fugier documents the ambiguous role played by the dandy in Parisian high society: he was an indispensable figure whose initiative created many of Paris's favourite elite amusements, but his flaunting of taste and refinement was itself in questionable taste.[63] 'Taste' was clearly not a quality that all men would wish to claim for themselves, nor one for which they would wish to educate their sons.[64]

Aesthetic pleasure, then, was a dangerous indulgence for the bourgeois citizen. Amateur pursuit of painting or music associated him with female accomplishment or the dandy's effeminacy. His friends and colleagues might, as Flaubert suggested, be surprised that he dressed like everyone else, or suspect him of having no head for money. Flaubert's *Dictionary* suggests the answer: he was to abandon art for science; give up soft aesthetic judgement for hard fact; and trade inspiration for mechanisation. Just as Bouvard and Pécuchet devoted themselves to knowledge that could be definitively mastered and Flaubert himself delighted in the irony of abandoning poetic artifice for alphabetical order, bourgeois Frenchmen resolved to dedicate their leisure to the useful, the scientific and the unquestionably manly.

Science as a signifier of 'masculine' and 'useful' attached itself to a wide variety of activities in bourgeois scientific circles. Early nineteenth-century learned societies were enthusiastically encyclopedic, and by limiting themselves to 'science', their members in fact gave up very little. Poetry disappeared from their programmes, but most other realms of knowledge were recuperated for the cause of science. While asserting their selectivity and critical judgement, amateur scientists simultaneously pursued every lead that came their way and made room for every passing interest in their definition of science. Asserting that a particular activity had 'become a science' in the nineteenth century was a means of representing progress, and it suggested that, in the hands of bourgeois citizens, these activities could be of real use to the public. Thus, bourgeois Frenchmen formed associations dedicated to the pursuit of all manner of subjects asserted to be scientific: geology, horticulture, lifesaving, geography, history, or gymnastics all possessed some element of science that associations of bourgeois men sought to master and offer to the public.

History and archaeology, in particular, enjoyed great success among bourgeois scientists, in encyclopedic associations as well as in specialised societies that multiplied in the mid-nineteenth century.[65] Amateur historians and archaeologists affiliated themselves with science by virtue of their relationship to concrete objects: archives and artefacts. 'History' emerged from the engagement of the male intellect with the concrete, tangible documentary record.[66] Objects that could be placed in a museum or counted in a statistical table automatically associated disciplines like history and archaeology with science understood as a rational, concrete form of knowledge. Joseph Prudhomme, Henri Monnier's quintessential fictional bourgeois and an antiquities enthusiast, was typical in his appreciation of the concreteness of ancient monuments – into which he regularly carved his name.[67] 'Scientific' history and archaeology eliminated problematic relationships to text and produced evidence that displayed to great effect in provincial museums all over France. By virtue of being examined, classified and presented by rational male bourgeois for the enlightenment of others, anything could become an object of science.

This eclecticism and apparent inability to concentrate on the production of scientific knowledge in any one domain is the joke at the centre of *Bouvard and Pécuchet*. Other authors also mocked bourgeois willingness to see science in everything they touched. If we understand science as an element in the practice of bourgeois citizenship (rather than exclusively as a knowledge-producing activity), however, learned societies' eclecticism makes sense as well as comedy. Any reasonably well-educated bourgeois man could do science. The citizen-scientist did not need advanced mathematics, sophisticated laboratory equipment, or even a pressing interest in the natural world to count himself a scientist. Broadly inclusive definitions of science admitted the bourgeois with a classical education to the ranks of the civic-minded and useful citizenry.

The citizen-scientist's embrace of the scientific was not without its pitfalls, however. He was an amateur in an era when science, like art, was professionalising. Moreover, his science shared many of the qualities of female artistic hobbies: it was detail-oriented and small-scale and, ultimately, profoundly concerned with the aesthetics of presentation and display. The practices and artefacts of bourgeois science – confidently proclaimed to be the guarantors of civic manliness – were all too often infused with artistic judgements and aesthetic pleasures. As satirists of bourgeois life noted, it was sometimes difficult to tell the difference between the products of bourgeois science and female craft. Botany and flower painting on china had more in common then the citizen-scientist would care to admit.

Just as the gendered lines between the amateur and the professional hardened in the arts, the same categories emerged in the sciences. We can describe the activity of the bourgeois learned societies as 'amateur' precisely because of the contemporary development of a professional science – remunerative, university-based, and enjoying state patronage.[68] This distinction, however, was still far from clear in the early nineteenth century. Independent wealth, income from a variety of administrative positions, and domestic laboratories continued to characterise members of France's scientific elite, and many science professionals also pursued scientific hobbies.[69] Increasingly, however, the distinction between amateur and professional scientists classed bourgeois learned societies as amateur. As amateurs, they were also figures of fun.[70]

Ridicule of bourgeois science focused on the self-importance of the *savant*. Provincial newspapers, particularly those of the political opposition, recognised that learned society membership was a claim to local leadership and their coverage was often sardonic. In these accounts, members 'dress themselves in peacock's feathers' and 'perfume' one another's work with a 'cloud of incense'.[71] Making fun of bourgeois science was also relatively common in the national press. Even writers generally sympathetic to learned societies could not resist pointing out provincials' habit of 'exclaiming over broken-down bits of wall like Jeremiah over the ruins of Jerusalem' and of becoming so 'wrapped up in ... the philosophy of human progress that they wind up losing sight of chronology and grammar'.[72] The women's magazine *Les Modes parisiennes*, for instance, routinely filled a humour column with accounts of scientific follies such as a horticultural society's experiments with grafts (the pistachio-carnation, for instance) and a newly invented electric harpoon which, having killed several chickens and rabbits, promised to give whales such a migraine that they would simply turn themselves over to hunters.[73]

Flaubert was, not surprisingly, in the forefront of this tradition of mockery: *Bouvard and Pécuchet*, in particular, systematically lampoons amateur scientists' claim to local leadership. While asserting their expertise and scientific aptitude, Flaubert's erudites chased after whims and defined everything with which they came into contact as science. Rather than an inclusive body of knowledge in which all men of good will and liberal education could share, *Bouvard and Pécuchet* maps out an untidy jumble of derivative trivia and intellectual dilettantism. Flaubert's heroes missed the point of the eclecticism of bourgeois science. Their erudition did not establish a set of common values and social norms among their peers; rather, it isolated the two men, in thrall to their own obsessions, and it mystified their neighbours. Self-absorption and complacency, not citizenship, emerged from Bouvard and Pécuchet's scientific hobbies. Flaubert's other representations of bourgeois life, most notably *Madame Bovary*, mine similar veins of egotism running through bourgeois claims to civic responsibility and leadership.

Bouvard and Pécuchet routinely abandoned disciplines when faced with uncertainties, scholarly disagreements, and conflicting evidence.

Most French bourgeois were not so easily put off, however. Inability to discover the system at the root of a science did not count as failure, because it had not been the aim of the inquiry in the first place. The purpose of leisurely science lay less in its content and more in its form and presentation. Dissemination of scientific knowledge – what these men referred to as 'vulgarisation' – was a vital component of their activities. Although amateur scientists did engage in research and field work, more time and larger slices of learned society budgets went to the shaping and presentation of science. Learned society life was an endless round of preparation of tables and statistical treatments of local industry, water quality, mineral resources, archaeological sites, or, indeed, almost any object. Some items lent themselves to a more literal presentation and consequently appeared in the museums and expositions that multiplied in the provinces. These settings presented the products of local ingenuity to the astonished eyes of the lower classes and the gratified gaze of the local bourgeoisie. Originality was not the purpose of these learned presentations, which aimed rather at arranging acquired knowledge in a satisfactory and enlightening manner. Imitation and representation were the standard mode of bourgeois science, and to become a platitude was the final mark of success.

Imitation and reproduction, rather than discovery and innovation, thus formed the mainstay of the bourgeois scientist's activity. Members of the Emulation Society of Lons le Saunier, for instance, dedicated most of their budget to their museum collections – not an unusual choice for nineteenth-century citizen-scientists. Among the proudest achievements of the Emulation Society was the construction, in the mid 1860s, of a plaster-cast relief map of the department of the Jura. The map recorded all of the scientific data in the Society's possession in encyclopedic detail: local industries and soil conditions, rivers and current directions, mountains, types of trees, geological strata and towns were all painted on the map in such a fashion as to 'speak to the eyes of the population' and enlighten the most routine-bound peasant. In order to present such a wealth of natural and man-made detail, the relief map of the Jura covered 30 square metres with cast plaster. This reproduction of an entire department was a truly remarkable undertaking, but one justified by the utility of the finished product: from farmers to archaeologists and engineers, all men could usefully consult the Society's map. The project brought the wealth of the Jura and the dedication of its citizens to national attention when it was exhibited, and awarded a bronze medal, at the Paris exposition of 1867. With smaller sections of the map offered at moderate cost to village schools, even children could learn to appreciate the presence of science in their own neighbourhoods.[74]

Emulators in Lons le Saunier were not the only bourgeois citizens to locate science principally in meticulous reproduction. Horticultural societies collected wax fruits to set standards for local market gardeners,[75] and statistical compilations presented themselves as neutral facsimiles of reality.[76] Historical documentary collections, or catalogues of engravings of archaeological or natural history samples likewise emphasised accuracy of reproduction as the ultimate goal.[77] The ability to reproduce natural or human artefacts with a painstaking precision – the very quality that condemned women's art to second-rate status – guaranteed the truth and disinterestedness of male science.

Preoccupation with detail, another attribute of women's capacities, similarly characterised the bourgeois citizen's science. The multiplication of categories and subheadings and the intricacies of species and genera defined amateur interest in the sciences. The statistical compilations and museum collections of bourgeois men clearly relied on the assumption that meticulous and patient exposition of detail was the foundation of science. The bourgeois amateur, as a rule, did not generate grand theories or aspire to paradigm shifts. His self-appointed role as scientist was to elaborate taxonomies and to multiply corroborative detail. Bourgeois *savants* commonly dedicated themselves to the elaboration of intricate taxonomies, spending decades in exhaustive records of the lepidoptera of the department of the Doubs, the venomous plants of the department of the Jura, or the heraldic emblems of the province of the Franche-Comté.[78]

Fascination with scrupulous reproduction and statistical detail went hand in hand with an interest in presentation and spectacle. Museums and expositions were a staple of learned society life, and bourgeois interest in the display of science and the visual forms of knowledge suggests aesthetic, as well as scientific, judgement at work. Exhibiting information in a pleasing fashion mattered more than creating or contributing to it. Objects exerted an attraction not only because they suggested the concreteness of scientific proof but also because they were more liable to arrangement and display than, for instance, scientific theories. Colour, pattern, and design played as important a role as science in the arrangement of museum specimens. Nineteenth-century insect or butterfly displays, for instance, pleased the eye as or more effectively than they informed the mind. Exhibition spaces, like the room of the

Universal Exposition (Figure 2) dedicated to the demonstration of scientific progress in timekeeping, combined the aesthetic of the bourgeois parlour with that of the bazaar. Ostensibly abandoned in favour of science, aesthetic judgements and attention to detail nonetheless played a crucial role in the bourgeois amateur's understanding of science.

David Elliston Allen has drawn historians' attention to the complex relationship between aesthetic pleasure and scientific progress in the realm of natural history. Aesthetic 'tastes and crazes', he notes, shape natural history in particular, in which 'a delight in shapes and colours and patterns ... co-exists with the mere pleasure of acquisition or the sheer satisfaction of having the evidence for some additional item of knowledge'.[79] Investigating the Victorian fern craze, Allen points out the intersections between the discovery of the reproductive mechanism of ferns, research on exotic species, and neo-Gothic taste.[80] Improving on nature's looks – the work of shell or birds' egg 'doctors' – moreover, was a remunerative profession that provided an important service to bourgeois collectors.[81] Similarly, expert taxidermists prided themselves not only on their accurate and pleasing representations of animal life, but also on their ability to produce fake, but life-like, composite species that could fool other naturalists.[82]

Not only did aesthetic judgements find their way into bourgeois science; scientific artefacts could also migrate from the learned society museum to the bourgeois parlour. Commercial taxidermists, for instance, produced animals for both ornamental and scientific purposes; by the 1880s, stuffed birds even found their way onto fashionable ladies' hats (Figure 3 from *Les Modes parisiennes*). One historian of the trade suggests that some early museum bird taxidermy was deliberately dull and lifeless, displaying stiff birds against white paper backdrops, in order to distinguish museum from drawing-room specimens.[83] Henry Havard, arbiter of late nineteenth-century taste in interior décor, clearly approved of animals as ornament: his *L'Art dans la maison* shows bearskin rugs, heads and paws attached, not only in the study and the vestibule, but also the bedroom.[84] The manufacture of inexpensive glass encouraged the display of natural history in the drawing room. From the elaborate Wardian cases containing collections of living ferns to the simpler glass domes that protected stuffed birds from the accumulation of dust, readily available glass changed display practices in both museums and parlours. A vogue for aquariums sent both men and women to ocean-side tidal

Figure 2: from Jean-Luc Mayaud, *Besançon horloger, 1793–1914* (Besançon, 1994).

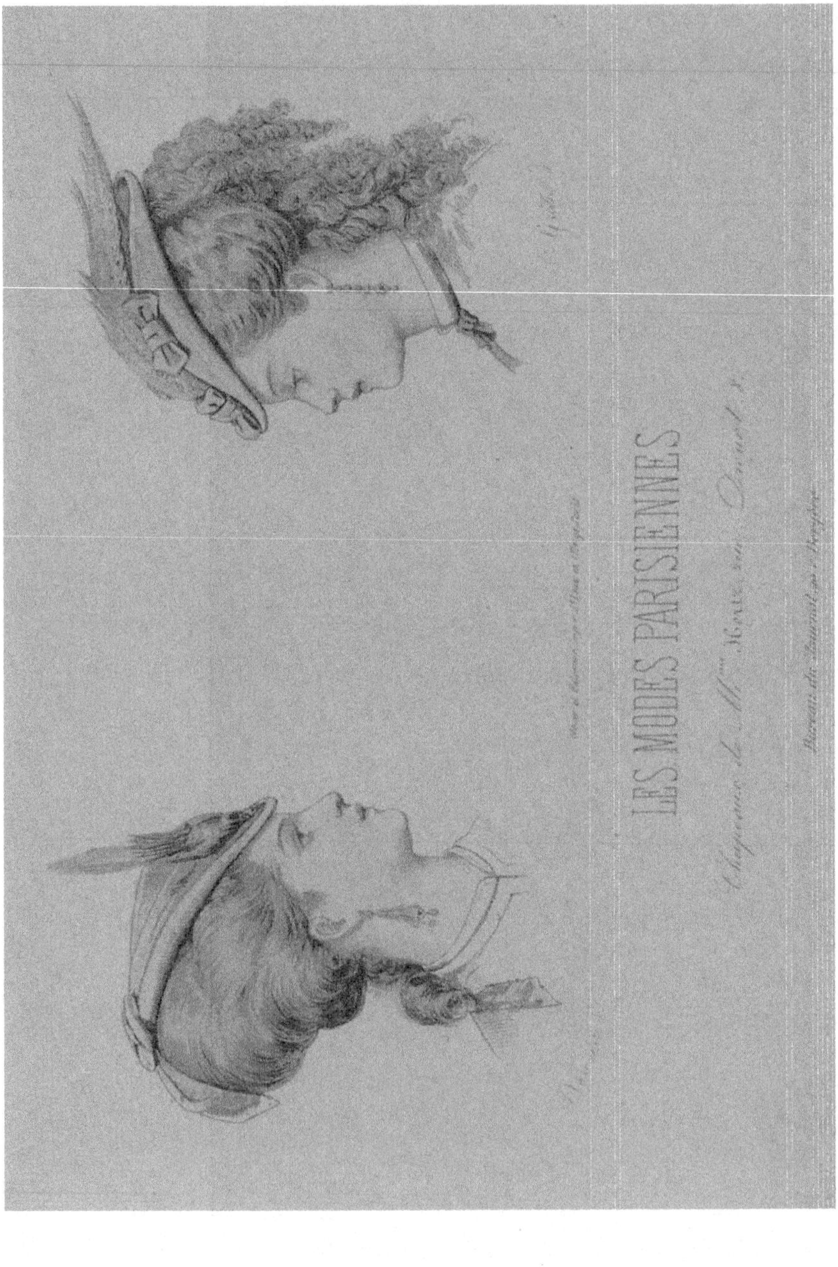

Figure 3: *Les Modes parisiennes*, 17 October 1868. Photograph courtesy of the Kent State University Museum.

pools in search of scientific and decorative sea life.[85] Pictures composed of pressed ferns, seaweed, feathers, and hair manipulated the raw materials of natural history for explicitly feminine and decorative ends.[86] The specimen exhibited in the bourgeois home, of course, was often arranged by the citizen-scientist's wife.

Natural history was not the only realm in which female craft and male science intersected. Studies of bourgeois women's arts, especially in France, are scarce. However, it does appear that the *petits riens* (crafts) that occupied women's idle hands often reflected the same values as the scientific collections with which their menfolk filled their spare time. Madame Celnart's *Complete Manual of Domestic Economy*, for instance, included a chapter on 'amusements' that told its female readers how to preserve dead birds and other animals for stuffing.[87] Her advice book for young ladies included detailed instructions for preserving the colour of butterfly wings and protecting them from other bugs.[88] Would-be botanists who could not draw could create accurate images of flowers and leaves by soaking the specimen in oil, holding it over a candle, then rubbing it between sheets of paper; readers who could draw could transform their work into an imitation engraving with ink, sugar and gum arabic.[89] Other crafts, not specifically oriented toward natural history, also produced imitations of the goods that were of scientific interest to bourgeois *savants*. Decoupage aimed at recreating Asian lacquer – the kinds of exotic imports or travel souvenirs that found their way into learned society museums.[90] Similarly, *potiche*, a craft which was briefly fashionable in the mid-nineteenth century, involved pasting images on the inside of glass vases and then painting the background in oils in an effort to imitate Chinese porcelain.[91] According to the *Journal pour rire*'s illustration (Figure 4), women interested in displaying a well-decorated mantelpiece needed *potiche*, Chinese figurines, and a well-dressed young gentleman as ornaments.

Satirical accounts of women's handicrafts recognised and exploited their similarity to male collections: by the early twentieth century, one commentator bemoaning the decline of taste suggested the establishment of a *musée à rebours* (inverted museum) or a *palais des vilains arts* (palace of the baser arts) to be dominated by women's *bibelots*.[92] Women's hobbies – pressed flowers, feather pictures, imitation lacquer, china painting, leather tooling – constituted an upside-down museum in which the public and universal values of bourgeois science were deployed as drawing-room decoration. The description

Figure 4: advertisement for the *Journal pour rire*, in *Les Modes parisiennes*, 6 March 1852. Photograph Courtesy of the Kent State University Museum.

is reminiscent of Flaubert's account in *A Simple Heart* of the maidservant's room, dominated by a stuffed parrot: Félicité's room 'simultaneously resembled a chapel and a bazaar, stuffed as it was with religious items and odds and ends'.[93] Henry Havard, in his dictionary of furniture styles, could only be grateful that 'the ravages' of *potichomanie*, which produced 'works of mediocre decorative value', were of short duration.[94] It is possible, however, that Havard's dislike of female craft lay in its adherence to and imitation of – not its distance from – the scientific collecting aesthetic.

The display cabinets of bourgeois homes and museums were filled by different methods – the *bourgeoise* shopped and painted and pasted while her husband wrested his trophies from nature or at least from an auction house.[95] Field collecting, in particular, was science conducted in the heroic mode.[96] Men who wandered the countryside collecting their own botanical specimens, lugged rocks across country, and refused to be deterred by the curiosity and derision of local peasants, understood 'natural phenomena through physical exertion and certif[ied] … understanding through risk'.[97] Many men opted for the heroic mode of science even when more modest techniques might produce better results: despite collecting manuals' recommendation that bird hunters use traps or poison, many preferred 'the delights of collecting with a rifle' even at the cost of damaged specimens.[98]

The heroic mode of scientific collection was not, however, immune to consumerism. The naturalist's equipment was increasingly standardised in the early nineteenth century, and the amateur scientist could purchase the most appropriate sample boxes, cork-lined cases, paper for pressing botanical specimens, and collecting jars.[99] Firms like the Maison Verreaux, the nineteenth century's largest commercial supplier of natural history specimens, could offer the scientist-consumer his choice of attractively mounted songbirds or impressive hunting trophies for display in his home.[100] Aesthetic choices did not disappear even for those men who shot their own game: Donna Haraway's recent study notes that scientific collectors looked for a 'typical' specimen, which they defined as a particularly large and handsome representative of the species, which behaved in such a way as to allow the hunter to get off a good, sporting shot.[101] Ironically, commercial suppliers for female crafts complicated the intersection between science and consumerism: women purchased their materials from catalogues that included *musée* (museum) in their titles and followed instructions published in the *Académie des dames*.[102]

Well before the dichotomy of professional and amateur science had established itself, satirists recognised the possibility of undermining the serious, scientific, virile world of bourgeois male sociability. Flaubert, in particular with his heroes Bouvard and Pécuchet, represented male leisure as persistently on the verge of the effeminate. Although these inquiring gentlemen were as sober, scientific, and methodical as any bourgeois amateur, their pastimes always threatened to intersect with the world of women. They sought to understand human psychology through romantic historical fiction; their enthusiasm for chemistry ended in disastrous experiments with food preservation; the study of theology resulted in the kind of emotional piety the nineteenth century associated with women; and their fascination with physiology directed them toward gymnastics and an objectification of their own bodies worthy of any dandy.[103] The antics of Bouvard and Pécuchet are funny, in part, because they always verge on the feminine. To cap it off, their one attempt at romance led to both scientists being duped by the women of their choice: Pécuchet catching a venereal disease from his innocent young servant girl and Bouvard nearly losing his farm to his devoted matronly neighbour.

Like Bouvard and Pécuchet, Jérome Paturot, the eponymous hero of an 1846 novel by Louis Reybaud, sought social position through scientific inquiry. Finding himself in a city rather than in the Norman countryside, Paturot joined learned societies:

> A quite excessive ardour for science suddenly seized me ... Thus, I became a member of philotechnical, entomological, oriental, phrenological, philomathic, numismatic ... geological, philanthropic, linguistical, and geographical societies; societies of antiquarians, of encouragement, of emulation, propagation, and improvement, of fine arts, of shipwrecks, of horticulture, of the history of France, of progressive education, of agricultural progress, of Christian morality; I became a member of all the academies, of all the athenaeums, of all the institutes ...[104]

These multiple memberships did introduce the social-climbing Paturot to the elite, but at the cost of having to sit through meetings where these *savants* 'discover[ed] the Mediterranean twelve times a year on the pretext that some distinguished members had, in their youth, taken part in the Egyptian campaign'.[105]

Like Bouvard and Pécuchet, the *savants* that Jérome Paturot met saw science (and hence their own competence) everywhere. Unlike Flaubert's heroes, however, Paturot had a wife who was not fooled by excessive scientific claims. When a member of the Statistical Society, covered with medals, attempted to convince her that she '[did] statistics without knowing it', Malvina refused to believe that her shopping lists constituted statistics and scornfully asked what sort of pleasure 'monsieur le savant' got out of all that counting. Undeterred, the 'apostle' of statistics announced that 'science is like fire: it purifies everything'.[106] Paturot himself eventually moved on to other pursuits in his search for social position. In the fiction of the mid-nineteenth century, amateur *savants* were muddled figures, full of self-importance, but ultimately unable to distinguish chemistry from cookery, statistics from shopping (Figure 5, Gavarni, scientists from *Le Tiroir du diable*).

By the last decades of the nineteenth century, the potential for mockery of the bourgeois *savant* had become commonplace. The division of the scientific world between amateur and professional had asserted itself, making the learned bourgeois into a comic figure – excessively self-important, blindly convinced of the social and scientific importance of his trivial amusements. Amateurism was not, however, intrinsically funny: the comedy lay in the possible effeminacy of a man who confused the decorative trappings of science for the real thing and who was too enamoured of detail to understand the difference between the scientific and the trivial. The bourgeois amateur definitively became a figure of fun when the professionals monopolised science

Figure 5: Gavarni, *Le Tiroir du diable*.

and defined it in gendered terms that implicitly feminised the non-professional.[107] Amateurs in late nineteenth-century science, like women, were capable of meticulous, repetitive, and imitative work, but not of real science.[108] Professionalisation denied the role of aesthetic pleasure in real science and exposed its fundamental position in the world of the amateur.

The growing status of professional science coincided with the development of a new consensus in favour of a meaningful universal manhood suffrage. Rejecting the Bonapartist formula of electoral manipulation by prefects and local notables, the Third Republic pursued policies to create a literate, and predominantly rural, electorate. By the end of the nineteenth century, republican laws had produced a more democratic male citizenship based on universal primary education rather than on *capacité* understood as an attribute of elite culture. Under such a regime, the earlier attempts of bourgeois *savants* to create an exclusive citizenship based on science and male rationality no longer served any useful purpose. Once the Third Republic was firmly established, no bourgeois man had any doubts about his standing as a full and complete citizen. While he might regret that he shared that status with so many of his social inferiors, amateur science offered him no possibility for remedying the situation.

Under the Third Republic the status of the scientist remained as high as ever, but the Republic's scientists were professionals who looked to universities and research institutes rather than to their local learned society to establish their credentials. Although learned societies survived the demise of the citizen-scientist ideal, they did experience a decline at the turn of the century.[109] Men wishing to claim scientific competence increasingly signed up as corresponding members of large Paris-based societies rather than joining their local learned assembly. These Parisian associations, which established ties to the world of professional science, maintained certain of the sociable traditions of the early nineteenth century, such as the male conviviality of annual banquets. They rejected, however, the notion that local civic leadership was a fundamental aspect of doing science. Moreover, Parisian scientific societies expected their correspondents to provide them with funds via journal subscriptions, not to submit the results of their research in scientific papers. Corresponding membership did not indicate that an individual was truly a scientist: the distinction between the real scientists and the enthusiasts was easily maintained in the *fin de siècle*.

Thus the bourgeois citizen-scientist was the product of the male anxieties generated by the politics of a period in which the universality of manhood suffrage remained in doubt. While science has remained a term to conjure with throughout the modern period, the instability of its social significance has meant that different groups have profited from its elevated status. The exceptional woman of the Enlightenment was briefly able to turn science to good account, using her acknowledged mastery of the subject to broaden her educational and social opportunities. During the revolutionary period, science was largely wrested from her hands, assigned to the public world of male citizens and universal values. Post-revolutionary bourgeois Frenchmen defined science as an element of citizenship and attempted to make both political and social capital from scientific activity. Their attempts to insulate scientific practice from the feminine and the domestic, however, were never completely successful, and by the last decades of the century they had clearly lost control of the rhetoric of science to the emerging professional elite. The principles that distinguished *bibelot* from specimen, masculine 'savoir' from feminine 'savoir-faire', real knowledge from the social niceties,[110] were never as clear as the rigorous application of gender dichotomy would suggest. Bouvard and Pécuchet did indeed discover that scientific method had many defects: among the most prominent, however, was its inability to maintain stable gender connotations for its amateur bourgeois practitioners.

Notes

I wish to acknowledge the assistance of Claire Goldberg Moses, Dena Goodman, Steve Harp, Nina Lerman, Laura Mayhall, the History Department of the Catholic University of America, Anne Bissonnette and Jean Druesedow of the Kent State University Museum, and the anonymous readers of *Gender & History*.

1. Quoted by R. Dumesnil, Introduction, in Flaubert, *Oeuvres* (2 vols; Gallimard, Paris, 1952), vol. 2, p. 704.
2. Geneviève Fraisse, *La Raison des femmes* (Plon, Paris, 1992).
3. Mary Sheriff, *The Exceptional Woman: Elisabeth Vigée-Lebrun and the Cultural Politics of Art* (University of Chicago Press, Chicago, 1996).
4. See especially Londa Schiebinger, *The Mind Has No Sex? Women in the Origins of Modern Science* (Harvard University Press, Cambridge, MA, 1989).
5. Ann B. Shteir, *Cultivating Women, Cultivating Science: Flora's Daughters and Botany in England, 1760 to 1860* (Johns Hopkins University Press, Baltimore, 1996); Pascal Duris, *Linné et la France (1780–1850)* (Librairie Droz, Geneva, 1993), pp. 182–9.
6. Schiebinger, *The Mind Has No Sex?*, pp. 41–4; Erica Harth, *Cartesian Women: Versions and Subversions of Rational Discourse in the Old Regime* (Cornell University Press, Ithaca, NY, 1992); Louis L. Bucciarelli and Nancy Dworsky, *Sophie Germain: An Essay in the History of the Theory of Elasticity* (D. Reidel, Dordrecht, 1980).

7.   Schiebinger, *The Mind Has No Sex?*, pp. 59–65; Harth, *Cartesian Women*, pp. 189–212; Elisabeth Badinter, *Emilie, Emilie: L'Ambition féminine au XVIIIe siècle* (Flammarion, Paris, 1983); Julie Candler Hayes, *Reading the French Enlightenment: System and Subversion* (Cambridge University Press, Cambridge, 1999), ch. 3.

8.   Dorinda Outram, 'Before Objectivity: Wives, Patronage, and Cultural Reproduction in Early Nineteenth-Century French Science', in *Uneasy Careers and Intimate Lives: Women in Science, 1789–1979*, ed. Pnina G. Abir-Am and Dorinda Outram (Rutgers University Press, New Brunswick, 1987), p. 23, notes the importance of salon society in scientific research. For a further account of salon sociability, see Dena Goodman, *The Republic of Letters: A Cultural History of the French Enlightenment* (Cornell University Press, Ithaca, NY, 1994).

9.   Lorraine Daston, 'The Naturalized Female Intellect', *Science in Context*, 5 (1992), pp. 209–35.

10. Krzysztof Pomian, *Collectors and Curiosities: Paris and Venice, 1500–1800*, trans. Elizabeth Wiles-Portier (Polity Press, Cambridge, UK, and Basil Blackwell, Cambridge, MA, 1990), p. 47.

11. Jean-Jacques Rousseau, *Politics and the Arts: Letter to M d'Alembert on the Theatre*, ed. and trans. Allan Bloom (Free Press, Glencoe, 1960), p. 101.

12. See especially Lynn Hunt, *The Family Romance of the French Revolution* (University of California Press, Berkeley, 1992); Sarah Maza, *Private Lives and Public Affairs: The Causes Célèbres of Prerevolutionary France* (University of California Press, Berkeley, 1993).

13. Olympe de Gouges, 'Declaration of the Rights of Woman', in *The French Revolution and Human Rights: A Brief Documentary History*, ed. Lynn Hunt (Bedford Books of St Martin's Press, Boston, 1996), p. 127.

14. Hunt, *Family Romance*; Joan B. Landes, *Women and the Public Sphere in the Age of the French Revolution* (Cornell University Press, Ithaca, NY, 1988); Olwen Hufton, *Women and the Limits of Citizenship in the French Revolution* (University of Toronto Press, Toronto, 1992).

15. Suzanne Desan, '"Constitutional Amazons": Jacobin Women's Clubs in the French Revolution', in *Re-creating Authority in Revolutionary France*, ed. Bryant T. Ragan, Jr, and Elizabeth A. Williams (Rutgers University Press, New Brunswick, 1992), pp. 11–35.

16. Daston, 'The Naturalized Female Intellect', pp. 220–21.

17. See especially Joan Wallach Scott, *Only Paradoxes to Offer: French Feminists and the Rights of Man* (Harvard University Press, Cambridge, MA, 1996); Claire Goldberg Moses and Leslie Wahl Rabine, *Feminism, Socialism, and French Romanticism* (Indiana University Press, Bloomington, 1993); Whitney Walton, *Eve's Proud Descendants: Four Women Writers and Republican Politics in Nineteenth-Century France* (Stanford University Press, Stanford, 2000).

18. Texts of 1814 charter and its 1830 revision in Irene Collins (ed.), *Government and Society in France, 1814–1848* (Edward Arnold, London, 1970), pp. 10–15, 90–1.

19. On the National Guard, see Pierre Rosanvallon, *Le Sacre du citoyen: Histoire du suffrage universel en France* (Gallimard, Paris, 1992), pp. 272–5. On workers' claims to citizenship, see William H. Sewell, Jr, *Work and Revolution in France: The Language of Labor from the Old Regime to 1848* (Cambridge University Press, Cambridge, 1980).

20. On the sociable practices of bourgeois citizenship, see Carol E. Harrison, *The Bourgeois Citizen in Nineteenth-Century France: Gender, Sociability, and the Uses of Emulation* (Oxford University Press, Oxford, 1999).

21. *Dictionnaire des idées reçues*, in *Oeuvres*, vol. 2, p. 1015. On science as a marker of rational masculinity in an American context, see Nina E. Lerman, 'The Uses of Useful Knowledge: Science, Technology, and Social Boundaries in an Industrializing City', *Osiris*, 12 (1997), 39–59.

22. Quoted by Rosanvallon, *Le Sacre du citoyen*, pp. 233, 232.

23. On moral distrust of the market, see Victoria Thompson, *The Virtuous Market: Women and Men, Money and Politics in Paris, 1830–1870* (Johns Hopkins University Press, Baltimore, 2000).

24. Both were included in the final text of the national electoral law of 19 April 1831 on condition that they paid at least half of the *cens,* the taxation threshold required for voting. (Rosanvallon, *Le Sacre du citoyen*, p. 241).

25. All were initially included in the government's proposal for the 1831 electoral law. (Rosanvallon, *Le Sacre du citoyen*, p. 241).

26. All were admitted to suffrage in municipal elections by the law of 21 March 1831. (Rosanvallon, *Le Sacre du citoyen*, p. 240).

27. Quoted by Rosanvallon, *Le Sacre du citoyen*, p. 239.

28. Guizot, quoted by Rosanvallon, *Le Sacre du citoyen*, p. 237.

29. Rosanvallon, *Le Sacre du citoyen*, p. 230.

30. Members of the *Institut* who paid half of the *cens* could vote in national elections, and members of approved learned societies could vote in local contests. Jean-Pierre Chaline, *Sociabilité et érudition: les sociétés savantes en France, XIXe–XXe siècles* (Editions du CTHS, Paris, 1995), p. 73.

31. Quoted by M. P. in 'Préface', *Travaux de la Société d'Emulation du Jura* (1919), p. xviii. On museum patronage under the Second Empire, see Daniel Sherman, *Worthy Monuments: Art Museums and the Politics of Culture in Nineteenth-Century France* (Harvard University Press, Cambridge, MA, 1989). For a discussion of the relationship between citizens and the state under Bonapartism, see Sudhir Hazreesingh, *From Subject to Citizen: The Second Empire and the Emergence of Modern French Democracy* (Princeton University Press, Princeton, NJ, 1998).

32. On nineteenth-century French learned societies, see Harrison, *The Bourgeois Citizen*, ch. 3; Chaline, *Sociabilité et érudition*; Gonzague Tierny, *Les Sociétés savantes du département de la Somme de 1870 à 1914* (Editions du CTHS, Paris, 1987); Robert Fox, 'Learning, Politics, and Polite Culture in Provincial France: The *Sociétés Savantes* in the Nineteenth Century', *Historical Reflections/Réflexions historiques*, 7 (1980), pp. 543–64, and 'The *Savant* Confronts his Peers: Scientific Societies in France, 1815–1914', in *The Organization of Science and Technology in France, 1808–1914*, ed. Robert Fox and George Weisz (Cambridge University Press, Cambridge, 1980), pp. 241–82; and *Les Sociétés savantes, leur histoire*, Actes du 100e colloque national des sociétés savantes (Bibliothèque nationale, Paris, 1976).

33. For a statistical treatment of learned society membership, see Chaline, *Sociabilité et érudition*.

34. The Industrial Society of Mulhouse, for instance, regularly offered prizes for technical improvements in cloth production, the town's main industry. Prize lists are in Archives départementales du Haut Rhin, 9 M 18. The 1865 water quality study was sponsored by the Emulation Society of the Jura. Correspondence in the Archives de la Société d'Emulation du Jura, 12 J 7.

35. Report of the jury for the watchmaking section of the Exposition of 1860, sponsored by Besançon's Emulation Society of the Doubs, in Archives Communales de Besançon F₃4.

36. Alphonse Deis, 'Barbizier à l'exposition', Bibliothèque municipale de Besançon, ms 1640, published as *Promenade à l'exposition universelle de Besançon* (P. Ducret, Besançon, 1860).

37. Chauvelot, 'Chronique', *Bulletin periodique publié par la Société d'agriculture et par la Société d'horticulture du Doubs*, 8 and 9 (1867).

38. Undated report on the zoology of the Jura by Dr Brillon, from the Archives de la Société d'Emulation du Jura, 12 J 1.

39. Speech from the 1857 annual banquet of the Emulation Society of the Doubs, in *Mémoires de la Société d'Emulation du Doubs* (1857).

40. On private and public interest, see William M. Reddy, *The Invisible Code: Honor and Sentiment in Postrevolutionary France, 1814–1848* (University of California Press, Berkeley, 1997).

41. My discussion of bourgeois citizenship as simultaneously universal and exclusive derives from Jürgen Habermas, *The Structural Transformation of the Public Sphere: An Inquiry into a Category of Bourgeois Society*, trans. Thomas Burger (MIT Press, Cambridge, MA, 1989), esp. pp. 85–7.

42. My discussion of the 'pressure of gender' draws on Dror Wahrman's account of roughly contemporary English anxieties, which he labels 'gender panic': 'Percy's Prologue: From Gender Play to Gender Panic in Eighteenth-Century England', *Past and Present*, 159 (1998), pp. 113–60. On the ideology of 'separate spheres' in France, see Bonnie G. Smith, *Ladies of the Leisure Class: The Bourgeoises of Northern France in the Nineteenth Century* (Princeton University Press, Princeton, NJ, 1981) and Michèle Perrot (ed.), *A History of Private Life*, vol. 4, *From the Fires of Revolution to the Great War*, trans. A. Goldhammer (Belknap Press of Harvard University Press, Cambridge, MA, 1990).

43. On masculinity and professionalisation, see Robert A. Nye, 'Medicine and Science as Masculine "Fields of Honor"', *Osiris*, 12 (1997), pp. 60–79.

44. Charles Louandré, 'Les Sociétés savantes et littéraires de la province', *Revue des deux mondes* (1846), p. 797. On old regime academies, see Daniel Roche, *Le Siècle de lumières en province: Académies et académiciens provinciaux, 1680–1789* (2 vols; Mouton, Paris, 1978). In the very first years of the century there was a vogue for poetry that took science as its subject. Jean Dhombres, 'La Gloire de la science: Culture et poésie vers 1800', *Revue d'histoire moderne et contemporaine*, 39 (1992), pp. 551–71.

45. Harrison, *The Bourgeois Citizen*, p. 220. Vocal music, however, spread rapidly throughout the *petite bourgeoisie* and the working class. See Paul Gerbod, 'L'Institution orphéonique en France du XIXe au XXe siècle', *Ethnologie française*, 10 (1980), pp. 27–44.

46. Raymonde Moulin, 'Les Bourgeois amis des arts: Les Expositions de beaux-arts en province, 1885–1887', *Revue française de sociologie*, 17 (1976), pp. 383–422.

47. 'Notice par M Demerson sur les plantes vénéneuses du Jura', *Travaux de la Société d'Emulation du Jura* (1842), Séance publique du 18 septembre 1842. 'Utility', in this case, was offered to the society's members as a discreet apology for the presentation of an extremely dull catalogue. On the notion of utility in scientific voluntary associations, see Michael A. Osborne, 'Applied Natural History and Utilitarian Ideals: "Jacobin Science" at the Muséum d'Histoire Naturelle, 1789–1870', in *Re-creating Authority in Revolutionary France*, ed. Bryant T. Ragan, Jr, and Elizabeth Williams (Rutgers University Press, New Brunswick, 1992), pp. 137–8.

48. *Dictionnaire des idées reçues*, in *Oeuvres*, vol. 2, p. 1000.

49. On bourgeois attempts to define leisure in productive terms by invoking the authority of science, see Douglas Peter Mackaman, *Leisure Settings: Bourgeois Culture, Medicine, and the Spa in Modern France* (University of Chicago Press, Chicago, 1998) and Arnold Thackray, 'Natural Knowledge in Cultural Context: The Manchester Model', *American Historical Review*, 79 (1974), pp. 572–709.

50. Whitney Walton, *France at the Crystal Palace: Bourgeois Taste and Artisan Manufacture* (University of California Press, Berkeley, 1992); Philippe Perrot, *Fashioning the Bourgeoisie: A History of Clothing in the Nineteenth Century*, trans. Richard Bienvenu (Princeton University Press, Princeton, NJ, 1994); David Kuchta, 'The Making of the Self-Made Man: Class, Clothing, and English Masculinity', in *The Sex of Things: Gender and Consumption in Historical Perspective*, ed. Victoria deGrazia and Ellen Furlough (University of California Press, Berkeley, 1996), pp. 54–78; and Leora Auslander, *Taste and Power, Furnishing Modern France* (University of California Press, Berkeley, 1996) all address aspects of the gendering of taste and display.

51. Sheriff, *The Exceptional Woman*, pp. 193–5.

52. Naomi Schor, *Reading in Detail: Aesthetics and the Feminine* (Methuen, New York, 1987); Jeffrey Kallberg, *Chopin at the Boundaries: Sex, History, and Musical Genre* (Harvard University Press, Cambridge, MA, 1996); Michael Fried, *Absorption and Theatricality: Painting and Beholder in the Age of Diderot* (University of Chicago Press, Chicago, 1980); Susan McClary, *Feminine Endings: Music, Gender, Sexuality* (University of Minnesota Press, Minneapolis, 1991), ch. 1. Early entomologists often found their studies dismissed as trivial because of their tiny subjects: Anne Larson Hollerbach, 'Of Sangfroid and Sphinx Moths: Cruelty, Public Relations, and the Growth of Entomology in England, 1800–1840', *Osiris*, 11 (1996), pp. 209–11.

53. On the astonishing numbers of women in nineteenth-century Paris who had some facility at the piano, see Arthur Loesser, *Men, Women, and Pianos: A Social History* (Simon and Schuster, New York, 1954), pp. 386–7.

54. Kallberg, *Chopin at the Boundaries*, pp. 41–3, and James H. Johnson, *Listening in Paris: A Cultural History* (University of California Press, Berkeley, 1995), ch. 13.

55. On women's self-representation in the visual arts, see Anne Higonnet, 'Secluded Vision: Images of Feminine Experience in Nineteenth-Century Europe', *Radical History Review*, 38 (1987), pp. 16–36, and Anne Higonnet, *Berthe Morisot's Images of Women* (Harvard University Press, Cambridge, MA, 1992), ch. 3.

56. On the early nineteenth-century vogue for female poets, see Anne Martin-Fugier, *La Vie élégante ou la formation du Tout-Paris, 1815–1848* (Fayard, Paris, 1990) ch. 9, and on Gay, see Walton, *Eve's Proud Descendants*. On the association of some forms of poetry with female competence, see Dena Goodman's account of a late eighteenth-century deliberation concerning the correct attribution of a poem, which concluded that it might have been written by a self-taught young girl because its subject was love (*The Republic of Letters*, p. 246).

57. Janis Bergman-Carton, *The Woman of Ideas in French Art, 1830–1848* (Yale University Press, New Haven, 1995). See also Higonnet, 'Secluded Vision', on female artists and fashion illustration.

58. Smith, *Ladies of the Leisure Class*; Anne Martin-Fugier, *La Bourgeoise: Femme au temps de Paul Bourget* (B. Grasset, Paris, 1983).

59. Thomas Crow, *Emulation: Making Artists for Revolutionary France* (Yale University Press, New Haven, 1995). See also Abigail Solomon-Godeau, *Male Trouble: A Crisis in Representation* (Thames and Hudson, London, 1997), pp. 46–61.

60. Sheriff, *The Exceptional Woman*; W. J. T. Mitchell, *Iconology: Image, Text, Ideology* (University of Chicago Press, Chicago, 1986), pp. 129–31; Anne K. Mellor, *Romanticism and Gender* (Routledge, New York, 1993).

61. Mary Jean Corbett, 'Producing the Professional: Wordsworth, Carlyle and the Authorial Self', ch. 1 of *Representing Femininity: Middle-Class Subjectivity in Victorian and Edwardian Women's Autobiographies* (Oxford University Press, New York, 1992), pp. 17–55; and Norma Clark, 'Strenuous Idleness: Thomas Carlyle and the Man of Letters as Hero', in *Manful Assertions: Masculinities in Britain since 1800*, ed. Michael Roper and John Tosh (Routledge, London, 1991).

62. By the *fin de siècle* professionalism and the marketability of the artist's production were no longer adequate guarantees against the suggestion of effeminacy. See Venita Datta, 'Intellectuals, Honor, and Manhood at the Fin-de-Siècle: The Literary Avant-Garde's Defense of Oscar Wilde', *Proceedings of the Western Society for French History*, 23 (1996), pp. 166–74.

63. Martin-Fugier, *La Vie élégante*, ch. 12. Note that 'effeminacy' rather than homosexuality was the charge levelled at dandies. Indeed, one of the often-deplored aspects of dandified life was the expenditure of large sums of money on mistresses. As scholars of homosexuality such as George Chauncey have suggested, early nineteenth-century understandings of manhood did not dichotomise themselves into a homosexual/heterosexual opposition. *Gay New York: Gender, Urban Culture, and the Making of the Gay Male World, 1890–1940* (Basic Books, New York, 1994), esp. pp. 12–14. On effeminacy, see G. J. Barker-Benfield, *The Culture of Sensibility: Sex and Society in Eighteenth-Century Britain* (University of Chicago Press, Chicago, 1992), ch. 3.

64. The effeminate connotations of 'taste' were not limited to the world of dandies. See also Auslander's discussion of male 'taste professionals' whose advice directed women in the furnishing of their homes and the decoration of their persons (*Taste and Power*, pp. 248–50).

65. Chaline, *Sociabilité et érudition*, pp. 189–93; Charles-Olivier Carbonnell, *Histoire et historiens: une mutation idéologique des historiens français, 1865–1885* (Privat, Toulouse, 1976), pp. 78–90.

66. Michèle Cohen's study of English education notes a similar definition of the grammar of
     dead languages as scientific and masculine as opposed to the feminine connotations of oral
     fluency in modern languages (*Fashioning Masculinity: National Identity and Language in
     the Eighteenth Century* (Routledge, London, 1996), p. 102.

67. Henri Monnier, *Mémoires de Monsieur Joseph Prudhomme*, vol. 2 (Librairie nouvelle, Paris,
     1857), pp. 28, 71–2.

68. In a large body of literature, see especially Robert Fox, 'Science, the University, and the
     State in Nineteenth-Century France', in *Professions and the French State, 1700–1900*, ed.
     Gerald L. Geison (University of Pennsylvania Press, Philadelphia, 1984), pp. 66–145.

69. Outram, 'Before Objectivity', pp. 28–9; Michel Hau, *L'Industrialisation de l'Alsace,
     1803–1939* (Association des Publications près les Universités de Strasbourg, Strasbourg,
     1987), pp. 406–7.

70. Jean-Pierre Chaline, 'Les Sociétés savantes au XIXe siècle', *Bulletin de la Société Libre
     d'Emulation de la Seine Maritime* (1993), p. 7.

71. *L'Impartial*, 12 August 1846 and *Le Patriote franc-comtois*, 18 March 1832. Both
     descriptions are of the Academy of Besançon, a notoriously conservative organisation that
     regularly drew fire from the liberal press.

72. Louandré, 'Les Sociétés savantes et littéraires de la province', p. 801.

73. 3 April and 26 June 1852.

74. Description of and correspondence concerning the map are in dossier 12 J 7 of the
     Archives of the Société d'Emulation du Jura.

75. President of the Société d'horticulture to prefect (Haut Rhin), 15 January 1864. Archives
     départementales du Haut Rhin 7 M 37. Most horticultural associations established
     patronage schemes for local market gardeners.

76. As an example of learned societies' statistical complications, see the *Statistique du Haut
     Rhin* (Mulhouse, 1833), produced by the Industrial Society of Mulhouse. See also Catherine
     Kudlick's account of changing uses of cholera statistics ('The Culture of Statistics and the
     Crisis of Cholera in Paris, 1830–1850', in *Re-creating Authority in Revolutionary France*,
     ed. Bryant T. Ragan, Jr, and Elizabeth A. Williams (Rutgers University Press, New
     Brunswick, 1992), pp. 98–124).

77. Carbonnell, *Histoire et historiens*, pp. 112–126, notes that it was not until the end of the
     century that learned societies moved from the 'édition passive' of historical sources to an
     'édition critique', which included notes, indices, and interpretative prefaces. Throughout
     the 1840s the Academy of Besançon depended on state support granted for an edition
     of the papers of Cardinal Granvelle, a sixteenth-century diplomat in Habsburg service.
     (Financial records in Archives départementales du Doubs, 1 T 462.) The Academy also
     made reproductions of all medieval Franc-Comtois seals.

78. The Jura and the Doubs are two departments of the former province of the Franche
     Comté, which is on the Swiss border. Bruand's catalogue of the caterpillars of the Doubs
     dominated all issues of the *Mémoires de la Société d'Emulation du Doubs* from 1841 to
     1851. See 'Notice par M Demerson' for venomous plants and Jean Cousin, *L'Académie
     de sciences, belles lettres et arts de Besançon, Deux cents ans de vie comtoise (1752–1952) essai
     de synthèse* (J. Ledoux, Besançon, 1954), pp. 166–70. Cousin's work itself fits into this
     taxonomic tradition.

79. David Elliston Allen, 'Tastes and Crazes', in *Cultures of Natural History*, ed. N. Jardine,
     J. A. Secord, and E. C. Spary (Cambridge University Press, Cambridge, 1996), p. 394.

80. David Elliston Allen, *The Victorian Fern Craze: A History of Pteridomania* (Hutchinson,
     London, 1969). Obsession with ferns appears to have been largely an English phenomenon.

81. Allen, 'Tastes and Crazes', pp. 395–6. By the early nineteenth century, collectors rejected
     repaired or 'doctored' shells and concentrated instead on elaborating techniques for
     maintaining a more 'natural' beauty (S. Peter Dance, *Shell Collecting: An Illustrated History*
     (University of California Press, Berkeley, 1966), pp. 80–1, 128–9). See also Larson
     Hollerbach's discussion of English conchology, in which the desire for attractive shells won
     out over a concern with killing living specimens ('Of Sangfroid and Sphinx Moths', p. 206).

82. Karen Wonders, *Habitat Dioramas: Illusions of Wilderness in Museums of Natural History* (Almqvist & Wiksell International, Uppsala, 1993), pp. 26, 33. Wonders also notes that the early nineteenth-century spread of French technical innovations, in particular the use of arsenic preparations to protect stuffed animals from bugs, was crucial to taxidermy's popularity (p. 25).

83. Wonders, *Habitat Dioramas*, p. 27. Susan Leigh Starr argues that taxidermy's explicit aesthetic concerns helped prevent its emergence as a formally organised profession ('Craft vs. Commodity, Mess vs. Transcendence: How the Right Tool Became the Wrong One in the Case of Taxidermy and Natural History', in *The Right Tools for the Job: At Work in Twentieth-Century Life Sciences*, ed. Adele E. Clarke and Joan H. Fujimora (Princeton University Press, Princeton, 1992), pp. 257–86).

84. Henry Havard, *L'Art dans la maison (grammaire de l'ameublement)*, 4th edn (E. Rouveyre et Librairie illustrée, Paris, n.d. (1883?)), plates facing pp. 292, 352, 388.

85. David Elliston Allen, *The Naturalist in Britain: A Social History*, 2nd edn (Princeton University Press, Princeton, 1994), pp. 112–13. On seaside social practices, see Alain Corbin, *The Lure of the Sea: The Discovery of the Seaside in the Western World, 1750–1840*, trans. Jocelyn Phelps (University of California Press, Berkeley, 1994).

86. Allen, 'Taste and Crazes' and *The Victorian Fern Craze*. On taxidermy as interior decoration, see Anne Larsen, 'Equipment for the Field', in *Cultures of Natural History*, ed. N. Jardine, J. A. Secord, and E. C. Spary (Cambridge University Press, Cambridge, 1996), pp. 358–77. Peter Wagner, 'Flower Gardens, Flower Fashions, and Illustrated Botanical Works: Observations from a Botanist's Point of View', in *Flowers into Art: Floral Motifs in European Painting and Decorative Arts*, ed. Vibeke Woldbye (SDU Publishers, The Hague, 1991), pp. 9–23, notes that while botanical art – both for scientific and decorative purposes – was held in high esteem by both sexes in the late seventeenth and early eighteenth centuries, it was increasingly feminised by the late eighteenth century. Fewer deluxe editions of botanical prints sold, botanical motifs disappeared from male dress, and china painting became the major outlet for floral art. See also, in the same volume, Charlotte Paludan, 'A Beguiling Similarity: A Contribution to the History of Artificial Flowers', pp. 116–26.

87. Madame Celnart (Elisabeth-Félicie Bayle-Mouillard), *Manuel complet d'économie domestique, contenant toutes les recettes les plus simples et les plus efficaces sur l'économie rurale et domestique, à l'usage de la ville et de la campagne*, 2nd edn (Roret, Paris, 1829), pp. 244–7.

88. Madame Celnart (Elisabeth-Félicie Bayle-Mouillard), *Manuel des demoiselles ou Arts et métiers qui leur conviennent et dont elles peuvent s'occuper avec agrément, tels que la couture, la broderie, le tricot, la dentelle, la tapisserie, les bourses, les ouvrages en filet, en chenille, en ganse, en perles, en cheveux, etc., etc.*, 5th edn (J. Dewaet, Brussels, 1830), pp. 301–5.

89. Celnart, *Manuel de l'économie domestique*, p. 232.

90. Dee Davis, *Decoupage: Paper Cutouts for Decoration and Pleasure* (Thames and Hudson, New York, 1995), ch. 1. In the eighteenth century, decoupage appears also to have interested men. The Lennox sisters enlisted their sons who made the grand tour to select engravings for print rooms (Stella Tillyard, *Aristocrats: Caroline, Emily, and Sarah Lennox, 1740–1832* (Farrar, Straus and Giroux, New York, 1994)) and one Parisian journal claimed that 'no one speaks of anything but decoupage … Whenever a gentleman appears in a lady's house, he is given a picture, he pulls his scissors out of his pocket and starts on the decoupage. Knowing how to do decoupage is a new kind of merit' (*Mercure* of December 1727, quoted by Henry Havard, *Dictionnaire de l'ameublement et de la décoration* (4 vols; Quantin, Librairies imprimeries réunies, Paris, n.d.), vol. 2, pp. 52–3.) See also Jean Grand-Carteret, *Vieux papiers, vieilles images: Cartons d'un collectionneur* (A. Le Vasseur, Paris, 1896), pp. 295–7.

91. Davis, *Decoupage*, ch. 1.

92. Georges de Montenach, *La Formation du goût dans l'art et dans la vie* (Fribourg, 1914), quoted by Martin-Fugier, *La Bourgeoise*, p. 172. Ironically, avant-garde art – which would

ultimately reclaim handicraft techniques such as decoupage and china painting for fine art – was to be exhibited next to female handicraft in this exposition of bad taste.

93. Flaubert, *Oeuvres*, vol. 2, p. 617.

94. Havard, *Dictionnaire*, vol. 4, p. 572, and vol. 2, p. 54.

95. On the gendered implications of shopping and male collecting, see Auslander, *Taste and Power*, pp. 295–302.

96. On the 'heroic mode' of science, see Naomi Oreskes, 'Objectivity or Heroism? On the Invisibility of Women in Science', and Bruce Hevly, 'The Heroic Science of Glacier Motion', both in *Osiris*, 11 (1996), pp. 87–113 and 66–86; Roy Porter, 'Gentlemen and Geology: The Emergence of a Scientific Career, 1660–1920', *Historical Journal*, 21 (1978), pp. 809–36.

97. Hevly, 'The Heroic Science', p. 84. On the ridicule that wandering naturalists attracted, see Allen, *The Naturalist in Britain*, pp. 137–8, and Larsen, 'Equipment for the Field', pp. 373–5.

98. Larsen, 'Equipment for the Field', p. 370. Larsen also notes that the appeal of birds was aesthetic as well as scientific, as birds (unlike, for instance fish and insects) held their colour after death. See also Allen, *The Naturalist in Britain*, p. 127, who notes that the introduction of the percussion principle during the Napoleonic Wars improved the utility of guns for shooting birds (previously the flash of igniting powder had warned birds of danger before the shot was fired). Further improvements (in particular, breech-loading, developed in France in the 1850s) made shooting even more practical for the collector.

99. Bouvard and Pécuchet's hobbies invariably required sending off to Paris for a long list of tools and equipment. See Larsen, 'Equipment for the Field'; Allen, *The Naturalist in Britain*, pp. 113–4 (on microscopes), 137–40; Dance, *Shell Collecting*, pp. 126–9.

100. Wonder, *Habitat Dioramas*, pp. 34–7.

101. Donna Haraway, 'Teddy Bear Patriarchy: Taxidermy in the Garden of Eden, New York City, 1908–1936', in *Culture/Power/History: A Reader in Contemporary Social Theory*, ed. Nicholas B. Dirks, et al. (Princeton University Press, Princeton, NJ, 1994), p. 66.

102. On the periodical literature of the *musée*, see Chantal Georgel, 'The Museum as Metaphor in Nineteenth-Century France', in *Museum Culture: Histories, Discourses, Spectacles*, ed. Daniel J. Sherman and Irit Rotgoff (University of Minnesota Press, Minneapolis, 1994), pp. 113–22. Georgel also notes that museums and department stores borrowed display techniques from one another. The *Académie des dames: Livre des arts faciles* was the bonus offered to subscribers of *Les Modes parisiennes*.

103. *Bouvard et Pécuchet* in *Oeuvres*, vol. 2, pp. 826–7 on psychology; pp. 758–61 on food preservation; pp. 920–44 on Catholicism; and pp. 879–82 on gymnastics.

104. Louis Reybaud, *Jérome Paturot à la recherche d'une position sociale* (J.-J. Dubochet Le Chevalier et cie., Paris, 1846), p. 278.

105. Reybaud, *Jérome Paturot*, p. 275.

106. Reybaud, *Jérome Paturot*, p. 274.

107. Bonnie Smith has recently described this process in the historical profession: *The Gender of History: Men, Women, and Historical Practice* (Harvard University Press, Cambridge, MA, 1998).

108. Oreskes, 'Objectivity or Heroism?'

109. Fox, 'Learning, Politics, and Polite Culture in Provincial France', pp. 557–8.

110. Martin-Fugier, *La Bourgeoise*, p. 166.

The Rhetorics of Slavery and Citizenship: Suffragist Discourse and Canonical Texts in Britain, 1880–1914

Laura E. Nym Mayhall

In a June 1912 editorial in the suffragette newspaper *Votes for Women*, Christabel Pankhurst, leader of the controversial Women's Social and Political Union (WSPU), explained the rationale behind suffragette militancy. 'Women', she wrote, 'are essentially moral beings. In asking them to adopt a militant policy, it is not enough to convince them that the policy is expedient and effective. They must also be convinced that it is morally right.' Pankhurst then recited a litany of justifications for women's resistance to state authority in their struggle for the parliamentary vote, culminating in a paean to Italian nationalist leaders Garibaldi and Mazzini that drew explicit parallels between the causes of British suffragism and Italian nationalism. Pankhurst's statement is worth quoting at some length:

> Now Woman Suffrage is not an international matter; it is a civil matter. It is not a case of one nation being held in bondage by another nation. It is a case of one sex being held in bondage by the other sex. It is not the freeing of Italy that is in question; it is the freeing of women. Yet the principle at stake is the same. Just as Italy was kept down by the strong hand, so women are kept in subjection by the strong hand. Provided there is not active and effective challenge of the political supremacy of the other sex, the fact is hidden, but let that challenge be offered, and at once the physical force measures at the disposal of the state are brought into play ... We have said that whether the domination complained

of be that of a nation by a nation, or a sex by a sex, the principle at stake is the same, and by that we mean that just as active resistance to that domination is needed in the one case, so it is needed in the other.[1]

Pankhurst's formulation, the moral necessity for active resistance to the domination of women by men, remains central to historians' explanations for British suffragettes' use of militancy after 1903. Motivated by an essentially spiritual impulse, militancy manifested itself in various acts of bodily sacrifice, most notably the suffragette hunger strike.[2]

Careful attention to the language with which Pankhurst articulated these demands, however, suggests a different trajectory for militancy's origins and subsequent development. Following political theorist Linda Zerilli, who has defined politics 'as a realm of speech', and the citizen 'as a speaking being',[3] this article explores the nineteenth-century roots of suffragettes' political language by placing in dialogue two texts central to the shaping of suffragist subjectivities in Britain: John Stuart Mill's *The Subjection of Women* and Giuseppe Mazzini's *The Duties of Man*.[4] Read and discussed by three generations of feminists, these two texts shaped the rhetorical and strategic possibilities of the campaign for women's parliamentary enfranchisement in Britain. Reading Mill and Mazzini in dialogue made available to suffragists new ways of thinking about women in relation to the realm of the political. Slavery and tyranny operate by analogy in both texts to limit and expand the domain inhabited by women.

Recovering the significance of particular texts to the making of political subjectivity remains a speculative pursuit.[5] That *The Subjection of Women* and *The Duties of Man* were read widely by political activists, including suffragists, in the late nineteenth and early twentieth centuries can be established easily. Both books went through numerous editions in the years between publication and the outbreak of the First World War. *The Subjection of Women*, completed in 1861 but not published until 1869, was released simultaneously by publishers in London, New York, and Philadelphia. A second edition was issued in London in 1869, with five more British editions by 1883.[6] With renewed interest in the question of women's suffrage in Britain at the turn of the century, a new edition of the text was released in 1906, with introductory comments by Stanton Coit, president of the West London Ethical Society and husband of a member of the militant suffrage organisation the Women's Freedom League. This edition was re-issued in 1909 and again in 1924.[7] *The Subjection of Women* was published again in 1912, in an edition introduced by Millicent Garrett Fawcett, and reprinted some fourteen times by 1974. *The Duties of Man* underwent a similar schedule of publication and re-publication after its appearance in 1858. Translated by Emilie Ashurst Venturi and published in English for the first time in 1862, Mazzini's text was picked up by J. M. Dent and Sons' series Everyman's Library, and was issued first in 1894, then again in 1907, 1910, 1912, 1915, and on until 1955. *The Duties of Man* was also available from 1890, in a six-volume set of Mazzini's writings issued by a London publisher.[8]

The intellectual influence of Mill's text has been well documented. Controversial at the time of its release, the text was welcomed enthusiastically by feminists and was to shape feminist argumentation well into the twentieth century.[9] Virtually every major player in nineteenth- and twentieth-century women's suffrage campaigns attests to Mill's significance. In 1884, suffragist Millicent Garrett Fawcett lauded Mill for drawing attention to the artificiality of women's disabilities. Looking back at her political commitments from the vantage point of the 1930s, Helena Swanwick confirmed the role played by *The Subjection of Women* in bringing her to feminism. Suffragette praise for Mill's text continued even into the more violent stages of militancy, with Christabel Pankhurst and Emmeline Pethick-Lawrence, prominent members of the WSPU, asserting its singular influence. And at least one militant suffrage organisation, the Women's Freedom League, organised annual processions to Mill's statue in Victoria Tower Gardens on the occasion of his birth well into the 1920s. Anti-suffragist writings provide yet further evidence of Mill's influence as they routinely referred to *The Subjection of Women* as 'the Suffragist's Bible'. One opponent of women's suffrage noted of the text in 1912: 'Nothing in their cause is not contained in its pages, and everything that can be said in favour of their cause is there said much better than they themselves can say it.'[10]

The impact of Mazzini's *Duties of Man* on nineteenth- and twentieth-century suffragism is documented less clearly. Certainly, as historians Margot Finn and Eugenio Biagini have shown, Mazzini was embraced as a 'prophet of democracy' by working- and middle-class radicals alike, male and female.[11] Evidence of Mazzini's influence is seen also in frequent references to his writings and life throughout suffragist publications. The National Union of Women's Suffrage Societies embraced Mazzini as a supporter of women's suffrage in 1912; Charlotte Despard, socialist and president of the Women's

Freedom League, wrote eloquently of his influence on her own understanding of political struggle.[12] It appears that Mazzini had achieved
canonical status within certain circles of British radical thinking, for
suffragists frequently appealed to his authority without making the
kind of careful textual citation that would indicate the derivation of
an idea from a specific text.[13] This is clear, for example, in Emmeline
Pethick-Lawrence's 1907 pamphlet *The Meaning of the Woman's
Movement*. Pethick-Lawrence stands on Mazzini's authority when she
argues that man and woman are two halves of humanity, an idea well
developed in *The Duties of Man*, but present in other of his writings as
well.[14] Two dicta attributed to Mazzini appear regularly throughout
suffragette writing in the early twentieth century: his definition
of democracy as 'the progress of all through all under the guidance of
the wisest and the best', and his admonition that 'War is the eternal
law that stands between the master and the slave'.[15]

At first glance, reading Mill and Mazzini in dialogue would appear
to bring together dichotomous ways of thinking. Much twentieth-
century scholarship on Mill posits a philosophy entrenched in the
ideological excesses of individualism, representing the moral bankruptcy
of liberalism, especially that associated with laisser-faire economics.
Late twentieth-century feminists have been quick to excoriate Mill
for his less radical positions, as measured against those held by his
wife Harriet Taylor Mill.[16] In contrast, Mazzini, as Margot Finn has
demonstrated, stood for 'a philosophy that emphasized the primacy
of duties over rights ... [appealing] to radical artisans by advancing
the nation's collective claims alongside (and at times above) those of
the individual, who figured in Mazzini's thinking less as an autonomous
agent than as a component of the Commonwealth'.[17] However, more
recent scholarship on Mill as a public moralist, to borrow Stefan
Collini's phrase, points to affinities between the writings of the two
men that captivated nineteenth- and twentieth-century suffragists,
particularly a belief in the ennobling effects of participation in public
life, for men and women.[18] Both men embraced what Frances Power
Cobbe in 1884 would describe as politics as 'a branch of ethics'.[19]
Both texts also grapple with questions fundamental to late-Victorian
and Edwardian campaigns for women's parliamentary enfranchisement: What role does force play in constituting the authority of the
state? And how best to reconstitute the state in order that the consent
of the governed, and not force, should underlie the state's authority?
Fundamentally, both texts rely upon extensive engagement with the

ideas of slavery and tyranny to move women from the realm of the
social to the political. It is in the bosom of the family that political
life resides; both Mill and Mazzini argue in favour of using the family
as leverage to vault women from the domestic to the political narrowly
conceived. Both men attribute the subordination of women to
custom and a lack of education.[20] Both men share the insight that the
private realm of family life lies embedded in the heart of public life,
and that it is in this realm that previously underexamined relations of
dominance and subordination must be corrected. Mazzini insists that
the 'scope and object of the Family is to educate [men/women] as
citizens', and Mill argues that 'the family, justly constituted, would be
the real school of the virtues of freedom'.[21]

Central to Mill's argument in *The Subjection of Women* is a belief
that the root of all tyranny is in the family, specifically within the
sexual subordination of women. He writes in chapter 1, 'Not a word
can be said for despotism in the family which cannot be said for
political despotism,' suggesting that the family is the nation, writ
small. Whatever tyranny exists in the state mirrors the tyranny enacted
in the family.[22] Feminist argumentation after 1869 followed from
the fundamental insight that the source of tyranny was in the home.
Suffragists' argument that relations between women and men in the
family were analogous to those between women and the state owed
much to their readings of Mill.

Mill's arguments are inflected as well by a long tradition in liberal
and radical thinking of what historian Thomas Holt has called 'the
problem of freedom', the central idiom of which is slavery.[23] A number
of historians have recently established the tenacity of the language of
slavery and its metaphorical appeal in Unitarian, radical, and feminist
campaigns of the nineteenth century.[24] Much remains to be said about
the purchase of slavery on British feminists' imaginations, however.[25]
Certainly, institutional and organisational connections between abolition-
ists and feminists in Great Britain contributed to the appeal of the
language of slavery within suffragist discourse.[26] The idiom of slavery,
however, underwent transformation within British feminist discourse
in the nineteenth and twentieth centuries. The emancipation of slaves
in the United States, the passage of a set of Married Women's Property
Acts in 1870, 1882 and after, and repeated usage of the language of
slavery in anti-prostitution campaigns of the late nineteenth century
had imbued any use of the analogy of women with slaves with a
different set of associations by 1914 than had existed in 1861.[27]

Mill's use of the analogy of slavery in *The Subjection of Women* proved to be especially important to suffragists' arguments for their inclusion in the franchise. Mill asserted myriad similarities between married women and slaves: custom dictated women's acceptance of the marital state as their lot; women's legal personalities became subsumed under their husbands' upon marriage; husbands had virtual powers of life and death over their wives. Mill referred to notorious contemporary cases of abuse, noting that wives had no legal right to refuse their husbands sexual relations, or to separate from abusive husbands without complicated legal manoeuvres entailing the establishment of desertion or cruelty and adultery.[28] Mill's enunciation of the slavery of women was calculated to chill the blood of its readers. He wrote that 'no slave is a slave to the same lengths, and in so full a sense of the word, as a wife is', and that woman is the 'personal body-servant of a despot'.[29] Political theorist Mary Lyndon Shanley has argued that Mill's critique of the institution of marriage as slavery, a depiction of the institution radically different from the sentimentalised portrayals by his contemporaries, 'demonstrated the great complexity of establishing that any presumed agreement was the result of a free volition, and the fatuousness of presuming that initial consent could create perpetual obligation'. In asserting that women were coerced by social pressures and legal disabilities to marry, and were not, therefore, truly freely consenting, Shanley argues that Mill's analysis raised 'by implication, the legitimacy of many other relationships, including supposedly free wage labor agreements and the political obligations of enfranchised and unenfranchised alike'.[30] Yet, the analogy of slavery is not, as Shanley suggests, the only mechanism delineating the limits of consent theory within this text. Rather, consent turns on a double analogy: Mill's use of slavery as analogous to women's condition is overlaid with an older political imagery of tyranny and despotism going back to eighteenth-century radicalism. In *The Subjection of Women*, slavery stands in contrast to radical liberal notions of freedom and individuality, originating within another strand of the imagery of slavery in liberal political discourse, its foundational position as freedom's 'other'.[31]

Thus, while Mill's use of the analogy of slavery draws upon the great metaphorical energy of slavery in the nineteenth century, that analogy remained inextricably linked with his understanding of the historical development of liberalism, in Britain as well as in Europe. Chapter 1 argues forcefully for a teleology of freedom within which women's political enslavement in nineteenth-century Britain appeared archaic. Mill asserts that 'the case of women is now the only case in which to rebel against established rules is still looked upon with the same eyes as was formerly a subject's claim to the right of rebelling against his king'.[32] This analogy, with the whiff of 1789 about it, suggests that women's subjection could be ended by rebellion against tyrannical authority, an option not available to them were they merely enslaved. For nowhere else in the widespread and divergent use of the Victorian idiom of slavery does the claim of resistance to oppression hold the same legitimacy as it did when oppressed subjects were encouraged to overthrow despotism. While deprecation of the institution of slavery and its attendant miseries was a staple of the Victorian discourse on slavery, nowhere was encouragement given to enslaved peoples to overthrow their oppressors. Mill's text, written in 1861 and brimming with outrage at the persistence of slavery in the USA, understands those enslaved peoples to be of African descent. The implication of blackness within the idiom of slavery thus restricts its metaphoric power to the identification of oppression, without leaving open the possibility of active resolution on the part of the oppressed, even as the historic dependence of liberal political theory upon the juxtaposition of freedom and slavery allows the analogy to serve double duty.

Mill's double analogy posited women as enslaved while raising the possibility that their condition might be ended through women's own exertions. The overlaid analogy of tyranny/despotism made visible the possibility of resistance, something which remained impossible within the analogy of slavery. Indeed, allusions to the necessity of women's resistance to their enslavement run throughout British suffragist discourse. Byron's maxim, 'he who would be free must strike the first blow', was frequently asserted by suffragists in the nineteenth and twentieth centuries.[33] Resistance as a possibility to end the subjection of women lies folded within much nineteenth-century suffragist discourse, but it is always set against a racialised (white), middle-class analogy: tyranny and despotism. In other words, the idiom of slavery remained useful up to the point of resistance. It provided the metaphoric power of sentiment and outrage, but it could not serve as incitement for women's own resistance. It is striking in fact that the analogy of women to slaves in British suffragist discourse consistently resonated, after 1865, with the emancipation of the slaves, that is, their liberation from bondage, yet the initiative of slaves and former slaves to free themselves from servitude features nowhere within British suffragist discourse.[34] British suffragists instead mapped their perceived sexual enslavement onto the Whig narrative of the gradual overthrow of tyranny through resistance to illegitimate government, a constitutional narrative available and relatively safe to use. And here the necessity for the double analogy becomes apparent. If the nineteenth-century discourse of slavery positioned slaves as helpless dependants of their liberators,[35] British suffragists operated under different constraints. They, too, were limited by a liberal political discourse that gave women no claim to political enfranchisement on the grounds of natural right,[36] but their relation to their oppressors, as wives, mothers, daughters, of the (white) men to whom they appealed, offered them different possibilities for resolution. Suffragists were constrained merely by sex. Blackness, in contrast, although increasingly encoded as gender, proved to be an insurmountable barrier to the assertion of political agency.

As a consequence, the juxtaposition of the idiom of slavery with that of tyranny in *The Subjection of Women* underwrites a gendered dichotomy within the problem of emancipation and bondage: slavery is to tyranny as the feminine is to the masculine. Slavery and tyranny resonate in Mill's text with gendered implications for the exercise of political agency. In order to elevate women to the sphere of the political, Mill must first render their oppression in masculine terms. Arguing by analogy, therefore, he removes their oppression from the sphere of the merely domestic and offers them the possibility of exercising their own will. Women must assert the masculine characteristic of independence, central to discussions of the franchise since the early nineteenth century.[37]

The dilemma posed by Mill's juxtaposition of slavery and tyranny achieved a kind of resolution in Giuseppe Mazzini's *Duties of Man*, which would explain why suffragettes found it so useful to their political thinking. It is striking that while Mill was cited with approval by suffragists of all stripes, Mazzini appears to have been read most enthusiastically by suffragettes, or women who would become suffragettes. Here the term 'suffragist' includes all women in late nineteenth- and early twentieth-century Britain engaged in the campaign for women's parliamentary enfranchisement, and the term 'suffragette' describes those women who had come to believe that resistance to existing government provided the only legitimate means of redressing women's exclusion from the franchise.[38] Mazzini's ideas about the morality of resistance in *The Duties of Man* transformed suffragist thinking about what women could do to end their own oppression. His articulation of that oppression within a liberal political discourse in which slavery and tyranny become the plight of subject nationalities made possible the exercise of women's political agency in the form of suffrage militancy.

Mazzini's use for suffragettes poses intriguing issues of interpretation, as well as reading practice. Female readers of Mill's text faced different challenges than did those encountering *The Duties of Man*. Mill's prose engaged at what one Edwardian commentator called a 'high level'. 'The essay', wrote Stanton Coit in 1906, 'is a broad expanse of generalisations concerning human nature, universal principles of character and conduct, and far-reaching prophecies'.[39] Less euphemistically, historian Stefan Collini has characterised Mill's prose as 'didactic and forensic', not entirely disagreeing with Thomas Carlyle's description of Mill's prose as 'sawdustish'.[40] These comments suggest that reading *The Subjection of Women* was a challenging experience for many nineteenth- and twentieth-century female political activists; Stanton Coit's twenty-two-page outline of Mill's argument preceding the 1906 edition of the text would confirm this assessment. Yet despite the complexity of Mill's writing, his message resonated with relevance to women readers. Their subjection, after all, provided the subject of examination, analysis, and critique. Mazzini's prose, in contrast, engages its audience through the device of directly addressing the presumed reader, the Italian working man. While dedicated to the 'sons and daughters of the people', the text at several points makes clear that the intended audience was the working man, as the address to the reader, 'You are Men', would indicate. This would appear to have the effect of rendering problematic a reading of the text by a British suffragist. Critical imaginative leaps would be necessary to overcome the gendered, class, and national distinctions inherent in such a reading.

Historian Jane Rendall's analysis of Mazzini's use of the language of altruism suggests one way suffragists in the 1860s could overcome the distinctions confronting female, middle-class British suffragists reading *The Duties of Man*. Mazzini's emphasis upon duties over rights provided an appropriately self-sacrificing language within which women could lay claim to citizenship.[41] Initial engagement of feminist readers with the text immediately upon publication of its first English translation alone, however, does not explain its significance to suffragists

in Britain over the following four decades. Rather, Mazzini's use of
language familiar to British suffragists from their own arguments
by analogy enabled them to read his text by analogy as well.
A suffragist reading Mazzini's charge to Italian working men, 'If you
would emancipate yourselves from the arbitrary rule and tyranny
of man, you must begin by rightly adoring God,' would not require
immense political acumen or metaphoric agility to apply that dictum
to herself.[42] And because Mazzini's uses for Italian nationalism were
understood by suffragists and other British progressives as arising
naturally from within a liberal discourse of the emancipation of
struggling nations, suffragists could find yet another way to argue by
analogy for their own cause.[43]

It is on the question of consent and the individual's relation to
the state that Mazzini's text most clearly offered a solution to the
problems identified by Mill's. Both texts argue that the domination
of one group by another was a moral and political problem, yet Mill's
resolution, in the end, was to criticise 'custom' as the force sub-
ordinating women to men. Mill's solution was marital friendship,
not legal reform. Men and women, he urged, were to form ethical
relations of equality. In contrast, Mazzini's critique offered women
more public agency in redressing their subjection. Mazzini's positing
of oppression as a moral problem allowed him to articulate a political
solution in ethical terms. Appealing to laws not grounded in human
institutions, but in divine law, Mazzini urged that resistance to those
who coerced, or enslaved, was not a right, but an obligation. He
writes: 'Nothing is of Caesar unless it be such in conformity with the
law of God. Caesar – that is to say, the Temporal power, or Civil
government – is but the administrator and executive … of the design
of the Almighty. Whensoever it is false to its mission and trust, it is, I
do not say your *right*, but your *duty* to change it.'[44] Posing an essentially political problem in moral terms, Mazzini provided a solution
for British suffragettes, whose political demands had originated
within a constitutional, or legal, framework, but whose repeated failure to gain admittance into the citadel of parliamentary enfranchisement had forced them to rethink their relationship to the state and
the authority underlying its laws.

Clearly, one could point to Mazzini's encouragement of violent
nationalist actions during the 1850s as evidence for his belief in the
moral necessity for resistance to illegitimate authority. More telling,
perhaps, were links both men made between the political categories

of blackness, gender, and nationality. As historian Catherine Hall has argued, Mill could simultaneously criticise British suspension of law and its protections in Jamaica with the imposition of martial law in 1865 (and ultimately, the creation of a crown colony the following year), while believing that blacks and women, 'those who had only recently come under "civilized influences"', required further educating before they would be deemed fit for participation in representative government.[45] Mazzini, in contrast, quite explicitly linked national emancipation, of Italy, Hungary, Switzerland, and Poland, with struggles for the abolition of slavery in the United States. Despite his desire for American support, one Edwardian commentator observed, Mazzini 'refused to dissimulate his horror of American slavery and denounced it again and again'.[46] Upon Mazzini's death, the American abolitionist William Lloyd Garrison praised him for his unwillingness to separate the liberty of his nation from that of the slaves. Mazzini never, Garrison wrote, 'tried to propitiate us by silence respecting our great national sin'.[47]

Both texts, then, employed the analogy of slavery as a means of drawing upon the moral energy and outrage of contemporaries to insist that women's oppression likewise should not remain a relationship embedded within the private realm but should be a matter of concern within the public. And both texts then mapped slavery onto great liberal narratives of the nineteenth century, those of the rise of the middle class and the emergence of the nation. But Mill's analogy with tyranny and Mazzini's with subject nationalities point to different solutions. In the final analysis, male actors resist tyranny in Mill's account, and their resistance takes a specifically British national form, for ultimately Mill could not endorse the French Revolution as a model for political change. In contrast, Mazzini's model of enslavement/subject nationalities allows women the agency to resist, to rebel as men do, or should.

Historian Maura O'Connor has noted the strong identification mid-Victorian English middle-class feminists had with Italian nationalist politics.[48] This identification continued into the Edwardian period, many years after Italian unification in 1871. Identifying women's subjection with that of oppressed nationalities transcended the limitation inherent in any specifically British use of the idiom of slavery. Opponents of women's suffrage had, from the beginning, rejected Mill's analogy of women to slaves. By the Edwardian period, a sophisticated reading of the meaning of slavery underwrote these criticisms. In a review essay on 'Woman Suffrage' in the January 1909 *Quarterly Review*, jurist A. V. Dicey proposed 'to make woman suffrage the subject of calm argument'. Developing a systematic etymology of the word 'emancipation' as used to discuss English women, Dicey argued that 'the women of England cannot now be "emancipated", for they have never been slaves ... They cannot be emancipated, because they are born free, are free, and will remain free whether they obtain parliamentary votes or not.' Keen to distinguish between personal and political liberty, Dicey urged that 'personal freedom has little or nothing to do with participation in sovereign authority', noting that 'a person's claim, in short, to govern himself is a totally different thing from his claim to govern others'.[49] Women, he concluded, held no claim to participation in communal political life. 'The claim to civil rights or private rights never has been and never can be placed on the same footing as the claim to political rights, or, in other words, duties.'[50] Dicey further denied that progress would result from extension of political rights to women. Real progress, he asserted, lay in the expansion of civil or private rights, and in that arena, he argued strenuously, women had been well treated. Conceding that 'deprivation of civil rights may amount to slavery', he claimed that the lack of political rights might be, for the individual, 'of the most trifling consequence'. Dicey equated the enfranchisement of women with adult suffrage, a prospect he found terrifying. Adding 'feminine emotion' to 'democratic passion' could only bring ill.[51]

Dicey thus read the analogy of slavery as embodying personal liberty; tyranny he read through a wider political framework, one offering women (and working-class men) the prospect of ruling others. Mazzini's earlier formulation had denied any such division. Connecting personal actions with the good of the state, suffragettes interpreted Mazzini as making no distinction between personal liberty and sovereign authority. Mazzini asked working men, 'You have no right of citizenship, nor participation – either of election or vote – in those laws which are to direct or govern your life. How can you feel the sentiment of citizenship, zeal for the State, or sincere affection for its laws?' He encouraged them to struggle for inclusion, not in order to improve their material prospects, but in order that they might live more virtuously.[52] Suffragettes and their supporters embraced this ethic and implemented it in their practice of citizenship. The Revd F. Lewis Donaldson urged in 1905 that 'in regard to citizenship, freedom means the removal of disabilities. For we are not free as citizens – nay, we are not strictly citizens at all – if we are governed without governing.'[53] Looking back from the 1940s, former WSPU member Frederick Pethick-Lawrence commented on Mazzini's inspiration for his political commitments, quoting from Mazzini's published work. 'Life is one: the individual and society are its two necessary manifestations; life considered singly, and life in relation to others. Flames kindled upon a common altar, they approach each other in rising, until they mingle in God.'[54]

Yet some Edwardian pamphleteers, drawing inspiration from Mazzini, accepted the persuasiveness of the analogy of tyranny over that of slavery, especially as the former empowered men to act on behalf of women. Ronald H. Kidd's pamphlet *For Freedom's Cause: An Appeal to Working Men* reproduces the rhetorical effects of *The Duties of Man* as it urges working-class British men to work toward attaining the parliamentary vote for women. From its opening salutation, 'Comrades!', to its repetitive address to the reader, 'you', Kidd's argument and rhetoric mirrors Mazzini's. The predominant imagery throughout Kidd's work is that of the struggle against tyranny waged by men against despots in preceding centuries. The analogy of slavery is given very little play. Kidd instead emphasises women's similarity to working-class men, and he employs the language of radicalism, struggling against 'privilege and monopoly' and the evils of class and sex rule.[55]

As Kidd's deployment of the analogy of tyranny to enlist working-class men in the struggle for women's votes suggests, suffragette discourse of the twentieth century held a dialogic relationship with nineteenth-century texts. Suffragettes embraced simultaneously Mazzini's 'Deification of duty', in the words of an Edwardian critic, and Mill's philosophy of individual rights in making arguments for their own enfranchisement. Mazzini's arguments complemented Mill's in the creation of a citizen identity for women, for, read in dialogue, these texts legitimated both citizenship's rights and its obligations. Both Mazzini and Mill connected the private realm with that of the public through the institution of the family, as in Mazzini's characterisation of the family and the country as 'the two extreme points of the same line'.[56] Suffragettes similarly connected state and family, urging that 'the State is the family with its boundaries extended, and the ethics of the smaller human family must also be the ethics of the larger'.[57] Suffragettes refused to see their lack of voting rights as a private matter, or to accept exclusion from the duties of citizenship. Reading by analogy thus offered women the opportunity to imagine a different relationship to the realm of the political. Embracing Mill's analysis of women's sexual subordination as the pivot on which enslavement within the family rested, and by extension, women's political oppression within the state, suffragettes understood *The Subjection of Women* and *The Duties of Man* as offering new resolutions to the problem posed by men's tyranny so perceived: resistance to illegitimate authority. Slavery and tyranny thus understood enabled suffragettes to connect family, state and citizenship within the realm of the political, and offered remedies for their political exclusion.

....

Notes

I would like to thank Judith Allen, Leora Auslander, Antoinette Burton, and Michael Dunn for their perceptive comments on earlier drafts of this essay.

1. Christabel Pankhurst, 'Methods of Violence', *Votes for Women*, 7 June 1912, p. 8.
2. Martha Vicinus, *Independent Women: Work & Community for Single Women, 1850–1920* (University of Chicago Press, Chicago and London, 1985), pp. 247–80; Barbara Green, *Spectacular Confessions: Autobiography, Performative Activism, and the Sites of Suffrage, 1905–1938* (St Martin's Press, New York, 1997).
3. Linda M. G. Zerilli, *Signifying Woman: Culture and Chaos in Rousseau, Burke, and Mill* (Cornell University Press, Ithaca, NY, 1996), p. 3.
4. References are culled from the following editions: John Stuart Mill, *The Subjection of Women*, edited with an introduction by Susan Moller Okin (Hackett Publishing Company, Indianapolis and Cambridge, 1988); Giuseppe Mazzini, *The Duties of Man*, translated by Emilie A. Venturi (Chapman & Hall, London, 1862).
5. See Kate Flint, *The Woman Reader 1837–1914* (Clarendon Press, Oxford, 1993), pp. 235–49; Laura E. Nym Mayhall, 'The Making of a Suffragette: The Uses of Reading and the Legacy of Radicalism, 1890–1918', in *Singular Continuities: Tradition, Nostalgia, and Identity in Modern British Culture*, ed. George K. Behlmer and Fred M. Leventhal (Stanford University Press, Stanford, CA, 2000), pp. 75–88.
6. Presses publishing *The Subjection of Women* in 1869 were Longmans, Green, Reader and Dyer (London); D. Appleton and Company (New York), and J. B. Lippincott and Company (Philadelphia). Longmans released a second edition in 1869, and subsequent editions in 1870, 1878, and 1883. Millicent Garrett Fawcett wrote an introduction to *Three Essays by John Stuart Mill*, which included *On Liberty, Representative Government*, and *The Subjection of Women* (1912; repr. Oxford University Press, Oxford, 1974).
7. John Stuart Mill, *The Subjection of Women*, ed. with introductory analysis by Stanton Coit, PhD (Longmans, Green, and Co., London, 1909).
8. *The Life and Writings of Joseph Mazzini* (Smith, Elder and Company, London, 1890).
9. For reception at time of publication, see William James, '*The Subjection of Women*', *North American Review* (1869). Historians have commented on the text's significance for liberal feminists; see Jane Rendall, 'Citizenship, Culture and Civilisation: The Languages of British Suffragists, 1866–1874', in *Suffrage and Beyond: International Feminist Perspectives*, ed. Caroline Daley and Melanie Nolan (New York University Press, New York, 1994), pp. 144–5; Olive Banks, *Becoming a Feminist: The Social Origins of 'First Wave' Feminism* (University of Georgia Press, Athens, GA, 1990), p. 7; Barbara Caine,

'John Stuart Mill and the English Women's Movement', *Historical Studies*, 18 (1978), pp. 52–67.

10. Millicent Garrett Fawcett, 'England: The Women's Suffrage Movement', in *The Woman Question in Europe: A Series of Original Essays*, ed. Theodore M. Stanton (1884; repr. Source Book Press, New York, 1974), pp. 2–3; Helena Swanwick, *I Have Been Young* (Victor Gollancz, London, 1935), p. 169; Eunice Murray, 'Prejudices Old and New' (Scottish Council of the WFL, Edinburgh, 1912); Christabel Pankhurst, *New Statesman*, 1 November 1913; Emmeline Pethick Lawrence, *My Part in a Changing World* (Victor Gollancz, London, 1938), p. 216. For reports of annual processions by members of the Women's Freedom League to Mill's statue in Victoria Tower Gardens, see *The Vote*, 28 May 1910 and 14 April 1911. These processions continued into the 1920s; see *Report of the Women's Freedom League from April 1927 to April 1928*, Fawcett Library, London Guildhall University, p. 10. For the anti-suffragist view of Mill, see Harold Owen, *Woman Adrift: The Menace of Suffragism* (Stanley Paul & Company, London, 1912), p. 219.

11. Margot Finn, *After Chartism: Class and Nation in English Radical Politics, 1848–1874* (Cambridge University Press, Cambridge, 1993), pp. 159–72; Eugenio F. Biagini, *Liberty, Retrenchment, and Reform: Popular Liberalism in the Age of Gladstone, 1860–1880* (Cambridge University Press, Cambridge, 1992), pp. 46–50.

12. 'Is this Equality? A Reply to Miss Violet Markham' (National Union of Women's Suffrage Societies, London, 1912), in NUWSS leaflets to 1914, Fawcett Library, London Guildhall University; Charlotte Despard, 'In the Days of my Youth', unpublished manuscript (no date), p. 15, D2479/4/7, Public Record Office of Northern Ireland, Belfast.

13. One ironic aspect of the making of a canonical text would appear to be the virtual cessation of actual readings of the text; see Stefan Collini, *Public Moralists: Political Thought and Intellectual Life in Britain 1850–1930* (Clarendon Press, Oxford, 1991), pp. 330–2.

14. Emmeline Pethick-Lawrence, *The Meaning of the Woman's Movement* (Women's Press, London, 1907).

15. See for example, Charlotte Despard, 'Ideals and Future of the Women's Freedom League', *The Vote*, 28 January 1911, p. 159; Christabel Pankhurst, 'Methods of Violence', *Votes for Women*, 7 June 1912, p. 8.

16. Collini has traced the origins of the analysis of Mill as 'an "old-fashioned Liberal"' to the decades immediately following his death; see *Public Moralists*, pp. 323–41. The critique of Mill as laisser-faire individualist continued well into the twentieth century, but has been modified in recent years; see W. H. Greenleaf, *The British Political Tradition*, vol. 2, *The Ideological Heritage* (Methuen, London, 1983), p. 104, and Michael Bentley, '"Boundaries" in Theoretical Language about the British State', in *The Boundaries of the State in Modern Britain*, ed. S. J. D. Green and R. C. Whiting (Cambridge University Press, Cambridge, 1996), pp. 29–58. Feminist critiques argue that Mill's analysis did nothing to alter the traditional division of labour within the household; further, Mill is taken to task for holding 'less radical' positions on marriage than did his wife; see Leah D. Hackleman, 'Suppressed Speech: The Language of Emotion in Harriet Taylor's *The Emancipation of Women*', *Women's Studies*, 20 (1992), pp. 273–86; Carol Dyhouse, *Feminism and the Family in England, 1880–1939* (Basil Blackwell Ltd, Oxford, 1989), p. 40; Jennifer Ring, 'Mill's *The Subjection of Women*: The Methodological Limits of Liberal-Feminism', *The Review of Politics*, 47 (1985), pp. 27–44; Susan Moller Okin, *Women in Western Political Thought* (Princeton University Press, Princeton, NJ, 1979), pp. 226–30; Julia Annas, 'Mill and *The Subjection of Women*', *Philosophy*, 52 (1977). Two notable exceptions are Kate Nash, *Universal Difference: Feminism and the Liberal Undecidability of 'Women'* (St Martin's Press, New York, 1998), and Susan Hekman, 'J. S. Mill's *The Subjection of Women*: The Foundation of Liberal Feminism', *History of European Ideas*, 15 (1992), pp. 681–6.

17. Finn, *After Chartism*, p. 166.

18. Collini, *Public Moralists*, pp. 122–69; see also S. J. Heans, 'Was Mill a Moral Scientist?', *Philosophy*, 67 (1992), pp. 81–101; H. S. Jones, 'John Stuart Mill as Moralist', *Journal of*

the History of Ideas, 53 (1992), pp. 287–308; Bruce L. Kinzer, Ann P. Robson and John M. Robson, *A Moralist In and Out of Parliament: John Stuart Mill at Westminster, 1865–1868* (University of Toronto Press, Toronto, 1992); Bernard Semmel, *John Stuart Mill and the Pursuit of Virtue* (Yale University Press, New Haven, CT, 1984).

19. Frances Power Cobbe, Introduction, in *The Woman Question in Europe,* ed. Theodore M. Stanton, p. xiv. The disjunction between Mill and Mazzini that appears so obvious today was not apparent to Edwardian radicals. For example, John MacCunn's *Six Radical Thinkers* (Edward Arnold, London, 1910) suggested affinities between the intellectual agendas of Jeremy Bentham, J. S. Mill, Richard Cobden, Thomas Carlyle, Giuseppe Mazzini, and T. H. Green. And H. M. Hyndman read Mazzini and Mill, suggesting important connections between nascent socialism and emergent feminist movements of the 1880s; see Finn, *After Chartism,* p. 317.

20. Mazzini, *Duties of Man,* p. 99; Mill, *Subjection of Women,* pp. 16, 22, 44.

21. Mazzini, *Duties of Man,* p. 98; Mill, *Subjection of Women,* p. 47.

22. Kinzer, Robson and Robson argue that Mill gained this perspective through his wife's published writings (see *A Moralist In and Out of Parliament,* p. 117).

23. Thomas Holt, *The Problem of Freedom: Race, Labor, and Politics in Jamaica and Britain, 1832–1938* (Johns Hopkins University Press, Baltimore, 1992).

24. See especially Kathryn Gleadle, *The Early Feminists: Radical Unitarians and the Emergence of the Women's Rights Movement, 1831–1851* (St Martin's Press, New York, 1996), pp. 62–70; Antoinette Burton, *Burdens of History: British Feminists, Indian Women, and Imperial Culture, 1865–1915* (University of North Carolina Press, Chapel Hill, 1994), pp. 77–9; Moira Ferguson, *Subject to Others: British Women Writers and Colonial Slavery, 1670–1834* (Routledge, New York, 1992); Clare Midgley, *Women against Slavery: The British Campaigns, 1780–1870* (Routledge, London, 1992); Jane Rendall, *The Origins of Modern Feminism: Women in Britain, France and the United States, 1760–1860* (Macmillan, London, 1985).

25. For the range of meanings attached to the idea of slavery in nineteenth-century feminist discourse, see Carl Plasa and Betty J. Ring, *The Discourse of Slavery: Aphra Behn to Toni Morrison* (Routledge, London, 1994); Myra Jehlen, 'The Family Militant: Domesticity Versus Slavery in *Uncle Tom's Cabin*', in *Reading with a Difference: Gender, Race, and Cultural Identity,* ed. Arthur F. Marotti, et al. (Wayne State University Press, Detroit, 1993), pp. 227–44; and Anne Summers, 'The Constitution Violated: the Female Body and the Female Subject in the Campaigns of Josephine Butler', *History Workshop Journal,* 48 (1999), pp. 1–16.

26. Sandra Stanley Holton, '"To Educate Women into Rebellion": Elizabeth Cady Stanton and the Creation of a Transatlantic Network of Radical Suffragists', *American Historical Review,* 99 (1994), pp. 1112–36.

27. Stanton Coit affirmed the continuing saliency of the analogy despite these changes in his 1909 introduction to *Subjection of Women,* p. 26.

28. Mary Lyndon Shanley, 'Marital Slavery and Friendship: John Stuart Mill's *The Subjection of Women*', *Political Theory,* 9 (1981), pp. 229–47; Shanley, *Feminism, Marriage, and the Law in Victorian England* (Princeton University Press, Princeton, NJ, 1989), pp. 62–7; Carole Pateman, *The Sexual Contract* (Stanford University Press, Stanford, CA, 1988), pp. 116–88.

29. Mill, *Subjection of Women,* p. 33.

30. Shanley, 'Marital Slavery and Friendship', p. 234.

31. Orlando Patterson, 'Slavery: The Other Side of Freedom', in *Out of Slavery: Abolition and After,* ed. Jack Hayward (Frank Cass and Co. Ltd, London, 1985), pp. 26–8.

32. Mill, *Subjection of Women,* p. 84.

33. See Mayhall, 'The Making of a Suffragette', p. 86.

34. For example, the 1865 Morant Bay riots in Jamaica nowhere feature as possible models for resisting servitude, even as slaves were emancipated in the USA; see Holt, *The Problem of Freedom,* pp. 179–307.

35. See Ferguson, pp. 299–307; Burton, pp. 38–9, 77–9, 96.

36. Joan Scott, *Only Paradoxes to Offer: French Feminists and the Rights of Man* (Harvard University Press, Cambridge, MA, 1996).

37. See Anna Clark, 'Gender, Class and the Constitution: Franchise Reform in England, 1832–1928', in *Rereading the Constitution: New Narratives in the Political History of England's Long Nineteenth Century*, ed. James Vernon (Cambridge University Press, Cambridge, 1996), pp. 239–53; Catherine Hall, Keith McClelland, and Jane Rendall, *Defining the Victorian Nation: Class, Race, Gender and the Reform Act of 1867* (Cambridge University Press, Cambridge, 2000).

38. For elaboration upon this point, see Laura E. Nym Mayhall, 'Defining Militancy: Radical Protest, the Constitutional Idiom, and Women's Suffrage in Britain, 1908–1909', *Journal of British Studies*, 39 (2000), pp. 340–71.

39. Coit's introduction to the 1909 edition, page 1.

40. Collini, *Public Moralists*, pp. 131–2.

41. Rendall, 'Citizenship, Culture and Civilisation', pp. 137–8.

42. Mazzini, *Duties of Man*, p. xii.

43. Eugenio Biagini likens Italian liberation to the 'Irish Question', in 'Introduction: Citizenship, Liberty and Community', in *Citizenship and Community: Liberals, Radicals and Collective Identities in the British Isles, 1865–1931*, ed. Eugenio F. Biagini (Cambridge University Press, Cambridge, 1996), pp. 10–17. Catherine Hall demonstrates how race and ethnicity shaped the limits of these analogies in discussions of Ireland and Jamaica around the 1867 Reform Act; see Hall, McClelland, Rendall, *Defining the Victorian Nation*, pp. 179–233.

44. Mazzini, *Duties of Man*, p. 44.

45. Catherine Hall, 'Rethinking Imperial Histories: The Reform Act of 1867', *New Left Review*, 208 (1994), p. 20.

46. Henry Demarest Lloyd, *Mazzini and other Essays* (G. P. Putnam's Sons, New York and London, 1910), p. 9.

47. William Lloyd Garrison, Introduction, *Joseph Mazzini: His Life, Writings, and Political Principles* (Hurd and Houghton, New York, 1872), pp. xiv–xv.

48. Maura O'Connor, *The Romance of Italy and the English Political Imagination* (St Martin's Press, New York, 1998), pp. 108–9.

49. A. V. Dicey, 'Woman Suffrage', *Quarterly Review*, January 1909, pp. 285, 286.

50. Dicey, 'Woman Suffrage', p. 298.

51. Dicey, 'Woman Suffrage', p. 290.

52. Mazzini, *Duties of Man*, pp. 22–3.

53. F. Lewis Donaldson, 'The Religion of Women's Suffrage' (Central Society for Women's Suffrage, London, 1905), p. 7.

54. Frederick Pethick-Lawrence, *Fate has been Kind* (Hutchinson, London, 1943), p. 54.

55. Ronald H. Kidd, *For Freedom's Cause: An Appeal to Working Men* (London, c. 1911–1912).

56. Mazzini, *Duties of Man*, p. 98.

57. Mrs Winton Evans, 'The Mother as a Factor in Human Progress', *The Vote*, 9 September 1911, p. 248.

Imagining Female Citizenship in the 'New Spain': Gendering the Democratic Transition, 1975–1978

Pamela Beth Radcliff

Spain's transition to democracy in the late 1970s has become a crucial reference point, not only for Spaniards recovering from a legacy of civil war but for 'transitologists' seeking models for successful transitions. Spain occupies a privileged place in much of this transition scholarship, at last offering an exemplary role model of political integration rather than disintegration. Scholars have sought to explain how, forty years after a bloody civil war, Spain was able to create a democratic political consensus. However, as feminist scholars have pointed out more generally, the mainstream scholarship on democratic transitions does not factor gender into its questions or its models. What impact do democratic transitions have on existing gender ideologies, or conversely, how does gender shape the process of transition itself?

Transitions provide fertile territory for a gender reassessment because they are special moments when the rules of the game are questioned and redefined. As Jane Jacquette puts it, under such circumstances 'there is a general willingness to re-think the bases of social consensus'.[1] Such an opening can give rise to more vigorous or contested debates about questions of identity, whether of nation, race or gender. In democratic transitions, these identity questions may be linked to the need to define or redefine the central concept of citizenship.[2] As individuals' and groups' relationships with each other and with the state are reinvented, so men's and women's relationships with each other and the nation may be re-evaluated.

Such a moment occurred in Spain, during the heady years between the death of dictator Francisco Franco in November 1975, and the institutionalisation of the new democracy in December 1978, when the Constitution received voter approval. As the parameters of the 'new Spain' were evolving, it was clear that the official Francoist ideal of womanhood did not belong there. For decades, the Franco regime had promoted a traditional model of the mother and housewife, supporting the nation through her powers of reproduction and her religious faith.[3] But if this ideal seemed anachronistic in the new democratic Spain, what kind of woman should replace her? What, in other words, should the new female citizen look like?

This question generated a rich, if submerged debate on female citizenship in the political discourse of the transition. Although it lurked below the surface of more high-profile debates about the integration of workers or Catalans into the nation, the relationship between women, the nation and the new democracy was a powerful theme in the general political discussion over the shape of the 'new Spain'. A close reading of this discourse, as it emerged in the democratic political press, reveals a range of competing images of potential female citizens, from the Francoist housewife to the feminist and the consumer activist. On one level, these competing images simply illustrate Jacquette's point about the fluidity of the transition moment, when modes of belonging to and participating in the nation were renegotiated. On another level, however, they reveal the flourishing contradictions surrounding the conceptualisation and recognition of female citizenship. This article will explore these contradictions, focusing in particular on the image of feminist citizenship and its problematic integration into a broader framework of Spanish democratic citizenship.

The issue of gender and citizenship has barely been broached in relation to Spain's democratic transition, and indeed it remains marginal in the more general transition literature. In general terms, this literature has sought to explain why and under what conditions transitions occur, according to two different approaches: one that gives primacy to structural preconditions for democratic transitions and another which privileges the agency of individual actors. Since the 1980s, the dominant framework has been actor-focused, with scholars utilising models of rational choice and elite decision-making to explain outcomes.[4]

The Spanish case has suited this analytic framework very well, given the centrality of elite pact-making in its institutional transition. According to this model, Spain completed a successful transition because reformist elites from the dictatorship negotiated with the moderate opposition to create a workable compromise.[5] The less nuanced version of this story concentrates on the particular skills and pragmatism of individuals like King Juan Carlos or Adolfo Suarez, the architect of the *ruptura pactada* (negotiated break).[6] More nuanced versions try to ground elite decision-making in a broader context, whether elites were responding to popular pressure or exploiting the greater room for movement in an authoritarian vs. a totalitarian regime.[7] For all these scholars, though, elite negotiation was the key to the transition. Within this framework, there is little room for the problematising of citizenship, which remains a formal category of rights and obligations granted by the new state.

While the importance of elite pacts in completing the Spanish transition is undeniable, critics of the 'rational choice' model complain that this version impoverishes the history of the transition, both by leaving out other actors and by ignoring the impact of elite decisions on the rest of society. In contrast to the elite-focused approach to the transition, therefore, other scholars have chosen to foreground the context in which elites made those choices. In particular, Victor Pérez-Díaz argues that a broader democratic culture had to be in place before elites could even imagine making certain choices.[8] In this theory, democratic traditions like mutual tolerance, bargaining and multiple voices both evolve gradually out of the unconscious actions of many people and are actively invented. In either case, the locus of this 'web of traditions' is civil society, the realm of public independent activity between the state and the family.[9] While 'pact' scholars recognise the role of civil society, in most cases they see it as a result, not a cause, of the transition.[10]

Pérez-Díaz's work opens up the study of the transition, beyond both the handful of elite leaders and the narrow institution-building to a broader realm of cultural discourse where democratic mentalities are established. It also points to an enriched reading of the process of democratisation itself, one which transcends the establishment of basic political institutions and rules. It is in this realm of process and discourse that the renegotiation of citizenship takes place. However, Pérez-Díaz's work remains uninformed by the gendered critiques of the public sphere made by scholars like Nancy Fraser.[11] In other words, Pérez-Díaz portrays civil society as a realm of autonomous activity without recognising the gender power relations that structure that activity.

Gendering the process of transition requires several parallel shifts in perspective which relate to the conceptualisation and practice of citizenship. As some feminist scholars have argued, the very categories of democratic participation and political activity must be redefined in order to recognise how women contributed to the transition process. Instead of the exclusive focus on the realm of elite high politics and formal institutions, these scholars have turned the spotlight on different forms of popular mobilisation and incorporated it into a broader model of politics.[12] As Carole Pateman puts it, a political sphere exists 'whenever citizens gather to make political decisions'.[13] Women were much more likely to be involved in social movements organised around neighbourhood issues or human rights, and feminist scholars have argued that they were key to undermining the legitimacy of authoritarian regimes and thus central to the transition process.[14]

In addition, these women participated not only in the transition but in the construction of a democratic citizenship. Rather than a formal status endowed by the new state, in this model citizenship is a dynamic interplay between active practice and formal rights and obligations. Drawing on revived notions of 'civic republicanism', which defines citizenship as active involvement in the affairs of the community, feminist scholars have argued that women's participation in social movements and popular mobilisations needs to be acknowledged as an alternative mode of action in which citizenship identities are constructed.[15] Conversely, this model of citizenship implies agency, not simply status.

At the heart of this argument is a critique of traditional frameworks of citizenship. Caught in the paradox between equality and difference, most citizenship models either ignore gender difference by defining all 'women's issues' as particularistic, private concerns, or they embrace difference by assigning women and men distinct relationships to the nation, traditionally through the lens of private and public spheres. In the first case, the rights and obligations associated with citizenship, even in the modern civic republican tradition, are all located within a narrow version of the political sphere and constrained by a restrictive definition of the public interest. The result, as Susan James argues, is that citizenship has excluded all that is traditionally female: 'the cluster of activities, values, ways of thinking and ways of doing things which have long been associated with women are all conceived as outside the world of citizenship'.[16] In the second case, there are two tracks of citizenship, as in the Franco regime, which defined women's citizenship, and their contribution to the nation, through their acceptance of the private role of motherhood.

To break down this paradox, the analysis of gender and citizenship requires a process of re-imagining and redrawing of boundaries in order to recognise the subject. Even then, citizenship is not a fixed status but a dynamic process, created at the intersection not only between rights and actions but also between the meanings ascribed to them. Thus, it encompasses high politics, collective agency and discourse and the way they interact across the boundaries of public and private interests. What occurred in Spain in the mid 1970s was a reconfiguration of these components of citizenship. The political transition gradually repealed much of the discriminatory Francoist legislation that restricted women's social and political role and replaced it with laws and a constitution that promised equal political, civil and social rights. That is, the new regime moved from a difference-based towards an equality-based legal framework for citizenship. At the same time, women mobilised around these issues and others, in feminist movements and consumers' groups, inventing their own practice of citizenship on the ground. And finally, a new discourse about what constituted female citizenship emerged as part of the efforts to invent and discover a 'new Spain'. These historical changes thus establish an ideal context for exploring the tensions and contradictions in the (re)construction of female citizenship.

What created these tensions in the Spanish transition was the disjuncture between new rights and modes of participation and a discourse that had trouble assigning meaning to them. The category of female citizenship remained a problematic one in the emerging democratic culture, despite an avowed desire to embrace equality as a potent symbol of the modern world Spain was about to join. An examination of the emerging democratic 'idiom' identified by Pérez-Díaz reveals that it was infused with markers of gender difference that clashed with the new egalitarian rhetoric. This conceptual confusion over equality vs. difference was not surprising or unique, but it does provide an opportunity to articulate the exact nature of the contradictions and how they shaped contestation over the construction of female citizenship.

One of the best places to investigate the place of gender in Spain's emergent democratic culture is in the political press of the transition. The press was a central building block of the revived public sphere, which began to take shape in the mid 1970s as censorship declined and the circulation of information reached a critical 'take-off' point.[17] At that moment there were few public forums that could facilitate such circulation of information, given the state control of new mass media such as television and movies. Although the majority of the press was also directly tied to the regime, a minority of newspapers and news magazines appeared in the early and mid 1970s with the explicit agenda of helping to guide a democratic transition.[18]

This independent press has been celebrated as a 'paper parliament', an 'effective instrument of dialogue and social collaboration at the moment of change'.[19] It was in the pages of the democratic press that the new democratic elite tried out their ideas, filling pages with 'articles ... propounding new practical and theoretical ideas about constitutional and political matters on which to base the building of a new state'.[20] In addition to providing a locus for elite discourse, the new democratic media also contributed, it has been argued, to the formation of a new democratic citizenry, by introducing them to the assumptions and expectations of democratic behaviour.[21] In other words, the press was a major site for the articulation of a new democratic political culture. The question is, what lessons about gender and citizenship did these publications teach?

Of the handful of ground-breaking publications, I have chosen to focus on two that carried special weight as interlocutors of the transition. The first, *Cambio 16*, launched in 1971 by 'sixteen people focused on change',[22] became the most important news magazine in the country after 1975.[23] A magazine of centrist opinion, Europeanist and liberal in public morals, it achieved an unprecedented circulation for a news magazine in Spain.[24] The other publication is *El País*, a newspaper that appeared in May 1976 and quickly achieved canonical status, becoming the 'dominant reference' for the independent Spanish media world.[25] Its editorial slant was centre-left, Europeanist and secular, but it also regularly aired leftist views as well. To balance these two centre/left sources, I have also consulted the more conservative daily, *ABC*. An independent monarchist newspaper with a large circulation, *ABC* was suspicious of change but open to the cautiously reformist wing of the Francoist regime.

Even with the addition of *ABC* to balance the political perspectives of *El País* and *Cambio 16*, these three papers do not provide a full spectrum of political opinion. The regime-controlled press, which was still government-subsidised until 1977, occupied one side of the spectrum, while the revolutionary left-wing press occupied the other. What these publications do reveal fairly well, however, is the dominant mode of discourse that took shape in the years between Franco's death and the approval of the Constitution, a discourse focused on consensus, negotiated change and the 'lessons' of the Civil War.[26] In other words, all three of these publications both represented and shaped the contours of the hegemonic democratic culture that came to define the 'New Spain'. As such, they are ideal sources for an analysis of the mainstream discourse on gender and citizenship in Spain's transition to democracy.

The discourse of citizenship took place in a context of dramatic political changes that affected both men and women. Basic political and civil rights which had been suppressed for forty years, like meaningful suffrage, freedom of speech, the right to association and to strike, the formation of political parties, and so on, became the fundamental conquests of a new democratic citizenship. The most contentious issues revolved around social and economic rights, especially in regard to labour unions, and around competing national identities, but the vaunted consensus produced workable compromises, at least in theory.

For the most part, it was automatically assumed that all these new rights would apply to both men and women. While there was dissent around the edges, most democratisers agreed that women's subordinate legal and civil status had to be addressed, although women's mobilising around these issues helped push the question into the public eye. With a few exceptions, in 1975 women were still legal dependants of their husbands and fathers. Thus, women could not sign a legal contract, make major purchases, apply for a job or take a trip without their husband's or father's permission. In the Civil Code, their status equalled that of the mentally incapacitated. By most standards, women lacked the basic legal autonomy required of a free citizen. On a more cultural level, the Franco regime and the Catholic Church defended a strict division of public and private spheres, in which women were discouraged from pursuing higher education, from participating in politics, from joining the work force or from seeing their mission in life as other than motherhood. While some women did pursue public roles, they carried no meaning within a framework of female citizenship that depended entirely on their private-sphere duties.

In contrast, the Constitution of 1978 explicitly proclaimed a set of political, civil, social and economic rights that applied to both men and women. Article 14 established equality before the law and forbade discrimination on the basis of gender or other categories. Articles 32 and 35 spelled out a series of rights that apply to both sexes, including the right to property and privacy, the right to work and to judicial appeal, and other rights previously denied women (with the major exceptions of reproductive rights and the right to ascend the throne).[27] How such rights would be applied in practice (and in the subsequent reform of the Penal and Civil Codes) and how to recognise inequality under the law has still not been resolved, but the Constitution created a new framework in which arguments over how to define equality took the place of an openly differential citizenship.

If men and women were supposed to be integrated into a single model of citizenship, what did it look like? Beyond the enumeration of rights, which fall in line with the general western European model, the specific context of the transition shaped the articulation of democratic citizenship in Spain. Bryan Turner has developed a typology of citizenship that runs along two axes, the public/private and the passive/active, which, he argues, describe the ideal and practice of citizenship in different countries.[28]

In Spain, citizenship during the transition seemed to develop along the passive/public axis. Turner defines passive citizenship as being granted 'from above' by the state, as opposed to being demanded 'from below' via more localised participatory civil institutions. While there was popular mobilisation in favour of democratisation before and during the transition, it was limited in scope and intensity. More importantly, popular initiative from below was discouraged by elites of all political stripes, who were by and large committed to an orderly, peaceful transition process. Streets full of noisy protesters evoked images of the chaos and discord that had led the country to civil war. In other words, the democratic idiom that emerged in Spain valued unity and order (the vaunted consensus) over popular participation. The 'lessons' drawn from the Civil War made mass mobilisation suspect and encouraged a passive model of citizenship in which plebiscitary acclamation of elite decisions was the preferred mode of participation.[29]

Along the other axis of Turner's model, democratic citizenship in Spain was defined by a clear identification with the public arena. Not only was the public the locus of moral actions in pursuit of the general good, but it was the origin of common interests. Because of the Franco regime's suppression of the public sphere and its praise of the private as the locus of moral citizenship, the private life of home and family was linked symbolically to the dictatorship. In contrast, the recovery of the 'public' and the freedom to participate in it were linked to democracy (in contrast to eastern Europe). While the rhetorical boundaries separating public and private spheres were becoming less significant in postwar social democratic societies, their symbolic importance in Spain actually increased at this moment of transition when the conquest of the public carried specific political meanings. In the framework of Turner's model, the correlation of public and passive produced an image of citizenship that we might call communitarian passivity.

While Turner's theory is useful for historicising citizenship practice, however, it does not take into account the gendered structure of public and private or recognise the contradictions that arise from it. The dominant transition discourse of 'gender-neutral' citizenship was in fact imbued with gender codes that made it difficult to recognise and identify female citizens. The result was a contested arena of female citizenship, in which women's groups struggled to define their practice within a general discourse of citizenship that did not comprehend them.

Most obviously, the negative image of the private affected women more than men, because of the key role that motherhood played in female citizenship identity under the Franco regime. As a result of this historical link, the *ama de casa* (housewife) was represented as backward and politically retrograde because of her particular rootedness in the private sphere. Because of this rootedness and the historical association of the private with Francoism, the *ama de casa* was clearly viewed as more saturated with the values of the regime. Thus, she emerges in the discourse as more than just a housewife; she was the emblem of an entire life on the brink of extinction. For the right, women embodied the essential bedrock of the nation that should be preserved, while, for the left, they had to be 'modernised' before the nation could move forward to democracy. The 'two Spains' (traditional and democratic) were thus gendered as the conflict between a mismatched couple, as in the later play *Cuplé* (written in

1986, after the transition itself), by Ana Diosadado, in which a progressive male intellectual hero is juxtaposed against a female 'Carmen', who symbolises traditional Spain.[30]

At the same time, and in direct contradiction, the framework linking women to the nation through the family was such a powerful one that it remained largely unquestioned, even in the democratic press. Despite the negative image of the *ama de casa*, women's access to politics and thus citizenship seemed to come through the family. That is, when women appeared in the 'political' news in *El País* or *Cambio*, it was usually simply by virtue of their spousal relationship to a prominent male political figure. The collective message, which seemed to be that women were politically significant only through their husbands, relied on a family metaphor of female participation, which in turn maintained a 'difference' model of citizenship at a moment of transition to an egalitarian legal framework.

While the observation that women were linked to the nation through the family is neither remarkable nor uniquely Spanish, in this context it created special problems for redefining female citizenship because of the close identification between the old undemocratic regime, the private sphere and women. That is, it exposed a contradiction between a comfortable framework in which women's access to citizenship came through the family and an emerging assumption that women in the family were incapable of democratic citizenship because of the corruption of the private sphere under Francoism.

On the other hand, the citizenship model of 'communitarian passivity' was equally problematic for assigning meaning to women who left the home and mobilised in the public sphere, like the feminists. On one level, feminist demands for the expansion of civil, political, social and reproductive rights to women harmonised with a notion of citizenship as a status granted from above. On the other hand, their implicit practice of citizenship collided with expectations of communitarian passivity. Their noisy public disagreements among themselves, in addition to their vociferous defence of what were considered special (i.e. women's) interests placed them at odds with the 'public good', a concept which often, as Ruth Lister notes, imposes a 'homogeneity that suppresses group differences in public'.[31] The pact-driven consensus model of transition further marginalised any 'difference' from the realm of public interest, leaving feminists in a public netherworld of particularity. While the tensions that arose from these clashing images of citizenship were not always articulated directly, the presence of minority feminist voices in the democratic press created more of an open debate than was the case for the more prevalent but largely voiceless *ama de casa*. The upshot of all these tensions was a contradictory discourse, replete with competing images, hidden frameworks and unrecognised categories.

Of all the competing images of women as citizens, the feminist in many ways corresponded most closely with Spain's emerging democratic culture. As in Latin America (and in contrast to eastern Europe), women's rights were a point of differentiation with the socially conservative authoritarian regime, and thus were congruent with and symbolic of the larger political transformation.[32] More specifically, women's rights carried the European caché that embodied modernity and democracy in the Spanish transition.[33]

In making the case for these rights, the Spanish feminist movement took shape and visibility during the same years that the country's new democracy was being forged, and left an indelible imprint on the process. The movement took off after the first UN conference on women, held coincidentally in December 1975 in Mexico City two weeks after Franco's death.[34] Feminists made important contributions to debates about birth control, adultery, abortion, divorce, pornography and the treatment of women in the Constitution. They argued that women needed several layers of rights, in the tradition of T. H. Marshall, in order to become full members of the new democratic Spain. Furthermore, this basic argument seemed to be accepted as axiomatic in the progressive political discourse and some of these rights were institutionalised in laws or the Constitution itself before the close of the transition period. The observation made by feminist scholars that improvements in women's status often play an iconic role in discourses of national progress certainly fits the Spanish case.[35] As one feminist editorialist noted, all political parties, even the conservative Acción Popular, had felt the need to include the theme of gender equality in their electoral campaigns, leading to an acceptance of what she called generic feminism.[36] In other words, general principles of legal equality, defined as 'feminism', became a significant marker of Spain's modernity.

And yet, the relationship between feminists and the transition was an ambivalent one. While feminism received significant coverage in the democratic press, reporters and commentators did not always view the movement itself favourably. Ironically, though many of the basic feminist precepts were accepted, feminists themselves came off badly in mainstream democratic discourse. Feminists attained high visibility in the press, but their visibility only highlighted their anomalous status. Once again, there was no conceptual framework that made sense of their presence. They were women outside the family metaphor and the private sphere, but they were not perceived as truly 'public' because of their pursuit of 'selfish' interests at a moment when Spaniards were building a historic consensus.

Thus, feminists' confrontational stances were juxtaposed with the 'civility' of communist and liberal deputies shaking hands around the negotiating table. And the feminist movement's own internal divisiveness, fully publicised in the press, contrasted starkly with the ability of former Francoists and Republicans to reach agreements. While (a version of) feminism was celebrated as a civic principle, the feminist movement was represented as speaking for private, sectional interests rather than the 'common good'. The historical connection between women and the private, which was celebrated under the Franco regime and maintained during the transition in implicit frames of reference like the family metaphor, provided the interpretive lens for this representation. As a result, certain feminist principles came to embody the ideals of democracy, yet the feminist herself did not stand as a role model for female citizenship.

To put it another way, feminism received positive press when it was something done *for* women rather than *by* them, or granted from above rather than demanded from below. Carlota Bustelo, one of the few prominent feminist deputies in the constituent assembly, made this point in an editorial entitled 'En favor del feminismo', in which she sought to give feminists credit for the recent slate of legislative changes benefiting women.[37] She pointed out the discrepancy between people's image of feminists as crazy, sexually frustrated lesbians, and the general acceptance of feminist demands as just. More importantly, she reminded readers that, although it was feminists who forced women's rights onto political platforms and into constitutional debates, when it came time to take credit for new laws, deputies rarely mentioned either women or the feminists. Rather than being the object of these progressive laws, she implied, women were their agents. Bustelo, then, tried to articulate a language of feminist citizenship practice, of feminists engaged in active political creation of women's role in the new democracy.

In contrast, most of the favourable press coverage of feminism was not about women's agency (i.e. citizenship as practice) but about specific injustices that had to be corrected for Spain to join the world of modern democracies (i.e. citizenship as a political status granted to women). As in the question of women's suffrage in 1931, feminism was discussed in the context of Spain's identity, not female empowerment.[38] The question posed by Susan Sontag in an interview with *El País* (28 May 1978) echoed the shame connected with the anachronistic legislation of the Francoist regime. Sontag, an American and self-defined feminist, told of her surprise when informed that until recently a Spanish woman could not open a bank account or get a passport without her husband's permission. 'What can one think about a country where women can't legally travel without their husband's permission?', she asked. This question clearly loomed behind much of the discussion about improving or 'modernising' women's situation in the new Spain. As one article noted approvingly, 'the Spanish woman is awakening from a long lethargy and is taking giant steps to catch up with the most advanced societies in the world'.[39]

Nearly everyone agreed that some change was necessary. While conservatives and progressives clashed over hot-button issues like abortion, divorce and birth control, by the end of the transition even conservatives generally accepted the need to end legal discrimination and to give women equal citizenship rights. This point is illustrated in a set of interviews published in a *Cambio 16* article (5 March 1978) on the 'state of womanhood' in Spain. The interviews, with a priest, a military officer and the president of the Francoist Parents' Association, articulated what seemed to be variations on the typical conservative position. The priest advocated social equality for women and participation in all aspects of life, while the officer supported the expansion of women in the military. He called himself a lover of women rather than a feminist, but believed in the equality of women. The president of the Parents' Association endorsed greater recognition of women, both within and outside the home, and interpreted liberation for women as their ability to reach their full potential. At least rhetorically, these assertions were far removed from the official Francoist model of womanhood.

Beyond such rhetoric, most conservatives even seemed to support the general judicial and penal reforms proposed to end direct discrimination of women. Thus, *ABC* signalled its approval of the May 1975 law that established an equality of rights and duties for spouses, as well as the concept of further marital law reform, by acknowledging that it corresponded to the 'social reality' and the 'mentality of our time' (31 August 1978). A similar evolutionary argument was made by a non-feminist editorialist in *El País* (12 September 1976) who supported changes in the laws regulating adultery, infanticide, statutory rape and *patria potestad* (child custody). While these inequalities may have made sense originally, she asserted, they were out of sync with a twentieth-century family built around the concept of the equal couple. Typical of the conservative position of the time, she warned that if Spain did not incorporate these legitimate feminist principles, it would only provide ammunition for the feminists' more extreme demands.

One of the first 'legitimate' feminist issues to become a matter of public debate during the transition was adultery. As a result of a handful of *cause célèbre* prosecutions, feminists and supporters exposed the anachronistic double standard of the Francoist legal system to the light of democratic scrutiny.[40] In the first major case to be publicised, a woman separated from her husband nearly lost custody of her child when she took a trip with a male friend and was prosecuted for adultery by her spouse. With the full support of the progressive press, feminist organisations raised a ruckus about the indignity of a law that condoned extramarital sex for men but punished women with up to six years in prison, and the woman was eventually acquitted.[41] In another case, a man who had abandoned his wife and child several years earlier decided to press adultery charges in order to vindicate his honour. In response, hundreds of women demonstrated and feminist organisations collected petitions demanding the decriminalisation of adultery.[42] As long as feminists demonstrated for the end to basic discrimination or inequality, they were lionised, especially by the progressive press.

Another issue that provoked general agreement was the need for rape law reform. In a big article on the issue, *Cambio 16* (4 September 1977) outlined the inadequacies of a legal framework constructed around a code of honour rather than sexual freedom, with 'sidebars' about recent advances made in France and Italy. The article included angry feminist voices calling for castration, as well as male gynaecologists describing the extent of physical injuries sustained by rape victims. The piece ended by pointing out the irony that the most recent victim, Theresa, had been raped in a dark corner of a street where the walls were covered with graffiti calling for democracy and liberty. Rejecting the Francoist code of sexual honour as anachronistic, the article pointed towards a new language linking sexual and political liberty. And, at least implicitly, the piece suggested a broader reading of citizenship rights that would include such liberties.

The progressive press pushed this broader vision of citizenship rights even more, in its embrace of reproductive freedom as a signifier of democracy and modernisation. For example, in *Cambio 16*'s major survey of the state of Spanish womanhood, on 26 February 1978, it blamed restrictions on divorce, abortion and birth control for the continued marginalisation of women. Implicit in the article's logic was the feminist argument that women required reproductive rights in order to be fully integrated into society and to become full and equal citizens of the nation. Even so, such an argument still implied that the issue was the reception of rights, not the creation of new identities. Women's citizenship was to be granted from above by a new social democratic state.

The most vigorous assertion of the connection between reproductive rights and modernity used the familiar language of the 'two Spains' to define positions on the issue.[43] Thus, the conflict between traditional and modern Spain was dramatised in the encounter between the 40-something women (the *amas de casa*) and (young) feminists distributing birth-control literature on the street, whom they harassed. The 'two Spains' metaphor was also evoked to portray the class divide between the thousands of wealthy Spanish women who flew to London to secure abortions or who could readily find birth control in the pharmacies of the tony Salamanca district, and the 300,000 poorer women who underwent illegal and often unsafe abortions at home.

While the 'two Spains' metaphor harked back to dangerous images of polarisation, the dominant interpretation presented a generally successful gradual evolution of attitudes, in which Spaniards were converging, not stuck in opposing camps. For example, one article on the cultural and social changes since Franco's death interviewed one 40-something doctor from a Francoist family who admitted that, little by little, things had been changing at home; he would fold laundry, or clean his own shoes, and not be upset when his two-course dinner was replaced by a sandwich.[44] Significantly, he felt the need to insist that his wife was not a 'militant feminist', and this seemed to be part of the larger message. Gradual individual change on the part of men and women within the private sphere of the home could complement the bestowal of new rights from above and avoid the more disruptive transformations demanded by 'radical' feminist movements. Such a message was congruent with the larger themes of political consensus and communitarian passivity that characterised the transition.

This point was underscored by a couple of cultural anecdotes, printed in the gossipy 'personal' pages of *Cambio 16*, that seemed designed to illustrate the quiet process of adaptation that was changing the face of the 'new Spain'. In one case, when a male singer and his wife were seen in the airport, the fact that she was loaded down with the bags while he was holding their son's hand was considered worthy of comment. Before women were liberated from the masculine yoke, quipped the article, men used to carry the bags.[45] In another story, a woman who was capriciously pulled over by a police officer argued her case, and witnesses supported her version of events. In the old days, the story noted, when a woman driver was stopped by a police car, she would simply submit, even if she thought she was in the right.[46] Once again, the story drove home the point that significant changes in gender roles were occurring alongside the larger political transition. Notably, these small changes were private and individual, as opposed to public and collective, once again reinforcing the model where gender is associated with the private sphere. While in themselves these stories were insignificant anecdotes about two encounters out of millions, the very anecdotal nature of the account reinforces the particularity of the issues and differentiates them from matters of general interest. Whereas feminists dragged these issues into the public, they were best resolved in the private realm of everyday life.

These small and private changes contrasted dramatically with the public and often radical image of many feminist groups and movements, even in the democratic press. Despite the general acceptance of many feminist principles in democratic discourse, it is clear that feminists themselves occupied a more ambivalent place in the rosy picture of laundry-folding doctors and luggage-carrying women. If the democratic press endorsed feminist principles as an enhancement of 'universal' citizenship rights, it feared the practice of the radical feminist as a destabilising and vindictive citizen. The militant feminist lurked as the potential threat, evoked to prod resisters into accepting 'reasonable' change. Thus, the angry feminist demand for castration in the rape article posed the unwelcome alternative to basic legal changes. The violence and extremism associated with feminists clashed with the 'lessons of the Civil War'.

Images of feminist extremism abounded in both conservative and progressive commentaries. One strand of the discourse identified feminists as abnormal or marginal. For example, in an editorial urging centre-right political parties to take feminism seriously, the prominent conservative historian Ricardo de la Cierva argued that the advance of feminism was being hindered by the 'eccentrics', the representatives of 'abnormal feminism'. For the movement to progress, he averred, it must be led by 'normal women', not 'viragos, sexual deviants, neurotics and other exceptional personalities'.[47] Even a sympathetic survey of the state of the feminist movement reached a similar conclusion, claiming that the majority of Spanish women found feminists incomprehensible and 'exotic'.[48]

More indirectly, in 'deviance through association', feminists were often linked discursively with other outsiders. The theme emerged explicitly in a story about a demonstration against the anti-gay law of 1970 in which feminists, lesbians and gays claimed sexual freedom. As if referring to one more odd-ball sexual orientation, the article added that, as a 'finishing touch', *even* prostitutes were invited.[49] Another piece, commenting on the proliferation of naked bodies on the news stands during the transition, listed those opposed to the trend as: 'feminists, puritans, old people, sexually frustrated individuals, supporters of the "bunker", the repressers and the repressed'.[50] As opponents of pornography, feminists were here dramatically linked to the bastions of the old Spain. From a more sympathetic point of view, Francisco Umbral chided gays, feminists and regionalists for their self-imposed marginalisation that prevented the 'straight Castillian men' from identifying with the broader struggle.[51] Whether imposed or self-defined, feminists' perceived links with other marginalised groups enhanced the sense that they were outside the mainstream of Spanish society inhabited by 'straight Castillian men'. Once again, feminists seemed to speak neither for the conventional private interests of the family nor for the assumed collective good that was implied in the transition's language of consensus.

A more common image of feminists during the period portrayed them as harsh, angry and intimidating, an unwelcome strident voice in a sea of civility. For example, a notice introducing the new feminist publication *Vindicación Feminista* used a play on words to quip that all 'vindictive feminists' should buy the new magazine.[52] Likewise, a report on Catalan feminists used the term 'intellectual terrorism' to describe how they intimidated writers on their 'blacklist'.[53] In another example, a book review of Eugenio Detti's *The Feminist Lunacy* featured a photo of the cover, a woman's hands holding an ear of corn and slicing off two large onions, a clear analogy to castration.[54]

The reviewer commented that the book helped explain the nature of feminist extremists.

This device of turning feminists into the oppressors instead of the victims appeared most directly in the account of a feminist attack on the offices of *Interviu*, a Catalan magazine considered to be a member of the independent democratic press. The *Cambio 16* piece, provocatively titled 'How to Rape a Magazine', lambasted the hundred feminists who gathered in front of the offices, threw tomatoes and eggs, and shouted 'down with the macho press' and 'castration for rapists'. The specific issue was the magazine's ad asking for girls who had been raped to be interviewed for a story, but the feminists claimed it was part of a larger pattern of sensationalist, manipulative stories that preyed on female victims. Even the less sensationalist *El País* version of the story (4 October 1977) emphasised the demonstrators' hostility towards all the men around, including the journalists reporting on the story. Perhaps the most stinging rebuke came from the *Interviu* editor, who complained that it was the first time he had been hit by someone other than the Francoist police. As when feminists were associated with the 'bunker' in the piece on pornography, this time they were rhetorically linked with rapists and police officers rather than with the rape victims they were claiming to defend.

Another common criticism of feminists in coverage of their activities was their perceived hostility toward men. In reports on the 'Tribunal of Crimes against Women', held in Brussels, the two features of the event which attracted most comment were the exclusion of men from the proceedings and the moment when 200 lesbians rushed the stage to sing an ode to Sappho to the tune of Paul Anka's 'Diana' (the 'abnormal' again).[55] Likewise, in the coverage of the First Catalan 'Jornadas de la Dona' (Women's Days), the male reporter highlighted the demand by the most radical group that their 'enemy' 'oppressors', the men, be excluded from the proceedings.[56] While men were not in fact banned, a follow-up story the next day featured a photo of a panel of women, with the caption 'the Jornadas Catalanas do not want men'. Once again, at a moment when Spaniards were attempting to finally put the Civil War behind them, feminists were portrayed as opening a new schism in Spanish society.

Beyond the specific issue of man-hating, feminists suffered from the mainstream democratic circles' general rejection of radical options and agendas which evoked, once again, the mistakes of the Second Republic and Civil War. Feminists spoke the language of the radical left, of turning society upside down, pursuing revolution and rupture, not reform. As one reporter noted disapprovingly, feminists seemed to question the entire social organisation of a world that was irredeemably macho, and, in so doing, they sought to make a special claim on the feminine word, revolution.[57]

Articles in the mainstream democratic press often emphasised the links between feminist organisations and leftist political movements, like the Communist Party or the Spanish Workers' Party. As an article on the Catalan feminist movement noted, the left and extreme left, from anarchists and Trotskyists to socialists and communists, dominated the movement. As evidence, it cited prominent feminist lawyer and Barcelona city official Nuria Beltrán's statement that it was nearly impossible to be both 'right' and feminist.[58] Given the parameters of transition political culture, where pragmatism and flexibility were championed over idealism and scope of vision, the feminists, like the radical left more generally, were consistently presented as out of sync with the general political trend.

The criticisms made by a Spanish doctor of the famous *Hite Report* (on its translation into Castillian) sum up the general response to what was considered to be feminist 'extremism'. The report, he fumed, simply blames everything on men. Furthermore, the obsession with orgasms ignored the deeper emotional meaning of sex and taught women to be *insolidaria* (selfish), not cooperative.[59] From his point of view, feminist extremism was individualistic and divisive, an attempt to open old wounds rather than start the healing process. Once again, rather than championing the public good as noble citizens, feminists pursued the claims of a minority of disaffected individuals. While none of these images of feminists were particularly novel in modern political culture, they clashed even more dramatically with the specific Spanish framework of consensus, with its universalising elision of difference within a presumed unity of interests.

The divisive nature of feminism was the key message that emerged from news reports on the internal functioning of the movement. As one reporter writing on the Catalan feminist movement put it, atomisation was the first impression one got.[60] A similar story on the Catalan 'Jornadas de la Dona' emphasised the fractured nature of the feminist groups, and the difficulties of building a unified regional movement that could embrace both Christian and radical feminists.[61] In order to navigate the confusing feminist spectrum, periodic 'dictionaries' were composed to distinguish between a variety of groups, from the Democratic Association of Women (ADM) to the Feminist Collective and the Antipatriarchal Struggle of Authoritarian and Revolutionary Women (LAMAR).[62]

Strategic and theoretical disputes dominated reports on feminist meetings and symposia. For example, an article entitled 'It Continues to be Difficult to Unify Spanish Feminists' highlighted the rift in the movement between the adherents and detractors of 'double militancy'.[63] A pair of stories on the schism within the Colectivo Feminista of Madrid reported on the precipitating disagreement over whether women belonged to a separate oppressed class or were integrated into the economic class system. When the minority objected to the majority's definition of the organisation as 'cross-class', they seceded.[64] Another article announced a 'Crisis in the Catalan Women's Association', because independent feminists spurned control by the Spanish Workers' Party.[65]

Yet another report, on the Catalan 'Jornadas de la Dona', identified the divisions between socialist feminists and Catholic feminists as the defining characteristic of the proceedings. The headline announced that the 'Jornadas' offered a 'panorama of contradictions and confrontations among the 2,000 participants'. The author went on to describe the opening session as a virtual brawl between Catholic groups and militants like the Colectivo Feminista, who refused to let the moderates speak, going so far as to grab the microphone out of their hands. This polarisation set the tone, he noted, for many of the debates, in which the militant position was always dominant.[66]

Interestingly, we have a very different account of the 'Jornadas' from a feminist participant, who called it a positive, emotional experience for the majority of those in attendance, despite the differences of opinion. Instead of dissension, she stressed the image of 4,000 women cheering for five full minutes at the reading of the joint conclusions. Moreover, she pointed out that the participants reaffirmed democratic procedure after the Catholic women were denied the floor on the first day, and for the remainder of the session everyone was allowed to speak. Within this framework of democratic consensus, she then discussed the issues that divided them.[67]

In a more pointed attack on the interpretation of the original (male) reporter, a feminist editorial censured the press for focusing on scandalous anecdotes rather than tackling substantive issues, and for fixating on the divisions within the movement instead of the 'remarkable fact that 3,000 women with different points of view got together, talked and came up with majority conclusions'.[68] Beyond the discrepancy over numbers, these feminist interpretations of the event provide an alternative lens through which to view both the 'Jornadas' and the construction of feminist citizenship, but they were the exception that proved the rule. Whereas the feminist writers portrayed themselves as engaged in the democratic activities of cooperation, negotiation and consensus-building, the dominant viewpoint presented them in undemocratic postures of violence, polarisation and intolerance. Such a viewpoint not only negated feminist citizenship, it also once again denied them any role in the transition to democracy.

Such accounts of schisms and dissensions within the feminist movement conveyed an image of divisiveness that was clearly out of sync with the consensus-building rhetoric of the period. Part of the problem lay with the nature of the feminist movement itself, which was indeed linked with the radical left and was also deeply fractured along organisational and ideological lines. Qualities which may have been perceived in a positive light in another political context were destined for the margins at a time when success was defined by the occupation of the middle ground. In this environment, there was little chance that the feminist could become the blueprint for a new female citizen.

In this sense, the representation of feminists in the press, which focused on the radicalism, the divisions and the combativeness of the movement rather than on its potential for mobilising and empowering women, only reflected the broader sensibilities of the society at large, which was sceptical of any path to citizen empowerment. Nevertheless, as was made clear in the conflicting interpretations of the Catalan 'Jornadas', it is apparent that alternative narratives did exist, narratives which linked citizen empowerment with democratic practice and women's rights with the public good. However, the dominant narrative minimised women's potential agency and their contributions to the larger democratic transition. What came across was an implicit contrast between the activities of women as feminists (individualist, particularist, private) with the qualities of citizenship (public, cooperative, universalist), a contrast that negated their status as citizens. Within this framework, the feminist movement fell outside the parameters of the transition and its miraculous consensus, posing an obstacle to, rather than support for, the process of democratisation. Likewise, while the discourse about women's rights helped define a new female citizenship based on passive equal status, feminists' contribution to citizenship practice remained unacknowledged.

Where, then, did the female citizen fit in Spain's emerging democratic culture? In fact, there was no comfortable place in transition political culture for such a category. In contrast to the Franco regime, which created a clear and well-articulated place for women in their role as *ama de casa*, the emerging democratic discourse was full of contradictions and conflicts between equality and difference-based frames of reference. Thus, on one level, equality of the sexes was the watchword of the transition, while on a more unexamined level, markers of difference remained in place. This contradictory set of impulses provided the primary material for the imagining of a new female citizenship within the specific context of Spain's passive communitarian model of democratic citizenship. Within these parameters, it was difficult to create a framework that could recognise any of the collective activities of women who participated in the transition, in particular those of the feminist movement, as contributing either to the transition or to a democratic female citizenship. In most cases, their actions were identified with the private and the particular rather than with the public and the universal, qualities which were linked to citizenship practice in the post-Francoist democratic culture. Informing these evaluations was an unquestioned conceptual framework that linked women with the private and men with the public and political. As a result, women actors were written out of the contemporary narrative of the transition, cast as extras in a drama that they watched from the sidelines.

What, then, does this conclusion tell us about Spanish women and the transition? Although it is difficult to make the link between public discourse and individual mentalities, it can at least be argued that the majority of women (those who joined no movements) had no clear road map to follow in negotiating or appropriating the transition. If citizenship formation was one of the primary tasks of the emerging democratic press, guides for the practice of female citizenship remained murky at best and riddled with contradictions at worst. In this context, it is plausible to argue that women's well-publicised lack of political engagement could have stemmed in part from how politics were defined. If women's activities during the transition did not qualify them for citizenship, then perhaps citizenship was not that important. Rather than asking why women rejected politics, we might ask what kind of politics they rejected. Likewise, rather than assuming that women did not take part in the transition, we might ask in what different ways they did participate, redrawing the boundaries around their actions in order to recognise their contributions.

Beyond such speculation about women themselves is the broader question of how a gendered analysis of political discourse enriches our understanding of the transition, or of political culture in general. How do we make such cultural discourses relevant to the master narrative of the transition, with its focus on elite pacts and institution-building? If we acknowledge, as Pérez Díaz argues, that the cultural transformation of civil society provided the framework for elite decision-making and behaviour, then this analysis helps define the gendered markers in that framework. As the existing bases of social consensus were loosened, the emerging public sphere set the parameters for a new social consensus, which would eventually be institutionalised. As a result, what happened (or didn't happen) during this foundational moment set the terms for the future development of political identities and relationships. From this perspective, the broader politics of gender can be integrated into the conventional high politics of the transition.

The Spanish transition has been celebrated precisely for its success in moving from one social consensus to another without violence or disruption. However, new gender roles were not a part of the consensus, which implies that the vaunted process of integration was incomplete. As the editor of *El País* wrote in an editorial in 1983 entitled 'Women and the Transition', although women had achieved legal equality, the centres of decision-making in politics, art, economics and the media continued to be male-dominated. On the eve of Spain's first socialist government, the editor challenged the new administration to carry out a truly 'historic transition' of social relationships (2 January 1983).

Taking the argument beyond this assertion of unfinished business, one could argue that the underlying continuity of gender ideologies was a necessary part of the consensus-building process. While on the surface there seemed to be plenty of 'new women' for a 'new Spain', underneath the apparent distinctions with Francoist womanhood was a common framework that linked women to the nation through the family. The fact that this defining relationship was not questioned in the mainstream discourse seemed to have provided an unspoken bond between the Francoist elites and the new democratic elites. The implicit agreement not to push the re-examination of gender relationships created an important ground on which to build a political consensus. Thus, gender mattered to the transition, even as women were marginalised from its master narrative. This is not to say that the Spanish transition was a failure, but to (re-)affirm that the construction of female citizenship is still a problematic aspect of the transition to democracy, even in the late twentieth century.

....

Notes

I would like to thank several patient and insightful readers, whose comments greatly improved and enriched this piece: Robert Moeller, Temma Kaplan, Judith Keene, Victoria Enders, Elizabeth Munson, David Gutierrez and the editors of this volume, Kathleen Canning and Sonya Rose.

1. Jane Jacquette, Introduction, in *The Women's Movement in Latin America: Feminism and the Transition to Democracy*, ed. Jane Jacquette (Unwin Hyman, Boston, 1989), p. 13.

2. Guillermo O'Donnell and Philippe Schmitter, *Transitions from Authoritarian Rule: Tentative Conclusions about Uncertain Democracies* (Johns Hopkins University Press, Baltimore, 1986), 'Democracy's guiding principle is citizenship', p. 7.

3. The Francoist regime, like other traditionalist authoritarian regimes of the twentieth century, espoused a return to the domestic ideology of 'separate spheres' and a patriarchal ordering of society. This ideology was propagated both by the regime's cultural ally, the Catholic Church, and by the official women's movement, the Sección Femenina, which conscripted women into domestic 'tours of duty', and taught the gospel of domesticity. On Francoist gender ideology, see Mary Nash, 'Pronatalism and Motherhood in Franco's Spain', in *Maternity and Gender Policies: Women and the Rise of the European Welfare States, 1880s–1950s*, ed. Gisela Bock and Pat Thane (Routledge, London, 1991), and Aurora Morcillo, *True Catholic Womanhood: Gender Ideology in Franco's Spain* (Northern Illinois University Press, DeKalb, IL, 2000).

4. Guillermo O'Donnell, Philippe Schmitter and Laurence Whitehead (eds), *Transitions from Authoritarian Rule: Prospects for Democracy* (Johns Hopkins University Press, Baltimore, 1986). See also Larry Diamond, Juan Linz, and Seymour Lipset (eds), *Democracy in Developing Countries* (Lynne Rienner, Boulder, CO, 1988), and John Higley and Richard Gunther (eds), *Elites and Democratic Consolidation in Latin America and Southern Europe* (Cambridge University Press, Cambridge, 1992).

5. The story has been told many times, but a concise and cogent version can be found in José María Maravall and Julián Santamaría, 'Political Change in Spain and the Prospects for Democracy', in *Transitions from Authoritarian Rule: Southern Europe*, ed. Guillermo O'Donnell, Phillippe Schmitter and Laurence Whitehead (Johns Hopkins University Press, Baltimore, 1986).

6. Donald Share, *The Making of Spanish Democracy* (Praeger, New York, 1986).

7. Juan Linz and Alfred Stepan, *Problems of Democratic Transition and Consolidation* (Johns Hopkins Press, Baltimore, 1996).

8. Victor Pérez-Díaz, *The Return of Civil Society: The Emergence of Democratic Spain* (Harvard, Cambridge, 1993), pp. 6–7.

9. Pérez-Díaz differs from Habermas in his definition: 'the autonomous sphere of markets, associations and the public sphere' (*The Return of Civil Society*, p. 56).

10. See O'Donnell and Schmitter, *Transitions from Authoritarian Rule: Tentative Conclusions about Uncertain Democracies*, ch. 5, 'The Resurrection of Civil Society'.

11. Nancy Fraser, 'What's Critical about Critical Theory? The Case of Habermas and Gender', in *Unruly Practices: Power, Discourse and Gender in Contemporary Social Theory* (University of Minnesota Press, Minneapolis, 1989). See also Johanna Meehan (ed.), *Feminists Read Habermas: Gendering the Subject of Discourse* (Routledge, New York, 1995).

12. As an introduction to the extensive literature on this topic, see Barbara Laslett, Johanna Brenner, and Yesim Arat (eds), *Rethinking the Political: Gender, Resistance and the State* (University of Chicago Press, Chicago, 1995), and Judith Butler and Joan W. Scott (eds),

Feminists Theorize the Political (Routledge, New York, 1992). See also my own article, 'Women's Politics: Consumer Riots in Twentieth-Century Spain', in *Constructing Spanish Womanhood: Female Identity in Modern Spain*, ed. Victoria Enders and Pamela Radcliff (State University of New York Press, Albany, NY, 1999).

13. Carol Pateman, *The Disorder of Women* (Polity Press, Cambridge, MA, 1989), p. 110.
14. This approach has been particularly fruitful in Latin America, where social movements were very prominent in several transitions. See Jacquette, *The Women's Movement in Latin America*, and Jane Jacquette and Sharon Wolchik (eds), *Women and Democracy: Latin America and Central and Eastern Europe* (Johns Hopkins Press, Baltimore, 1998). Although the same types of social movements existed in Spain, the literature is not as well developed. See Giuliana di Febo, 'La Lucha en los barrios en los últimos años del franquismo', in *La Oposición al régimen del Franco: estado de la cuestión y metodología de la investigación*, vol. 2, ed. Javier Tusell, Alicia Alted, and Abdón Mateos (UNED, Madrid, 1990), pp. 251–60.
15. Ruth Lister, *Citizenship: Feminist Perspectives* (New York University Press, New York, 1997), and Wendy Sarvasy and Birte Siim, 'Gender, Transitions to Democracy and Citizenship', in *Social Politics*, 1 (1994).
16. Susan James, 'The Good-Enough Citizen: Female Citizenship and Independence', in *Beyond Equality and Difference*, ed. Gisela Bock and Susan James (Routledge, London, 1992).
17. Gerard Imbert, 'El Discurso de la representación', in *El País o la referencia dominante*, ed. Gerard Imbert and Jose Vidal Beneyto (Editorial Mitre, Barcelona, 1986), p. 25.
18. Antonio Sanchez-Gijón, 'The Spanish Press in the Transition', in *Spain in the 1980s*, ed. Robert Clark and Michael Haltzel (Ballinger Publishers, Cambridge, MA, 1987), p. 124, and Juan Giner, 'Journalists, Mass Media and Public Opinion in Spain, 1938–1982', in *The Press and the Rebirth of Iberian Democracy*, ed. Kenneth Maxwell (Greenwood Press, Westport, CT, 1983), p. 38.
19. J. Luis Cebrián, editor of *El País*, quoted in Giner, 'Journalists, Mass Media and Public Opinion', p. 33.
20. Sanchez-Gijón, 'The Spanish Press in the Transition', p. 129.
21. Imbert, 'El Discurso de la representación', p. 26.
22. Laura Desfor Edles, *Symbol and Ritual in the New Spain: The Transition to Democracy* (Cambridge University Press, Cambridge, 1998), p. 22.
23. Giner, 'Journalists, Mass Media and Public Opinion', p. 49.
24. Manuel Tuñon de Lara, et al., *Historia de España*, vol. 10, *Transición y Democracia: 1973–1985*, (Editorial Labor, Barcelona, 1992), p. 423.
25. José Vidal Beneyto, 'El Espacio publico de referencia dominante', in *El País o la referencia dominante*, ed. Gerard Imbert and Jose Vidal Beneyto (Editorial Mitre, Barcelona, 1986), p. 18.
26. See Edles, *Symbol and Ritual in the New Spain*, ch. 4.
27. For the exact text of these articles, see Carmen Pujol Algans, *Código de la mujer* (Instituto de la Mujer, Madrid, 1992), pp. 30, 35.
28. Bryan S. Turner, 'Outlines of a Theory of Citizenship', *Sociology*, 24 (1990).
29. On the 'lessons' of the Civil War as a context for the transition, see Paloma Aguilar Fernández, *Memoria y olvido de la guerra civil española* (Alianza Editorial, Madrid, 1996), and Edles, *Symbol and Ritual in the New Spain*.
30. The play is discussed in these terms by Ann Witte in *Guiding the Plot: Politics and Feminism in the Work of Women Playrights from Spain and Argentina, 1960–1990* (Peter Lang, New York, 1996), p. 33.
31. Lister, *Citizenship: Feminist Perspectives*, p. 30.
32. Jacquette and Wolchik, Introduction, *Women and Democracy: Latin America and Eastern Europe*, p. 8.
33. Laura Desfor Edles discusses the symbolic meaning of democracy in the Spanish transition; see *Symbol and Ritual in the New Spain*, pp. 52–8.

34. Monica Threlfall, 'The Women's Movement in Spain', *New Left Review*, 151 (1985); Colectivo Feminista de Madrid, 'El Feminismo español en la década de los 70', *Tiempo de Historia*, 3:27; María Angeles Dúran and María Teresa Gallego, 'The Women's Movement in Spain and the New Spanish Democracy', in *The New Women's Movement: Feminism and Political Power in Europe and the USA*, ed. Drude Dahlerup (Sage Publications, London, 1986).

35. See, for example, the introduction to *Gender and History*'s issue on nationalisms and national identity, volume 5 (Summer 1993).

36. *El País*, 29 June 1978.

37. *Cambio 16*, 21 May 1978.

38. Judith Keene, 'Into the Clear Air of the Plaza: Spanish Women Achieve the Vote in 1931', in *Constructing Spanish Womanhood: Women in 19th and 20th Century Spain*, ed. Victoria Enders and Pamela Radcliff (State University of New York Press, Albany, NY, 1998).

39. *Cambio 16*, 26 February 1978.

40. See Temma Kaplan, 'Women, Popular Democratic Movements and the Transition: the Anti-Adultery Campaigns of 1976', paper delivered at SSPHS, April 2000.

41. *El País*, 6, 7, 9, 10 October 1976.

42. *El País*, 12, 13, 17 November 1976.

43. *Cambio 16*, 24 April 1977.

44. *Cambio 16*, 26 June 1977.

45. *Cambio 16*, 9 August 1976.

46. *Cambio 16*, 12 December 1976.

47. *El País*, 16 February 1977.

48. *Cambio 16*, 22 January 1978.

49. *Cambio 16*, 25 December 1977.

50. *Cambio 16*, 9 October 1977.

51. *El País*, 28 June 1978.

52. *Cambio 16*, 19 June 1976.

53. *Cambio 16*, 24 April 1977.

54. *Cambio 16*, 23 July 1978.

55. *Cambio 16*, 22 March 1976.

56. *Cambio 16*, 27 May 1976.

57. *Cambio 16*, 14 June 1976.

58. *Cambio 16*, 24 April 1977.

59. *Cambio 16*, 23 October 1977.

60. *Cambio 16*, 24 April 1977.

61. *El País*, 27 May 1976.

62. *El País*, 17 February 1977. Monica Threlfall notes that there were already ninety women's organisations by 1977 ('The Women's Movement in Spain', p. 47).

63. *El País*, 17 June 1977. Supporters of double militancy argued for the need to work both in independent feminist movements and in the regular political parties. In contrast, groups like the Seminario Colectivo Feminista and LAMAR argued that feminism was a separate struggle that required its own political organisations. Another example of this debate is found in the report on a symposium on 'Women and Politics' organised by the Club de Convergencia (*El País*, 16 February 1977).

64. *El País*, 9 and 10 October 1976.

65. *El País*, 29 July 1977.

66. *El País*, 30 May 1976.

67. *El País*, 6 June 1976.

68. *El País*, 8 June 1976.

The Trial of the New Woman: Citizens-in-Training in the New Soviet Republic

Elizabeth A. Wood

> Our task consists in making politics accessible for every labouring woman and in teaching every [female] cook [*kukharka*] to run the government.
>
> — Vladimir Lenin, Third Congress of Soviets, 1918

The accusations were flying thick and fast against the defendant. She had pretensions to running the government and meddling in public affairs. She had taken part in strikes and demonstrations. She was trying to put all women on an equal footing with men. She had destroyed her own femininity, ceasing to be an object of beauty and pleasure for men, ceasing as well to raise her children and, instead, giving them into others' hands. All these things, it was alleged, contradicted woman's very nature, which was to serve as decoration in men's lives.

The setting was *The Trial of the New Woman*. The prosecution witnesses included a factory director, a lady secretary, a rich peasant, a priest, and a traditional family woman. The so-called 'bourgeois' court initially found the defendant guilty, but then workers appeared on stage, and her judges ran away. Her rights were restored, and she was recognised to be 'equal to men in all respects'.

This *Trial of the New Woman* was, of course, a mock trial, and the new woman herself emerged as the heroine of the play. It was staged under the auspices of the local women's section of the Communist Party in Voronezh, a provincial city in the Soviet Union, in late February 1921.[1] A few months later a similar *Trial of the New Woman* was performed in the Great Columned Hall of the House of Unions in Moscow, the same hall where the famous Moscow Show Trials would be enacted in the 1930s.[2] Other such trials of women and women's issues were held in provincial cities and in the countryside for the next six years.[3]

The mock trials emerging at this time were a new form of political education known as 'agitation trials' (*agitatsionnye sudy*). In the first half of the 1920s the central women's section of the party and local women's sections used these trials of new women as a vehicle to publicise the regime's claim of a revolutionary commitment to women's participation and equality.

Yet, as I will show, their representation in these dramatic works in fact served to undermine the Soviet assertion that women were fully equal citizens. Analysis of the portrayal of these heroines suggests instead that they should be characterised as citizens-in-training, i.e. as citizens who ostensibly enjoyed fully equal rights, but who nonetheless needed constant monitoring and training because they were not yet capable of being full members of the body politic.

This article is part of a larger study of agitation trials that were staged in a wide variety of contexts.[4] These courtroom dramas were performed by amateurs, including in this case political activists in the women's sections of the party. They put fictional characters on trial in order to condemn pre-revolutionary and, above all, 'backward' forms of behaviour. Sometimes, as in the cases of the *Trial of the New Woman*, the dramas were improvised along generally accepted political lines without a formal script. In other trials of women delegates formal scripts were usually twenty to thirty pages long. They were printed in inexpensive editions ranging from 3,000 to 100,000 copies.

The trial format permitted relatively easy staging by amateur actors at low cost. All that was needed was a red cloth to cover a table for the judge, a few benches for the accused and witnesses, plus a few incidentals such as a bell for keeping order, a carafe of water for verisimilitude. The actors went through the ritual motions of declaring the court in session, inviting the witnesses and the defendant to give testimony, presenting closing arguments, and pronouncing a final verdict.

The trials in which women and women's issues figure as the central subjects form a distinct minority of the scripts and accounts I have collected. Only nine accounts and texts are devoted to women's involvement in political issues.[5] Yet in this subset of the agitation trials one can see important assumptions about males and females, political consciousness and ignorance.[6]

On the surface, Soviet ideology was unambiguously committed to women's citizenship and full gender equality. The 'new woman' in these plays was not only acquitted; she was officially presented as the heroine who had endured much at the hands of men and other women who failed to understand her important new role in society. As Lenin himself noted in 1917, 'Unless women are induced to take an independent part in political life generally, but also in daily and universal public service, it is no use talking about full and stable democracy, let alone socialism'.[7] Revolutionary laws from the first decrees after October 1917 explicitly eliminated any gender inequalities in marriage, divorce and private property, in voting rights and land use, and in labour policies.[8] Soviet officials insisted tirelessly that they wanted women to be involved in politics and the public sphere. They did not want women to be trapped in the kitchen any more. As Lenin had noted, every female cook should be able to run the government.

In this article I argue that the revolutionary authors' depiction of their own heroines reveals an underlying ambivalence about women's emancipation and citizenship. In the Russian and Soviet context historians have tended to focus almost exclusively on official discourses of women's equality (i.e. pronouncements of the law, the party, or prominent women within the party). Yet what the new authorities gave with one hand in terms of the public announcement of women's 'objective' equality, they took away and undermined discursively with the other, in their 'subjective' representations of female characters, as we shall see. The trials turn out to be steeped in mixed messages, a combination of explicit, official ideological representations of women as equals, on the one hand, and competing presentations of women, even the heroines, as still locked in older behaviours that put them in need of special tutelage and restraint.

Citizenship itself is not a fixed and unitary term even in the most liberal of 'modern' societies. As scholars have been showing in rich detail recently, citizenship as a concept has to be viewed in both political and social terms. One must ask not only who can vote, but also who can receive social services from the state and on what terms, who is required to serve the state and in what capacities. Citizens 'belong' to their states, as historical sociologist Rogers Brubaker has shown; but, at the same time, states make certain promises to those citizens.[9]

The issue of Soviet citizenship is particularly complicated because of the nature of this new state, its history and ideology, and the often unexamined preconceptions of those involved in the actual creation and administration of the new polity.[10] Many scholars might argue that the term 'citizenship' should not be applied at all in the Soviet context because this was a quintessentially 'illiberal' state. It did not permit free and contested elections. Competing political parties were quickly muzzled. The state did not provide legal guarantees as basic as habeas corpus, freedom of speech, assembly. There was no separation of the branches of government, no independent judiciary, no freedom of the press.[11]

Yet the new Soviet authorities themselves began using the term 'citizens' from their very first decrees. They eliminated the older term for 'subject' (*poddannyi*), declaring that it deserved to be 'relegated to the museum of antiquities'.[12] In its place they substituted 'citizen' (*grazhdanin*) and reiterated everywhere imaginable that they were declaring citizenship without regard to race, religion, domicile, or sex. The Constitution of 1918 claimed a series of freedoms explicitly for citizens: freedom of religious and anti-religious propaganda; the right freely to hold assemblies, meetings, processions, etc.; the right to vote and to be elected to the soviets. It also declared 'the duty of all citizens of the Republic' to be labour on the premise that 'Whoever does not work shall not eat'.[13]

Are we to view this as entirely a matter of hypocritical self-serving, a ploy to deceive the Russian and non-Russian peoples who otherwise might reject the revolution? I don't think so. In the first place, these were revolutionaries who had been following in the footsteps of the French Revolution and the Paris Commune for almost half a century.[14] Lenin himself had written extensively on the two-stage nature of the revolution he and his colleagues were creating: first, they would create a bourgeois democracy, then proceed to a socialist revolution and a socialist state.[15]

The question of who actually had citizenship is, however, rather tricky. In 1929 the American scholar Samuel Northrup Harper published his now almost entirely forgotten *Civic Training in Soviet Russia*.[16] He had lived in Russia before the October Revolution of 1917 and then spent the summer and fall of 1926 investigating questions of 'civic education', 'civic cohesion', and the like. These were fashionable questions at the time, and the University of Chicago published an entire series on citizenship in different countries. Harper's conclusion, which I endorse, was that one can see a tripartite hierarchy in early Soviet Russia, with the *lishentsy* or non-citizens at the bottom, ordinary workers and peasants in the middle, and party members at the top. Those on the bottom, the *lishentsy* (or disenfranchised persons), were denied suffrage and citizenship on the grounds that they had been tsarist officials, members of classes that exploited the labour of others, officers in the tsarist army, religious personnel, those convicted of crimes by the courts, or mentally ill.[17] Ordinary workers and peasants in the middle, both male and female, could both elect and be elected. The top category of what Harper calls 'a kind of super-citizenship' consisted of comrades who fulfilled active duties at the request of the party. The ideal of this kind of citizenship, Harper noted, was 'the stalwart, revolutionary, Communist fighter'.[18]

The proof that a 'comrade' was a higher rank than a 'citizen' can also be seen in the courts themselves. By the early 1920s, court practice had established that the defendant and all the witnesses in a trial were to be referred to as 'citizens'. Only the court personnel itself could be referred to by the judges as 'comrades'.[19] The defendant now had no right to refer to the judge or anyone else in authority as 'comrade'. Thus, a person on trial was demoted to the position of a mere 'citizen' – in other words, a mere resident of the Soviet Republic.

An excellent example of this can be seen in an agitation trial in which a woman delegate named Cherepanova is ultimately vindicated by the courts and shown to be the real heroine of her village. The judge who has consistently addressed her as 'citizenness' (*grazhdanka*), a term emphasising her status as defendant, turns to her in his very last speech, for the first and only time calling her 'comrade':

> Comrade Cherepanova, you are now free. Go and work yet more for the benefit of the government, for the benefit of all toilers. Call others to follow you as well.[20]

As long as she occupied the liminal status of someone on trial (i.e. someone who had not yet been found either guilty or innocent), Cherepanova had to be addressed as 'citizenness'. Only once she had regained the ranks of those working for the Soviet state could she be referred to as 'comrade'.

In the agitation trials under study in this article, the main tension revolves around the issue of women's public service to the party through their roles as *delegatki*, i.e. female delegates. Invented in about 1919, the delegate meeting (*delegatskoe sobranie*) was intended to provide a place for women workers and peasants to meet and learn about current political affairs. Larger conferences of local women would elect the *delegatki* to serve for a year. During that time the *delegatki* would study political literacy; they would visit various model Soviet organisations (museums, factories, courts, day care sites); and they would support mobilisation campaigns that the regime was running. Sometimes they would hold what might be called 'office hours' in their factories to hear the problems of other women and try to help them out. At the end of their year of service they were supposed to report back to the constituents who had elected them.[21]

In practice the delegate meetings were entirely insular. In the first place, they were set up only for women workers and peasants, with no equivalent for men. Women were deemed to be particularly in need of remedial work in a way that men were not. (While it is true that 86 per cent of women were illiterate on the eve of the October Revolution, fully 67 per cent of men were illiterate as well.)[22] Secondly, these meetings were designed primarily for those women considered most illiterate and least involved in public campaigns.[23] So, clearly it was not the most capable and/or committed women who were asked to join these meetings and contribute their skills to political work. Finally, these delegate meetings did not actually report to anyone other than the women who elected them. In other words, they were a kind of self-sufficient political organisation. They were thus not designed to have any serious influence on the political process, even at the most local level. Rather they were intended primarily to teach a few women a few political skills. Even that training did not usually translate into increased party membership for women or increased political involvement. After their year of service in the delegate meetings, women workers and peasants typically did not join the party, although they might remain working in the kindergarten or public cafeteria where they had done an internship.

The women's section of the party usually took the lead in publishing agitation trials of women delegates. This set of trials tended to focus on the harassment of *delegatki* and women electors by local men. The stated goal was to show the harm this harassment could do and to vindicate the women, showing that they had triumphed over their male harassers. Fictional trials of the heroine *delegatka*, obviously, gave playwrights an opportunity to show the obstacles she faced and to turn the tables on her opponents, showing that they were in fact the ones hindering the new order.

At the same time, however, these trials reveal new assumptions that only public work and service made the individual a member of the new order. The woman delegate who is the ostensible heroine of the trials is never portrayed as having already *attained* full political consciousness. Even when she does break out of the clutches of the domestic sphere to become involved in the public sphere, she is nonetheless depicted largely in terms of traditionally negative 'female' qualities of indiscipline, meddling, gossip, and/or, their opposite, a kind of saintliness.

The male characters in these plays express stereotypical peasant misogyny.[24] Politics, for example, 'is no women's matter [*ne bab'e delo*]', says one peasant husband.[25] Another says his wife can't be a boss, because he is the boss, and because women have 'stupid heads'. If you let them run things, 'you might as well put your head in a noose'. If the women want to go off and form their own 'women's council', that's fine, but we don't need them in ours. It's also not women's place to wander idly into various reading huts (created by the regime to encourage literacy) and 'stick their noses' into news-papers.[26]

Women delegates in these plays themselves subscribe to many of these views. Before being put on trial for not fulfilling her responsi-bilities as a delegate, Maria Tikhonova herself thought she did not have a good enough head for politics. She was barely literate. She did not really understand that being elected as a delegate meant that she actually had to do work in that role. Everything would be taken care of by the woman organiser from the women's section of the party, she thought. After all, she noted, people had got along fine without women delegates before the revolution. Furthermore, she needed to go home right after work in order to take care of the house and the farming: 'My female responsibility is to get my work done and get home as soon as possible'.[27] Her neighbour defends her, saying, 'Look, from childhood no one bothered to teach us, so now what are we supposed to do? Once a female [*baba*], always a female.'[28]

The way out of this problem ('once a female, always a female') was to make women 'human', or so the intelligentsia had long believed. In the nineteenth century, radical members of the Russian intelli-gentsia had envisaged the solution to the 'woman question' as making women into 'people', giving each a personality (*lichnost'*), and in the process making them the equals of men.[29] Through careful intervention and tutelage by male members of the educated classes, women could be 'brought up to' the level of men. This was the starting point of the early Bolshevik government's stated commitment to women's emancipation, though the new leaders came to this issue somewhat reluctantly.[30]

In the agitation trials, women delegates invariably speak of themselves as having become fully human only through the outside intervention of the Communist Party, which has brought them a new consciousness. On the one hand, this fits well with Lenin's assertions, in his famous essay 'What Is to Be Done?', that social-democratic consciousness could be brought to the workers only from outside, only by the Social Democratic Party itself (known as the Communist Party from 1918).[31] Yet this transition from 'backward woman' to 'human being' also has striking overtones of a kind of Pygmalion myth. The party will infuse the inert, uninvolved woman with breath in the form of political consciousness, and she will come alive, now able to serve the revolution and society.

In *The Trial of the Peasant Woman Delegate*, Maria Cherepanova, whom we have met before, is accused by her husband of abandoning her household and children in order to attend political meetings. In her own defence at the end of the play she tells why she became a woman delegate. 'I didn't consider myself a person', she begins. For years she worked only for her family. But then Soviet power came, and 'they' (presumably Soviet authorities) began to explain everything. Instructors came from the women workers' section in the city. 'It was as if a bandage fell from my eyes, [...] as if I had been blind and now I saw everything'. When they sent in a rural organiser to set up delegate meetings for women peasants, she became involved. 'All of a sudden I felt that I was, after all, also a person, really a person, and that I have all the rights; but before that wasn't the case. I felt so good, so joyful.'[32]

The main foil to her character, who illustrates someone stuck in the 'old' way of life, is her elderly mother-in-law, aged sixty-five. A widow who must live with her children in order to receive support, the mother-in-law complains bitterly of how young people 'have become smarter than us', and how it is a 'disgrace' that this family conflict between Maria and her husband has come to court. What kind of a wife and housewife is Maria, she asks. She doesn't listen to her husband; she leaves her children. Of herself, she says that she never tried to teach her husband; and if he beat her, well, then that was his business. 'We tolerated everything. You'll never hear of a life more bitter than that of our women. But what can you do? That's our women's lot. It's obviously God's will. It's not made by us, and not up to us to redo it. [...] We suffered, and she should do the same.'[33]

Another example of a character who becomes 'a person' through the process of the courtroom trial is the wife, Anna Grigor'eva, who has been beaten by her husband, in *The Trial of the Old Way of Life*. Although she is described as a 'conscious woman worker', she has tolerated her husband's abuse because of the remains of her 'old, slavish habits'. Once she realises, however, that the bourgeois ideal of domestic bliss is really an illusion and once she has found the courage to bring a suit against her husband, then she becomes, in her words, 'a completely different person'. Where earlier she was terrified to speak out and act, now nothing frightens her. She is the first to arrive at every meeting, lecture, and political discussion circle.[34]

Though the plays speak of 'freedom' and even of 'rights' (words which are rather unusual in the context of later Soviet writings), the freedom and the rights of women are linked irrevocably in these trials to their responsibility to work for Soviet state and society. The crime of several husbands in these plays is in failing to see that their wives are 'conscious' women workers, that they are 'respected and trusted comrades at work'.[35] Working as a *delegatka* and in other public spheres becomes 'the duty of every honest, conscious woman citizen'.[36] Grigor'eva, the wife whose husband has been beating her, also comes to see that 'a woman is not a slave, not a bitch for breeding [*samka*], but a free person, *engaged just as much in productive labour as the man*, and capable of fulfilling the same public work as he is'.[37] In saying this, she asks for a divorce from her husband not in order to have some abstract rights or freedoms but so that she can engage in productive labour and public works. She promises that from now on she will engage in fighting for women's emancipation, for public cafeterias, for nurseries, cooperatives, and clubs. While these institutions clearly assist women, Grigor'eva and the other defendants are not being 'emancipated' for their own sake either as women or as individuals. Rather they are being emancipated so they can work for Soviet power.[38]

These plays rely for some of their drama on the contrast between husbands who try to 'teach' their wives by beating them and dragging them around by the hair, on the one hand, and the new Soviet authorities, on the other hand, especially the women's sections and the local executive committees, who take the women delegates in hand and teach them through example, showing them the new Soviet order. In the old world, God had allegedly created an order which obliged women to submit to their husbands. In the new world, women could divorce their husbands and become involved in building a whole new social order.[39]

Yet the women are always in need of tutelage. The local authorities, especially organisations like the village executive committee, play a crucial imaginary role in 'developing' them. Then the women can 'be transformed into good workers' (*vyrabatyvaiutsia iz nikh i khoroshie rabotniki*).[40] Once they are turned into those good staff members, even the nouns lose their gender designations: the *delegatki* (a marked, female noun) become *rabotniki* (a general word for worker or staff member which does not have a gender marking). It is the party and its political organisations which must show women the way. On her own, Cherepanova, for example, is characterised as having only 'an instinct, a feeling' (*instinkt, chuvstvo*) which 'makes her feel drawn [to the new life]' (*ona tianetsia k nei*). She does not have 'a clear striving, a knowledge of the essence of this new life'. If she's to be sentenced, the defence argues, it should be to a term in school, so she can learn more and gain in knowledge, so she can 'sow light among her co-citizens and awaken the peasant women'.[41] In none of the agitation trials of women delegates, even those who are acquitted and vindicated as 'useful citizens', are they portrayed as fully formed, ready to hold positions of leadership.

Ostensibly, the heroines share a common commitment to telling the truth and helping to clean up village life. They appear to be doing good by blowing the whistle on individuals' and groups' bad habits, habits such as moonshine distilling, hindering the new political processes, and failing to implement political directives from the centre. Yet at the same time, these heroines come across as not very likeable. The question is, how and why.

The main character in the play *The Trial of the Peasant Woman-'Delegatka'* is named Maria Gudkova, i.e. the whistle-blower (from the Russian word *gudok*).[42] If her actions were being tried in a US court of law today, the case would probably be considered at least partly a libel case, since the male plaintiff sues that she has publicly defamed his character. It is also in part a corruption case, since she is charged with bribe-taking. Her accusers, the plaintiffs Kosorotov (whose name means 'crooked mouth'), and his wife and daughter-in-law, note that she has called Kosorotov a 'bloodsucker' and a *kulak* (a derogatory term for a rich peasant). She has even drawn a picture of him on the wall newspaper in the official reading hut, portraying him with a fat belly. Kosorotov, who admits that he has a history of moonshine distilling, wants the court to free him from her harassment.

In the course of the trial Kosorotov's main charge in the case, that Gudkova took a bribe from a woman moonshine distiller, is proven to be false. A number of prosecution witnesses bring other charges, however. The men claim that she has been stealing their wives, 'stirring them up' to become involved in public affairs, making them 'contrary' and difficult. Kosorotov's nephew, for example, claims that his wife was just a female (*baba*) like any other. Now, though, Gudkova has 'commanded' her to learn to read and write, while he, the husband thinks her 'women's work' should be to attend to the house and fields; so, of course, they are quarrelling. In his view, Gudkova is usurping his male role: 'And I say, who is your husband – me or Maria Gudkova?' He's also upset that his wife might become literate and leave him behind: 'Am I supposed to be her fool then?'[43] Even his parents have been upset by all this. His father calls the wife a *bolshevichka* (female Bolshevik), while his mother, on the contrary, wants to follow Gudkova and become a *delegatka* herself.

The nephew's wife has a different perspective, however. For her Gudkova is nothing short of a saint.[44] 'She takes care of us, showing us the light, teaching us good things', she notes. She helps the downtrodden women of the village while fighting off their enemies, the *kulaks* who exploit them, say other witnesses. Even the woman distiller whom Kosorotov had tried to force to bear false witness against Gudkova recants and rues her own behaviour. 'Why should anyone do Maria harm for no reason?', she asks; 'she does us a good turn, but we do her wrong'. The woman Communist who is the organiser for the whole region comments too that Gudkova is doing her duty in 'revealing all falsehoods and wrongdoing, defending the poorest'.[45] In her own brief final speech, Gudkova declares that she is not afraid of the likes of Kosorotov: 'Where something is bad or unjust, I will reveal it, without fearing anyone.' She gives a simplistic account of her transformation to a *delegatka*: 'There was a time', she claims, 'when I was ignorant [literally 'dark'] and didn't know what needed to be done in order to make life better, but now I know, and I want to teach all women to fight for the new, bright life under the direction of our Communist Party.'[46]

Yet Gudkova's own words are barely recorded in the twenty-nine-page script of the trial. When she does say anything (aside from her final speech which is a scant one-paragraph long), it is often without permission, interrupting the plaintiff and speaking out of order. In response to this behaviour, the judge disciplines her verbally. 'You will speak when you are given the floor', he insists. Whilst the primary motivation of the judge's interventions is undoubtedly to show the court's impartiality (even the heroine could be rebuked for not following the court's rules), a secondary effect is to show Gudkova as impulsive and not in control of her own speech. 'I know, citizen judge,' she tells the judge, 'but I don't have any patience'.[47]

After she has been rebuked for the second time, Gudkova falls completely silent until the judge asks her for her final speech at the very end of the trial. This brief speech begins with Gudkova's confusion: 'What should I say?' Ostensibly her question refers to her insistence that she has not done anything wrong. Yet in the context of the judge's rebukes, it also appears that she has in fact been successfully silenced by the court. She may be the delegate in the village, the one who can blow the whistle on others' misconduct, but ultimately it is the judge who has the power of speech and the power to determine guilt and innocence.

Nor does the audience learn from her short final speech what her motivations were in choosing to become a *delegatka* and work for the state. The audience is told nothing of her personal situation. We never learn whether she is married or has children, whether she has parents whom she cares for and whether she has land (though we learn a great deal about the family situations of the other witnesses in the course of the trial). Instead she is inscribed primarily as a vehicle to help, and in fact push, others in the village to find their way to the reading huts, the schools, the cooperatives, and other Soviet institutions.

The image on the cover of the printed scenario reinforces a sense of the saintliness and mediating role of Gudkova (see illustration overleaf). It pictures a smiling peasant woman posing her hand on a boy's head and showing him the way to the schoolhouse. Above her are the judge with his bell and two people's assessors. Below her stand three peasant men with their fists clenched. With the help of the wise judge above (now a secular figure instead of God), she helps the

Cover of *The Trial of the Woman Peasant-Delegate* by
N. Bozhinskaia, with the heading 'The Little Library of the Woman
Worker and Peasant' (State Publisher, 1926).

ignorant peasants, and especially the youth, find their way to the institutions of the new, brighter world.[48]

The contrast between the presiding male judge and the female lay assessor in this play is also instructive.[49] The male presiding judge plays the central role of father in Gudkova's trial. He is described as having a grey beard and being very calm. Several characters address him as 'my father' (*otets rodnoi, batiushka*). When the woman distiller becomes frightened of speaking in court (because of the threat of retaliation from Kosorotov), the judge tells her not to be frightened of anyone. When she bursts into tears saying that Kosorotov (Mr Crooked Mouth) is really a wolf and not a person and will harm her if she speaks the truth ('he will eat me', she says), the same male judge adopts a reassuring tone: 'Don't be afraid. We have good shepherds [to protect you] against wolves'. The male judge is thus associated with the strong (Christian) father figure who will protect the hapless female (the sheep) against the evil (wolf-like) male peasant who threatens to eat her.[50]

The female lay assessor who is assisting the judge is, by contrast, like Gudkova herself, undisciplined in her comments. Several times she breaks into the dialogue to tell other characters how they should live their lives. She angrily instructs one witness to give maternity benefits to his peasant wage labourer despite the fact that she cannot work. She tells another he shouldn't be fighting with his wife. She warns a woman who does not want to send her children to school that if she does not help them attain literacy, 'your children will never thank you when they grow up'.[51] Unlike the male judge, her tone lacks impartiality. She intrudes in a meddlesome way that makes her appear an interloper instead of an authority figure.

Another moralising *delegatka* who threatens to disrupt all the men's plans appears in the play *The Trial of the Peasant Medvedev Who Wrecked the Election of the Women's Candidate to the Village Council*. From her first appearance in court, the woman delegate Gracheva (whose name means 'rook' or 'crow'), interrupts other characters, challenging their interpretations of events and procedures. In her first appearance in the scripted court scene, she angrily interrupts Medvedev, the defendant: 'Who then instructed the men to hold their women down by the braids at home during the elections?'[52] Gracheva presents herself as having lost all patience with the 'gang' of peasants (including a *kulak* and a priest) who want to keep women out of elections. She wants women to learn to read so they can learn their rights and go after the 'new lords', i.e. the *kulaks* who are making money off the people. She too thus appears to be protecting the poor and downtrodden, especially women, against the oppressions of their husbands who want to keep them from even learning to read and write.

The defendant Medvedev and his cronies, however, take a different view of Gracheva's 'righteousness': 'Why does she stick her nose in with her morality?', asks Zabubennyi, a former chair of the village council and now a freelance scribe (whose name means 'unruly' or 'dissolute'). He defends a law-and-order perspective on moonshining, arguing that one cannot simply go into any hut and search for illegal stills without a warrant, as Gracheva (according to him) has done. Others criticise Gracheva for gossiping to outsiders when they come to visit, telling them everything that is wrong with the village. When she hears foreign words such as *Mopr* (the acronym of an international Soviet propaganda agency at this time) and *Dobrolet* (a Soviet organisation dedicated to supporting the extension of the air force), she wants to know what they are and to introduce them into the village council even though the council already has too much work just taking care of the village's own affairs. Nor, they argue, does she know anything about the really important local matters of land divisions, peasants who want to separate from the commune and live on their own, and the running of tractors.[53]

The male defendants obviously need to find reasons to criticise Gracheva in order to protect themselves against the charges that they have hindered the elections of women as delegates. But Gracheva also betrays herself as a less than fully sympathetic character. She addresses her husband in a simultaneously patronising and threatening manner: 'Oh yes, my Akimushka [little Akim], I can abandon you and I can take you to court for beating me. The comrade judge will affirm that for you. But what I find much more painful than your beatings is your ignorance.' She berates him for not knowing anything and for letting the rich peasants take advantage of him. She takes a high moral tone too, in arguing that if the judges were to acquit the defendants, they would be directly attacking her, and with her the whole worker-peasant government. Often she uses the pronoun 'we': 'we'll figure out who should have their tax lowered and who should have it raised'. 'It's just too bad we don't respect moonshine,' she concludes, making it clear that she has no intention of respecting any village traditions. Instead – and this was what the Soviet government was clearly counting on – she is offering to come in and clean up the whole nest of those engaging in moonshining and illegal kickbacks.[54]

In general, the heroines are almost never granted full, flesh-and-blood characters. They can sing the praises of the party and state, but they cannot evince a broader range of interests and desires. Moreover, they can move seamlessly from the 'we' of the family into the 'we' of the state, extending their apparently maternal qualities to the whole collective. But they cannot do so in an authoritative fashion.

Nor do the trials depict the history of the heroines' development. The narrative trope that their eyes 'have been opened' is presented exclusively in a passive voice. The women show little agency of their own, never taking actions that are not directed by the party. While the plays do mobilise their female characters into the public sphere, they simultaneously undermine a sense of their competence. Many *delegatki* are marked by passivity and insecurity. Others show their intemperance, breaking in while other witnesses are speaking. Still others blow the whistle without regard for local customs or even for the law (Gudkova conducts searches without proper search warrants).

Ostensibly the *delegatki* are presented to the public as victims of harassment by others. Yet they themselves need to be counselled and restrained. The judges emerge as those with the power and the authority to determine who will speak, on what basis, and when. It is they who determine who can be elevated from the status of 'citizen', i.e. defendant, to the status of 'comrade', one who is the equal of those on the bench. The plays thus ultimately *tame* these activist women even as they allow them to have minimal roles as delegates in closed organisations that have little real influence.[55]

In the end this portrayal of women as not quite citizens in the agitation trials reveals an important aspect of Soviet citizenship in general. No one, male or female, was granted unconditional citizenship; and many individuals residing in the Soviet Union spent years trying to prove their worthiness to attain that status.[56] Citizenship could not be attained definitively through one's birth or residency (*jus sanguinis* and *jus soli*, to use the juridical terms). Since it was not defined by objective criteria, it could not, I would argue, provide closure in Rogers Brubaker's sense.[57] Where the French and German states at the turn of the twentieth century identified one set of persons as citizens and another as non-citizens, Soviet authorities, including the women's sections themselves, identified certain groups as something in between, as a kind of citizens-in-training.

For women this absence of fixed citizenship was especially problematic because in the absence of objectively defined and enforceable
rights and obligations, prerevolutionary misogyny and resistance to
women's participation in the political sphere could be mobilised by
opponents. It was easy to point to women's illiteracy, inexperience,
and intemperance as reasons to continue to exclude women from the
public sphere. While the rates of women's participation did rise over
the course of the 1920s, their representation in urban and village
soviets did not exceed 30 per cent of the total even as late as 1934.[58]
Only in the most local soviets in the 1960s and 1970s did women's
participation reach 40 per cent of all deputies. Still more tellingly,
in the whole history of the Soviet Union (up to 1977) women never
constituted more than 25 per cent of the membership of the
Communist Party.[59]

The agitation trials present what are essentially conversion stories.
Individuals 'see the light'. They 'find the truth'. They recognise
Soviet power. In this context women's stereotypical backwardness
provides more dramatic interest than would stories of competence
and creativity. Soviet power plays a tutelary role, bringing the women
delegates up to the level of 'becoming human'. As Cherepanova notes
in her final speech, she fell in love with Soviet power and the party of
the communists: 'They opened my eyes, taught me literacy, taught
me how to work – they made a person out of me.'[60]

Once such women delegates become at least partially conscious,
then they can begin to teach others. The defence lawyer for Cherepanova
praises her for 'sowing light among women peasants, as much as she
herself has become imbued with it'.[61] She should 'awaken the women
peasants who don't yet understand the truth/justice [*pravda*] of
the new life'.[62] Individuals, and especially women, who represent this
tutelary state can then take over husbands' traditional roles as teachers
and enforcers of discipline within the household. Kosorotov, as we
saw above, expresses fear that his wife is listening more to Gudkova
than to him: 'And I say, who is your husband – me or Maria Gudkova?'[63]
Emancipating women as citizens-in-training could thus provide a
wedge in the conservative household, a way for the Soviet state and
the new Soviet order to penetrate the countryside.

The state in these narratives is the ultimate Pygmalion creator,
permitting some women and men to attain citizenship while remand-
ing others to Soviet 'schools' such as literacy programmes and delegate
programmes for further development and transformation. Ironically,

the Soviet state in these plays is itself rather faceless. While the judges, the prosecution and defence do appear on stage, the organisers and party representatives who originally 'awaken' the heroines have always appeared before the narrative action of the plays takes place. They are also mentioned in vague terms, without reference to concrete persons, events, or institutions. In this way too the narratives illustrate not rules and procedures for attaining citizenship, or even common paths toward promotion, but rather indeterminate psychological states of 'unconsciousness' and 'consciousness'.

If citizenship can be analysed as a spectrum, as Nancy Cott has recently argued, ranging from nominal membership in the polity to full participation, then it may be that a person's or group's degree of citizenship must be measured not only by the laws of a country (which in this case declared women to be the full equals of men), but also by the practices of the day, the ways in which individuals' roles are or were scripted in public discourses.[64] The various agitation trials of the new woman and of the *delegatki* prove amply that even the new Soviet heroines had to be tamed and controlled by the authorities.

......

Notes

1. 'Sud nad novoi zhenshchinoi', *Pravda*, 38 (20 February 1921). The women's sections of the Communist Party were officially created in the fall of 1919 and served to draw women into the party until they were abolished in 1930. For more on their history, see Elizabeth A. Wood, *The Baba and the Comrade: Gender and Politics in Revolutionary Russia* (Indiana University Press, Bloomington, IN, 1997); Mary Buckley, *Women and Ideology in the Soviet Union* (University of Michigan Press, Ann Arbor, 1989); P. M. Chirkov, *Reshenie zhenskogo voprosa v SSSR (1917–1937 gg.)* (Mysl', Moscow, 1978); Richard Stites, *The Women's Liberation Movement in Russia: Feminism, Nihilism, and Bolshevism, 1860–1930* (Princeton University Press, Princeton, 1978); Gail Warshofsky Lapidus, *Women in Soviet Society: Equality, Development, and Social Change* (University of California Press, Berkeley, 1978); Carol Eubanks Hayden, 'Feminism and Bolshevism: The Zhenotdel and the Politics of Women's Emancipation in Russia, 1917–1930' (PhD dissertation, University of California, Berkeley, 1979); Carmen Scheide, '"Einst war ich Weib und kochte Suppe, jetzt bin ich bei der Frauengruppe": Das Wechselverhältnis zwischen sowjetischem Frauenalltag und Frauenpolitik von 1921 bis 1930 am Beispiel Moskauer Arbeiterinnen' (dissertation, Historische Seminar der Universität Basel, 1999).

2. A. Sergeev, 'Zhenskii samosud', *Pravda*, 265 (21 November 1921).

3. B. Kanatchikova, 'God raboty (na mestakh)', *Kommunistka* 16/17 (1921), p. 29; N. Tr-ii, 'Rabota sredi zhenshchin v Sibiri', *Pravda*, 8 (13 January 1923), p. 4; Delegatka M. Genert, 'Vypusk delegatok glavnogo Pochtamta', *Rabotnitsa i krest'ianka* (journal), 6 (1923), p. 25; Rossiiskii Gosudarstvennyi Arkhiv Sotsial'no-Politicheskoi Istorii (RGASPI, formerly the Party archives), f. 17, op. 10, d. 11, l. 244; f. 17, op. 10, d. 20, l. 2; *Biulleten' no. 15 Otdela TsK RKP po rabote sredi zhenshchin: Tezisy i rezoliutsii IV Vseross: soveshchaniia zavgubzhenotdelami* (Moscow, 1921), p. 21; 'Tsirkuliar TsK RKP 'Ob oktiabrskikh torzhestvakh: Vsem gubzhenotdelam' *Izvestiia TsK*, 34 (15 November 1921), p. 17.

4. The larger book project is entitled *Performing Justice: Agitation Trials in Revolutionary Russia* (University of California Press, Berkeley, forthcoming). For more on agitation trials see also Julie A. Cassiday, *The Enemy on Trial: Early Soviet Courts on Stage and Screen* (Northern Illinois University Press, Dekalb, IL, 2000), esp. ch. 2, 'The Mock Trial'; Julie A. Cassiday and Leyla Rouhi, 'From Nevskii Prospect to Zoia's Apartment: Trials of the Russian Procuress', *Russian Review*, 58, no. 3 (1999), pp. 413–31.

5. In addition I have found dozens of references to such trials being performed in a range of provincial cities and towns. Since the texts have not come down to us, however, it is impossible to provide detailed analysis of their content.

6. Other topics of agitation trials that were not specifically devoted to women's issues include political trials of Lenin and the Communist Party, army trials of soldiers who committed infractions of garrison regulations, trials of individuals who violated correct sanitation and hygiene, trials of farm animals, and trials of literary characters. All of these trials were used by political instructors and agitators to stimulate public discussion of contemporary social issues.

7. V. I. Lenin, 'Zadachi proletariata v nashei revoliutsii', *Polnoe Sobranie Sochinenii*, 5th edn (Gospolitizdat, Moscow, 1960–65), vol. 31, p. 165.

8. In addition to the sources listed above, see also Rudolf Schlesinger (ed.), *The Family in the USSR: Documents and Readings* (Routledge and Kegan Paul, London, 1949). Soviet Russia also pioneered the notion that marriage did not require a woman to take her husband's citizenship; instead the two could each make their own decisions about keeping or changing their citizenship, as well as deciding what citizenship they wanted for any children they might have (articles 103 and 147 of the Code on Marriage, the Family and Guardianship, *Sobranie uzakonenii i rasporiazhenii rabochego i krest'ianskogo pravitel'stva* (Gos. izd.-vo, Moscow, 1920), 1918, no. 76/77-818; discussion in S. S. Kishkin, *Sovetskoe grazhdanstvo* (Iuridicheskoe izd-vo NKIu RSFSR, Moscow, 1925), pp. 24–5).

9. Rogers Brubaker, *Citizenship and Nationhood in France and Germany* (Harvard University Press, Cambridge, MA, 1992); Susan Pedersen, 'Gender, Welfare, and Citizenship in Britain during the Great War', *American Historical Review*, 95 (1990), pp. 983–1006.

10. One of the few sources to address citizenship directly is Elise Kimerling, 'Civil Rights and Social Policy in Soviet Russia, 1918–1936', *Russian Review*, 41 (1982), pp. 24–45.

11. Laura Engelstein, for example, speaks of 'the pervasive disdain for the law' in tsarist Russia which 'came into its own as public policy after 1917' ('Combined Underdevelopment: Discipline and the Law in Imperial and Soviet Russia', *American Historical Review*, 98 (1993), p. 349). Of course, this view is substantially correct. Yet at the same time we must note in the phenomena of the agitation and show trials an extreme fascination with the ritual and, above all, with the *performance* of law. Law and courts constituted places of show, where the authorities could present examples of good and bad behaviour to the population at large. On the absence of democracy and hence of citizenship the literature is enormous. Some of the most important sources on the erosion of any meaningful notion of citizenship include Leonard Schapiro, *The Origin of the Communist Autocracy* (Harvard University Press, Cambridge, MA, 1954); Robert C. Tucker, 'Leadership and Culture in Social Movements', in *Political Culture and Leadership in Soviet Russia: From Lenin to Gorbachev* (Norton, New York, 1987); A. J. Polan, *Lenin and the End of Politics* (Methuen, London, 1984); Peter Kenez, *The Birth of the Propaganda State: Soviet Methods of Mass Mobilization, 1917–1929* (Cambridge University Press, Cambridge, 1985).

12. Kishkin, *Sovetskoe grazhdanstvo*, pp. 22, 74.

13. Articles 13, 15, 64, 18 of the Constitution (Fundamental Law) of the RSFSR of 1918, *Sobranie uzakonenii*, 1917–1918, no. 51-582.

14. On the French Revolution and citizenship, see Brubaker, *Citizenship and Nationhood in France and Germany*, ch. 2, 'The French Revolution and the Invention of National Citizenship', pp. 35–49. On Russian revolutionaries' fascination, and almost obsession, with the French Revolution, see Tamara Kondrat'eva, *Bol'sheviki-iakobintsy i prizrak*

termidora (izd. 'Ipol', Moscow, 1993); Dmitry Shlapentokh, *The French Revolution in Russian Intellectual Life, 1865–1905* (Praeger, Westport, CT, 1996).

15. Lenin, 'Two Tactics of Social Democracy in the Democratic Revolution', July 1905, *Selected Works* (Moscow, 1950–1952), vol. 1, book 2, pp. 48–142.

16. Samuel Northrup Harper, *Civic Training in Soviet Russia* (University of Chicago Press, Chicago, 1929).

17. For a brilliant discussion of the disenfranchised, see Golfo Alexopoulos, 'Rights and Passage: Marking Outcasts and Making Citizens in Soviet Russia, 1926–1936' (PhD dissertation, University of Chicago, 1996).

18. Harper, *Civic Training in Soviet Russia*, p. 17.

19. Andrei Sinyavsky, *Soviet Civilization: A Cultural History*, trans. Joanne Turnbull (Arcade Pub., New York, 1990), p. 212–13.

20. 'Politsud nad krest'iankoi-delegatkoi', in *Mezhdunarodnyi den' rabotnits*, ed. G. S. Maliuchenko (Rostov na Donu, 1925), p. 51.

21. For general discussion of *delegatki*, see Wood, *Baba and Comrade*, pp. 85–93, 172; Scheide, '"Einst war ich Weib und kochte Suppe"', pp. 138–43, 240–8; Chirkov, *Reshenie zhenskogo voprosa v SSSR (1917–1937 gg.)*, pp. 86–100; Buckley, *Women and Ideology in the Soviet Union*, pp. 71–82; Hayden, 'Feminism and Bolshevism', pp. 143–6, 151, 187–9, 199–203, 210–11.

22. Stites, *Women's Liberation Movement*, pp. 166–7.

23. Chirkov, *Reshenie zhenskogo voprosa v SSSR (1917–1937 gg.)*, p. 92.

24. The historical literature on changing intelligentsia images of the peasantry is rich and nuanced, showing how often members of the educated class tended to project their own ideas onto 'the people'. See especially Cathy A. Frierson, *Peasant Icons: Representations of Rural People in Late Nineteenth-Century Russia* (Oxford University Press, Oxford, 1993); Laura Engelstein, *The Keys to Happiness: Sex and the Search for Modernity in Fin-de-Siècle Russia* (Cornell University Press, Ithaca, NY, 1992); Richard S. Wortman, *The Crisis of Russian Populism* (Cambridge University Press, Cambridge, 1967); Esther Kingston-Mann, *Lenin and the Problem of Marxist Peasant Revolution* (Oxford University Press, New York, 1983). On images of peasant women, see Christine Worobec, 'Temptress or Virgin? The Precarious Sexual Position of Women in Postemancipation Ukrainian Peasant Society', *Slavic Review*, 49 (1990); and her 'Victims or Actors? Russian Peasant Women and Patriarchy', in *Peasant Economy, Culture, and Politics of European Russia, 1800–1921*, ed. Esther Kingston-Mann and Timothy Mixter (Princeton University Press, Princeton, 1991).

25. 'Politsud nad krest'iankoi-delegatkoi', p. 32.

26. *Sud nad krest'ianinom Medvedevym sorvavshim vybory kandidatki ot zhenshchin v sel'sovet* (Rabochee izdatel'stvo 'Priboi', Leningrad, 1925), pp. 12, 6–8.

27. Glebova, *Sud nad delegatkoi*, p. 11.

28. Glebova, *Sud nad delegatkoi*, p. 27.

29. Stites, *Women's Liberation Movement*; G. A. Tishkin, *Zhenskii vopros v Rossii 50–60e gody XIX v.* (Leningrad, 1984); Jane McDermid, 'The Influence of Western Ideas on the Development of the Woman Question in Nineteenth-Century Russian Thought', *Irish Slavonic Studies*, 9 (1988), pp. 21–36; Derek Offord, '*Lichnost'*: Notions of Individual Identity', in *Constructing Russian Culture in the Age of Revolution, 1881–1940*, ed. Catriona Kelly and David Shepherd (Oxford University Press, Oxford, 1998), pp. 13–25; Arja Rosenholm, 'The "Woman Question" of the 1860s and the Ambiguity of the "Learned Woman"', in *Gender and Russian Literature: New Perspectives*, ed. Rosalind Marsh (Cambridge University Press, Cambridge, 1996), pp. 112–28.

30. See Wood, *Baba and Comrade*, pp. 28–34, on the Bolsheviks' resistance to devoting attention to 'the woman question'.

31. V. I. Lenin, 'What Is to Be Done? Burning Questions of our Movement', in *The Lenin Anthology*, ed. Robert C. Tucker (Norton, New York, 1975), pp. 12–114.

32. 'Politsud nad krest'iankoi-delegatkoi', pp. 50–51.

33. 'Politsud nad krest'iankoi-delegatkoi', pp. 34–5.

34. Boris Andreev, *Sud nad starym bytom* (Doloi negramotnost', Moscow-Leningrad, 1926), pp. 15, 17–18. Her evolution is reminiscent of the title character in Gorky's novel *The Mother*.

35. Andreev, *Sud nad starym bytom*, p. 15.

36. 'Politsud nad krest'iankoi-delegatkoi', p. 46.

37. Andreev, *Sud nad starym bytom*, p. 14; emphasis added.

38. One trial even brought a fictional woman to court 'who did not use the rights given her by the October Revolution': 'Sud nad zhenshchinoi, ne vospol'zovavsheisia pravami Oktiabria', *Rabochii klub*, 7 (1924), p. 37.

39. 'Politsud nad krest'iankoi-delegatkoi', pp. 36–7.

40. 'Politsud nad krest'iankoi-delegatkoi', p. 39. This language is repeated by the defence at the end of the play which characterises Cherepanova as a 'very necessary, useful worker for her society' (p. 49); and by the judge who calls her a 'useful member of society'. Once she has become useful, her 'femaleness' falls away.

41. 'Politsud nad krest'iankoi-delegatkoi', pp. 47, 49.

42. N. Bozhinskaia, *Sud nad krest'iankoi-delegatkoi* (Moscow-Leningrad, 1926). In parts of pre-revolutionary Russia the verb *gudit'* also meant to reproach, find fault with, or defame someone (V. Dal', *Tolkovyi slovar'* (1978; Moscow-Petersburg, 1880), vol. 1, p. 405).

43. Bozhinskaia, *Sud nad krest'iankoi-delegatkoi*, pp. 15–16; he uses the Russian word *dura* for 'fool' which is female rather than the masculine form *durak*.

44. Gudkova's first name, Maria, may not be accidental. The author Bozhinskaia is probably descended from the clerical estate (since her last name contains the Russian word for God) and may have chosen the name Maria in order to create a secular heroine in place of Maria, the Mother of God.

45. Bozhinskaia, *Sud nad krest'iankoi-delegatkoi*, pp. 17, 25, 21.

46. Bozhinskaia, *Sud nad krest'iankoi-delegatkoi*, p. 28. For an account of nineteenth-century female revolutionaries who are portrayed as saintly and therefore rather bloodless, see Christine Faure, 'Une violence paradoxale: Aux sources d'un défi, des femmes terroristes dans les années 1880', in *L'Histoire sans qualités*, ed. Christiane Dufrancatel et al. (Paris, 1979), pp. 85–110.

47. Bozhinskaia, *Sud nad krest'iankoi-delegatkoi*, pp. 10–11.

48. This type of 'triptych' would have been familiar to Russian churchgoers. For more on the relationship between pre-revolutionary icons and post-revolutionary pictorial art, see Victoria E. Bonnell, *Iconography of Power: Soviet Political Posters under Lenin and Stalin* (University of California Press, Berkeley, 1997) and Stephen White, *The Bolshevik Poster* (New Haven and London, 1988). As I have noted, Bozhinskaia's own clerical background may have made her particularly cognizant of parallels to Russian hagiography.

49. Two lay judges or assessors usually presided in public trials, both real and agitational, as (untrained) associates of, and assistants to, the presiding judge. In some agitation trials these assessors were elected from the audience as people's representatives at the start of the trial.

50. Bozhinskaia, *Sud nad krest'iankoi-delegatkoi*, p. 26. Another (probably unconscious) inversion can be seen near the beginning of the play when Kosorotov claims that this 'baba' (Gudkova) has worn him out; literally, that she has 'eaten' him up (*zaela menia baba*) (p. 7).

51. Bozhinskaia, *Sud nad krest'iankoi-delegatkoi*, pp. 3, 9, 15, 14. While the judge addresses the witnesses using the formal 'you' (*vy*), the people's assessors tend to use the informal *ty*, suggesting that they (the people's assessors) are closer to the witnesses than is the judge (presumably an outsider) who can therefore have more impartiality.

52. *Sud nad krest'ianinom Medvedevym*, p. 7.

53. *Sud nad krest'ianinom Medvedevym*, pp. 19, 9, 18.

54. *Sud nad krest'ianinom Medvedevym*, pp. 22–3.

55. In some sense this ambivalence about women's participation in the public sphere can be seen as fairly overdetermined given the Russian language's ambivalence about 'public women' (*publichnye zhenshchiny*), a phrase which means prostitutes.

56. For one example, see Jochen Hellbeck, 'Fashioning the Stalinist Soul: The Diary of Stepan Podliubnyi (1931–1939)', *Jahrbucher für Geschichte Osteuropas*, 44 (1996), esp. pp. 348, 351, 354.

57. Brubaker, *Citizenship and Nationhood in France and Germany*, esp. ch. 1, 'Citizenship as Social Closure'.

58. G. N. Serebrennikov, *The Position of Women in the U.S.S.R.* (Victor Gollancz, London, 1937), p. 211.

59. Lapidus, *Women in Soviet Society*, p. 210.

60. 'Politsud nad krest'iankoi-delegatkoi', pp. 50–51. For a comparative discussion of conversions, see Igal Halfin, 'From Darkness to Light: Student Communist Autobiography During NEP', *Jahrbucher fur Geschichte Osteuropas*, 45 (1997), pp. 1–27.

61. 'Politsud nad krest'iankoi-delegatkoi', p. 49. Even this formulation expresses some doubt that a woman like Cherepanova has become fully imbued with the light of Soviet power.

62. *Pravda* in Russian means both 'truth' and 'justice'.

63. Bozhinskaia, *Sud nad krest'iankoi-delegatkoi*, p. 15.

64. Nancy F. Cott, 'Marriage and Women's Citizenship in the United States, 1830–1934', *American Historical Review*, 103 (1998), pp. 1440–74.

Enfranchised Selves: Women, Culture and Rights in Nineteenth-Century Bengal

Tanika Sarkar

British raj

Narratives of the acquisition of citizenship rights are often self-referential and self-grounded. A fully formed theory of rights emerges as the active subject of history, animating debates and initiating change in the direction of self-realisation. Such a theory of citizenship rights falls short when it is called upon to account for activities and ideas of people who are eventually to emerge as bearers of rights. For such people may seem from a western point of view to possess very imperfect approximations of the perfected concept. Their fitful progress towards what in hindsight may be summed up as 'rights-like' competencies seems to derive from struggles for very different entitlements.

If we examine how Indian women made themselves into citizens between the mid-nineteenth and the mid-twentieth century, the attainment of rights seems to be the consequence of a number of movements that did not aspire directly to procure citizenship for women: social reform, social legislation, female education, new religious sects, class struggles and anti-colonial mass movements. The expected trajectory of a suffragist movement actually accounts for very little of the process. Nor do we find in the course of the various social movements and reforms a clear and self-conscious articulation of rights as such.

In a sense, this peculiarity is useful. As an extreme Hindu right-wing consolidates its ascendancy over Indian politics today, subtly dismantling all manner of citizenship rights even within a formal democracy, it uses the logic and rhetoric of cultural nationalism very effectively. Rights, it is suggested, are an alien and colonising notion, meant to strip the Indian woman of her many-splendoured religious identity and to make her over into a grey, empty, disembedded and deracinated citizen, a clone of her erstwhile masters, her citizenship banishing her from her authentic roots. In order to escape from charges of mimicry, we need not deduce the history of rights from a singular theoretical construct that originated in western thinking. We can see this history, instead, as the eventual and uncertain point of coalescence for many different historical movements that resulted in legal personhood for the woman – underpinned by state guarantees for certain immunities and entitlements. Thus this analysis seeks to preserve the authenticity and distinctiveness of the Indian experience while conjoining it to conceptions of what Martha Nussbaum has identified as 'human capabilities' that are universal.[1]

John Rawls offers a political conception of justice that emanates from ideas that are latent in the public political culture of a society and that arise out of the implicit self-understanding of public actors. Ideas of justice, therefore, belong to the democratic political culture where they are articulated. Seyla Benhabib extends this vision much further by pointing out that there is actually no disembedded abstract individual subject – to whom rights will adhere – who is set apart from her larger social matrix, her inherited culture. She suggests that the subject attains an identity or constructs selfhood through a 'narrative unity' which can only occur through dialogues with society.[2] Habermas establishes a similar continuity between the individual and her lifeworld, unsettling the opposition between the two, and very pertinently recalling that all individual rights were acquired and sustained through collective social struggle.[3] These are powerful responses to the more communitarian arguments of Charles Taylor who would view notions of impregnable citizenship rights as a potential threat to minority cultures, and would advise a partial mitigation of the former in order to ensure the survival and continuity of such cultures.[4] In this essay I will reassess these positions in the light of the historical experience of Indian women.

Nancy Fraser points out that liberal democracy withholds effective citizenship rights from women by undermining their consent in the private sphere. Women's real subordination in this realm insidiously cancels out their formal rights in the public domain.[5] Examples from Indian history add a few twists to this framework. Colonialism withheld citizenship rights from men, while liberal reformism abbreviated their unlimited mastery over the lives and deaths of women in the private sphere. Moreover, self-determination and a fledgeling notion of something like rights – translated as a few immunities from sexual, physical or intellectual death – emerged as political values in the sphere of women's lives even before they were articulated in the public and political realms. What looks like dead-letter liberalism acquires different histories and possibilities in the Indian context.

We will focus on nineteenth-century Bengal, politically a very active province, which then housed the capital of the empire. In Bengal, struggles for certain immunities and entitlements for the Hindu woman unfolded alongside of simultaneous – at times overlapping and at others conflicting – struggles for Indian nationhood. Entangled with both, in complicated ways, were movements for an enlargement of the disciplinary rights of religious communities. As we shall see, very often all these demands converged and clashed over the bodies of dead women, on whose behalf liberal nationalists claimed immunity for their lives. Cultural nationalists would counter this claim by referring to the onslaughts of a triumphant western power-knowledge on the traditional bases of indigenous culture. Unless Hindu prescriptions were assured of power over the life and death of women, cultural nationalists claimed, their religious communities would be rendered fatally misshapen.

The other distinctive feature of Indian history was that all colonised Indians were disenfranchised people until the very end of British governance, before which a minuscule minority of rich and educated men obtained the right to vote. In this limited but important sense, disadvantages existed that were common to both women and men. As a consequence, among all shades of anti-colonial nationalist discourses, self-determination came to be generally accepted as an absolute political good, creating further complications in the relations between the community and women. Indeed, women themselves would often link self-determination with their own condition as they began to publish their experiences and to intervene in the public sphere. They thus took the edge off nationalist critiques of colonial power by pointing out that an anterior colonisation and subjection had already occurred in the realm of gender relations, for Hindu men ruled over their women as despotically as did their colonial masters.[6]

There was yet another complication in the Indian situation. Men lacked the privileges of high masculinity and were hence deprived of the possibility of administrative and military leadership or entrepreneurial opportunities. Furthermore, their rulers often accused them of physical weakness and effeminacy. They usually articulated their hegemonic claims on the basis of a perceived powerlessness of their class, rather than from a position of power, in order to claim representative rights over all classes of Indians. Colonialism thus denied men special claims to power, thereby further generalising their political disadvantages.

In this essay, I will analyse three related and overlapping fields in which a certainty about absolute immunities and entitlements for women began to emerge in the nineteenth century. In particular I will focus on three crucial acts of legislation which spanned the nineteenth century: in 1829, the abolition of the custom of burning or burying alive Hindu widows; in 1856, the legalisation of remarriage for Hindu widows; and, in 1891, the raising of the age of consent within and outside of marriage. All of them referred to Hindus, though the 1891 act also applied to Muslims. Each also required a collision with upper-caste Hindu religious prescriptive norms that increasingly provided the horizon of 'clean' practices for upwardly mobile segments of low castes as well.

Crucial to understanding these legislative acts is the division which British legislators and judges assumed within the colonial legal domain. The colonial Anglo-Indian law had a 'territorial' scope, and ruled over the 'public' world of land relations, criminal law and the laws of contract and of evidence.[7] It came to be accepted as a basic principle, at least from 1793, that 'in cases of succession, inheritance, marriage, caste, and religious usages and institutions, the Mahomedan Law [was] for the Mahomedans and the Hindu Law for the Hindus'.[8] According to one English judge, then, 'the law of the conquering nation was universally a territorial law, but the conquered nation retained its own as a personal law'.[9] Gibbon's reading of Roman law was used, for example, to retain a space of self-governance for the conquered nation. This space was primarily conceived as a domestic one and the question as to who would rule over this sphere was acutely contested in the debates about the three legislative acts that are under discussion in this paper. Indeed, the colonial state explicitly turned this domain over to the two major religious communities. Late nineteenth-century Hindu revivalist-nationalists insisted on the

lack of communication and agreement

absolute inviolate integrity of this domain, which simultaneously represented a trace of lost freedom as well as an anticipation of future nationhood. This meant the preservation of the full disciplinary regime of brahmanical gender norms. Liberal reformers, on the other hand, regarded the governance of this domain as an exercise of their own transformative capacity to redefine the community through their Indian initiative, otherwise denied in colonial times.

Each of the legislative acts analysed here related to the mandatory deaths of women: to their physical deaths in widow immolation, to the very low age of consent that led many child wives to die of the complications of premature intercourse, and, finally, to their social and sexual deaths in widowhood. All three of the acts originated in the conflicts between Indian liberal and conservative opinions, in which the state often reluctantly and belatedly responded to liberal arguments. The Indian reformist initiative shaped the legislation and provided its content as well as arguments for self justification. It was consolidated through intense debates in the emergent public sphere of the new print culture, vernacular prose and journalism, the public theatre, bazaar paintings and cheap woodcut prints, polemical tracts and popular farces. From the 1860s on, some women also began to articulate their opinions in print. The public sphere was organised largely around these issues, diverging therefore from the public/private divide that is assumed in western modernities. Domestic issues, more-over, were suffused with a public and political meaning.

Liberals and conservatives shared some discursive methods and practices. The state granted relative autonomy to religious beliefs and practices, allowing legislative change only if custom could be shown as violative of scriptural injunctions. Thus both liberals and con-servatives dealt in the currency of scriptural arguments and citations and both flaunted impeccable brahmanical learning and origins. How-ever, when they mobilised popular support for their arguments in the public sphere – a highly significant departure in the realm of norms that had not been necessary earlier – both strained to display an ethical face, going beyond the injunctions and prohibitions through which norms usually speak. More important, in matters of domestic norms, both began to use the argument of women's consent as a cen-tral reference point, which again marked a departure of tremendous significance. For the colonial condition and the Indian claim to a share of political rights and at least a consultative status in governance rendered self-determination a political value of significantly greater

mobilization of Hindu elite

importance than western liberal theories of social contract or general will. The difference between liberal and conservative positions lay above all in the definition of contemporary customs pertaining to domesticity.

Liberals claimed that existing domestic practices or customs ensured the subjection of women in the domestic domain, which, they argued, invalidated male claims to political rights. Although liberals frequently criticised sexual double standards in domestic practices, implicitly formulating an argument in favour of equality, they did not entirely elaborate its full potential. They chose to rest their case on the argument that custom abused and constricted women to such an extent that adherence to these customary rules would render Indians unfit for self-governance by any measure. Moreover, given the relative autonomy of the religious norms under colonial dispensation, liberals regarded this campaign as a possibility for self-transformation and self-fashioning which was absent in all other realms of life in which the state ruled arbitrarily.

Conservative arguments also underwent an important shift. Earlier, their defence of custom had sought to establish its scriptural underpinning as well as its larger humanity. Both widow immolation and celibate widowhood, they claimed, were based on consent, while child marriage led to conjugal bliss. By the 1870s and 1880s, however, a stridently nationalist note entered their discourse, which did not contest political subjection, but claimed complete cultural autonomy and immunity from colonial intervention. The man, they said, had already been transformed by alien knowledge, whereas the woman, still largely governed by religious-ritual norms, embodied freedom, cultural authenticity, and, ultimately, the nation of the future. She thus had access to unique political rights only by way of an entire embrace of the rule of custom. As long as she embraced custom, faith and culture would live in her and in her alone. If, however, norms required her death, a form of human sacrifice, then her death would only enlarge her political function. Faith and culture would survive colonialism only if the woman consented to die for them. Conservatives feared that the reform of faith and culture would close the circuit of colonisation to which the minds and lifeworlds of Indians were subjected.[10] Evoking a collective demand for cultural recognition, conservatives aimed at a 'reification of identity' that would mask internal power lines.[11]

What lay between the laws that liberals desired and conservatives refused was a system of non-consensual and indissoluble marriage that was performed before the girl entered puberty. Once puberty set in, she had to go through a life cycle rite of ritual cohabitation with her husband, without which her womb would remain polluted and the sons of the womb could not make pure offerings to ancestral spirits. Almanacs warned that offerings by such sons would as surely pollute ancestors as the drinking of menstrual blood.[12] To ensure the performance of this rite, marriage was essential in early infancy, for the exact moment of puberty was both uncertain and very early in warm climates. Marriage was a woman's only access to a sexual relationship.

Even if it was unconsummated or even after she was widowed, the woman needed to remain absolutely chaste, since the performance of the marriage sacrament made her the half-body – '*ardhangini*' – of her husband. Any other sexual relationship could only be an adulterous one, a crime under colonial law and a sin according to religious norms. Widow immolation was not obligatory, but it certainly signified rare and great virtue. Otherwise, the celibate widow was surrounded by ritual prohibitions and deprivations that signified a life of permanent inauspiciousness. In the nineteenth century there were many learned debates about the custom of '*ekadasi*', or ritual fasting without a drop of water every fortnight, even on her deathbed.[13]

Above all, Manu, the ancient, eponymous lawgiver, had declared that she must never acquire rights in her own person and that she must, rather, be ruled by father, husband and son at the different stages of her life. If she lived by these regulations, she was promised both power and honour within the household. Hence a valorisation, an aestheticisation of the discipline of norms took place. With the birth of cultural nationalism in the late nineteenth century, discipline was transfigured as authentic religion, culture and nation. I argue in this essay that this new rhetoric, which coupled independence with normative discipline, proved irresistibly resonant in the context of a more explicitly charged racist and authoritarian colonial governance in late nineteenth-century Bengal. The government's proposal to equalise the judicial powers of Indian magistrates, to the point of extending their jurisdiction over European subjects, had raised howls of naked racist agitations and propaganda in European circles.[14] A politics of recognition, even when cast in culturalist-conservative, rather than political terms, would produce enormous resonance and weaken the reformist impulse considerably. The Age of Consent Act reflected a temporary retreat from the self-interrogation that had strongly characterised the earlier reformist impulse of the liberals.

Despite the discursive strategies they sometimes shared, liberal reformers and conservatives deployed arguments regarding consent with quite different intentions. Prior to the criminalisation of widow immolation, the colonial state had evolved an elaborate mechanism for confirming the widow's consent to being burned alive, just before it took place. This act of consent was, however, often plagued by a dilemma. For sometimes the widow would not only consent to immolation, but would even insist upon it. Yet in some cases, once the pyre was lit and the burning began, widows sought ineffectively to escape the flames, proving that the experience of burning alive could not be fully anticipated beforehand. Consent or insistence prior to the act of burning was therefore based on ignorance.[15] The dilemmas surrounding widow immolation were resolved when the state passed an act abolishing it, which bypassed the issue of the widow's consent altogether. In the final act, the word 'consent' was used only to affirm that immolation would remain a criminal act even when it was carried out on the basis of the widow's full consent.[16] In order to protect widows from being burned alive, the state effectively disqualified their own will and opinion.

Endorsing this nullification of women's consent, reformers like Rammohun Roy noted that widow immolation was valorised by scripture, but only when the widow was in a perfectly serene and dispassionate frame of mind and expected no gain from the act. In reality, however, widows were either crazed with grief or tempted by expectations of eternal reunion with their husbands in afterlife when they consented to or requested immolation. Under these circumstances women could never fulfil the scriptural conditions for an authentic and permissible act of immolation. In his other writings, Roy would interrogate the entire prescriptive process of female socialisation that denied female intelligence, starved the woman of education and knowledge, incarcerated her in the kitchen, thereby ensuring her consent to a brutal disciplining.[17] The reformers, therefore, ignored the explicit consent of the woman in order to focus on its coerced production, and thus opened themselves up to a larger interrogation of an entire gender system. The conservatives, on the other hand, accepted explicit consent as an absolute given and used it to foreclose any such broader agenda.

A highly revolutionary clause of the act on widow remarriage of 1856 introduced an implicit but real violation of several basic tenets of Hindu marriage. Clause VII of Act no. XV of 1856 specified: 'In the case of a widow who is of full age or whose marriage has been consummated, her own consent shall be sufficient to constitute her remarriage lawful and valid'. This passage implied that the woman could dispose of her own person, indeed that she could give herself away. This clause thus violated the basic form of marriage in which the girl was always given away by her father to her husband as an object of exchange between two lineages, a transaction in which her consent was entirely immaterial. A further implication was that the woman herself had a right to her own person, a claim that entirely nullified Manu's strict injunctions against female autonomy. More importantly, the widow's consent opened up the possibility of an entirely different kind of conjugal relationship, based on premarital love and romance, as the widow was the only adult woman who now became available for a romantic, yet licit, relationship.

Accounts of such relationships were partially removed from the domain of scandalous stories, pornographic and misogynist literature, and acquired the status of serious and complex novels.[18] In the first book published by an Indian woman, *Chittabilashini*, by Krishnakamini Dasi, an imagined dialogue takes place between two widows who contemplate the possibility that they now would have to propose to men themselves, since their parents would hardly be inclined to arrange a remarriage for them. Indeed, in the life stories of several nineteenth-century widows, this radical transgression of feminine codes did occur and desperate widows did confess to their love of men, now that legitimate marriage was a distinct possibility on the horizon.[19] This reformist legislation thus enacted alternative imaginaries of female lifeworlds.

Ishwarchandra Vidyasagar, the inspiration behind the Act on Widow Remarriage, had contrasted the repeated remarriages of ancient widowers to nubile young wives, in order to point out both the sexual double standards and to justify female sexuality as natural and given, even when unanchored in a living husband. This notion of unconditional female sexuality as a part of the natural order of things met with violent resistance, waged in the name of a higher moral order in which sexual double standards were natural, and both male and female sexuality were conditional upon the nature of licit relationships. Otherwise, even incest would have been natural. An irrepressible female sexuality was caricatured to warn elderly and unattractive husbands that their dissatisfied wives might take to murdering them, now that they could be sure of the possibilities of remarriage. The resistance waged against this act hence negated woman's own consent on the ground that her body was her husband's private land that no one could fertilise without his consent and monstrous births would be the result of such a union.[20]

The nineteenth century was the century par excellence for reviewing the Hindu conjugal system. The debates on widow immolation had more or less split Hindu society right down the middle.[21] The agitations surrounding widow remarriage, in the 1850s, further widened these cleavages. On trial were the foundational texts of Bengali Hindu conjugality: the ancient sacred book of *Manusmriti* and the Dayabhaga modifications later undertaken by Raghunandan in the sixteenth century. The core conviction that held the system together was that the true wife remained faithful to her husband even after his death, for she was the *ardhangini* – the half-body of the husband. On that basis women were granted limited rights of usufruct to their husband's share of the joint family property under traditional Dayabhaga law.[22]

Upon this stable structure of marital asymmetry fell the massive blow of the 1856 act legalising widow remarriage. The full normative implications thereof were sorted out in legal case after case, even beyond the end of the nineteenth century. An interesting aspect of these legal contests was the conflicting judicial interpretation of the 'most enabling clause'. Some judges used this clause to allow low-caste widows to inherit their first husband's properties. Yet the act was drafted with high-caste widows about to remarry in mind, who had not had the right to remarry. In order to neutralise some of the orthodox outrage against the act, high-caste widows about to remarry had to renounce all claims to their first husband's property. Low-caste widows, by contrast, had been customarily allowed to remarry as well as to retain their share of their deceased husband's property, and now stood to lose that right under the new act. So some of the subsequent judicial rulings sought to maximise gains: for the upper-caste widow the right to remarry and for the lower-caste widow the right to share marital property.[23] This interpretation of legal application, that laws desired to maximise entitlements, served to undermine the prescriptions of custom and scripture.

Many criticisms were launched against this law, and against Ischwarchandra Vidyasagar, the reformer who agitated for it. Vidyasagar was himself bitterly disappointed by the results of the act, which in my assessment were more successful in the realm of normative thinking than in terms of practical or immediate effects.[24] As a result of the act, adult widows, not only infant, virginal widows, could now legitimately remarry. But as a more significant longer-term consequence of the act, the normative fit between absolute female chastity and wifehood was ruptured. It is worth noting, of course, that the previous normative convictions continued to rule. For the first time, however, norms had to cede ground to legal prescriptions that pulled in a different direction.

Indeed at this juncture a very interesting gap opened up between morality and legality. Widow immolation, the absolute proof of womanly virtue, was criminalised in 1829, while widow remarriage – a moral sin – was legalised in 1856. The new reformist laws did not carry much moral conviction, but they did have legal sanction, while much of the old moral order was now outlawed. In this historical moment the symbiotic relationship between morality and legality, their substantive unity and identity, were brutally ruptured. And the space that the rupture opened up allowed the appearance of a few tentative claims for immunities and entitlements within the public sphere.

This space was enlarged little by little, as legal loopholes continued to appear. The Kerry Kolitani vs. Moniram Kolita case of 1873 further complicated discussions of the Widow Remarriage Act.[25] A widow, under the law of Dayabhaga, enjoyed a usufruct on her husband's property only on the condition that her chastity was beyond question. Chastity, however, had to be proven at the time when widowhood commenced and then the widow was granted a share of the property. Under the older structures of morality, of course, her claims would be forfeited if she were subsequently to violate chastity, since she inherited only as her husband's half-body. But under the new laws, private property carried very different connotations that overrode the charge of 'unchastity'. In another case in 1873, a widow was accused of promiscuity after her inheritance was finalised, and the charge was proven in court. Her relatives argued that she would have to renounce her titles under Dayabhaga. The High Court, however, ruled finally that her claim was based on her state of chastity at the point of her husband's death. Since the charge of promiscuity referred to a period after she had inherited, the court ruled that it was not relevant to her claim. Once she had inherited the property, her title became absolute.

This sensational case acquired notoriety as 'The Great Unchastity Case' in Bengali Hindu circles. Yet the responses to the case were divided along interesting lines. While the newspaper *Murshidabad Patrika* thundered indignantly that the High Court decision would encourage immorality among widows,[26] Dacca Prakash admitted in 1873 that 'when once the widow has come into possession of her husband's property, it is no longer his but hers, and no one has any right to deprive her of that'.[27] At this point the newspaper the *Bengalee* made a significant intervention in the debate about the decision. Without challenging the absolute nature of private property rights, the *Bengalee* tried to salvage morality through a different route, implementing the argument of cultural distinctiveness and emphasising the alien nature of colonial law and judiciary. 'What we object to is the arbitrary interpretation put by judges on our ancient texts in the face of the opposition of the single native judge who had a seat on the court.'[28]

The High Court decision was a very bitter pill to swallow. In the discourse of cultural nationalism, a woman's monogamy was the stated condition for national distinctiveness, cultural excellence, political virtue, upon which the Hindu claim to nationhood depended. 'We are but a half-civilised, poor, sorrowful, subjected, despised nation. We have but one jewel, our chaste women, and that is the treasure of seven realms, a priceless jewel ... this so-called subjection of our women produces this sacred jewel of chastity which still glows radiantly throughout the civilised world, despite centuries of political subjection.'[29] Women's chastity, then, had a real and explicit political value, not merely a symbolic one. It was as if the lost nation had been pushed back into the small, precious, threatened sacred space of her vagina.

It was not then mainly a legal quibble that followed upon the case, nor did Hindu society regard it as such. One outcome was that the right to property had been secured as separated from moral conditions as interpreted by the community. A bourgeois notion of the absolute value of property had been given priority over scriptural discipline.

Moreover, too many seepages had opened up within the variegated public sphere for the moral order to remain intact. In a notorious murder trial of 1873, a few interlocutors questioned the fundamental certainty surrounding the question of who was a good woman. The case involved the head-priest of a powerful pilgrimage centre at

Tarakeswar who had raped the young girl Elokeshi with her parents'
connivance, and then had installed her as his mistress. Her husband,
then in Calcutta, heard of the rape upon his return home, and mur-
dered her in a fit of jealous rage. He confessed and the Indian jury
acquitted him on the grounds of insanity and in the face of overwhelming popular sympathy. The European judge demurred, the case
was sent up to the High Court, and the husband was sentenced to be
deported for life. There were unprecedented expressions of solidarity
on his behalf, and in 1875 he was given a royal pardon. The case is
interesting, for it was reported and discussed at great length in newspapers, depicted in Bazaar paintings and woodcut prints, and prompted
an outpouring of cheap farces and tracts. In fact, its enactment made
the fortunes of a public theatre company in Calcutta.[30]

The contention that Elokeshi had entered into a longstanding
adulterous relationship with the Mohunt was not in doubt.[31] Popular
representations of the case generally concluded that the woman's
husband was within his rights in taking the law into his own hands.
There was wide agreement that even though Elokeshi had been gravely
wronged, she had forfeited the right to live. But some voices argued
otherwise. A reformist newspaper sympathised with her husband's
fate, but upheld the High Court verdict: 'in sympathising with the
unfortunate Nobin (the husband) people forget that the victim was
not the man that he and all Bengal believe to be a vile seducer, nor the
still worse scoundrel who had bartered her daughter's virtue ... but a
girl of tender years ... What had she done to forfeit her young life?'[32]

Elokeshi had been unchaste but that no longer seemed to suffice
as an adequate reason for her death. For the polyphonic public sphere
had destabilised convictions by pluralising moral arguments. Casting
Elokeshi as a victim, not just of a 'vile seducer' but equally of her
wronged and justly enraged husband, marked a momentous shift in
the monolithic moral order. The new sensibilities unleashed by this
case did not become hegemonic, but they ruptured older certainties,
shaking up the rule of prescriptions that earlier required no self-
explanation in order to remain pertinent. Norms were thus peeled
away from religious commands that were beyond questioning. They
were prised apart from a common sense where they had lain submerged without questioning. They were rendered post-conventional,
but not defeated.

As norms lost their absolute moral certainties, and as certain basic
immunities began to acquire a moral basis of their own, the old

discipline of the community sought new arguments. It found them in the discourse of cultural nationalism. What was the life of a woman in comparison with the life of a culture? Were the new colonial laws that safeguarded the woman's immunity from death not endangering the culture and the community of Hindus? If the dispositions of women were to change, what would remain of the old moral order? If difference from alien values lay in greater pain and even death of the woman, then pain and death should be celebrated, not questioned. In the context of the death of a girl of ten from marital rape in 1890 and in the subsequent discussions about an increase in the age of consent within marriage, one participant noted: 'This discipline is the prize and glory of chaste women and it prevails only in Hindu society'.[33] What would justify this fidelity? It was the survival of culture against the designs of colonialism, they said: 'No, no, a hundred battles like Plassey, Assaye, Multan, could not in terribleness compare with the step Lord Landsdowne has taken ... The Hindu family is ruined.'[34] By comparing Lord Landsdowne's Age of Consent Bill with the battles that signified British territorial conquests, they suggested that real colonialisation, had, in fact, just commenced in the form of the take-over of culture.

The nineteenth century saw massive debates on the abolition of widow immolation, the legalisation of widow remarriage, and the increase of the age of cohabitation within marriage. The last issue, in particular, led to unprecedented nationalist mobilisation against the Age of Consent Act, which the state had pushed forward in 1891.[35] What is remarkable is that all these momentous controversies revolved around the death of the woman: her physical death in the cases of widow immolation and the age of consent, and her sexual death in the case of the widow remarriage issue.

More importantly, these cases became subjects of debate because the state had proclaimed that, in the matter of personal law, Hindus and Muslims would decide their own fate according to their own custom and scripture. Scriptural interpretation became a highly contested issue, upon which depended lives and deaths of women and of Hindu patriarchal culture. Even more significant were the debates enabled by the emergence of a public sphere after Christian missionaries introduced cheap vernacular printing presses. At the same time, a serviceable and supple Bengali prose was fashioned to enable little-educated, ordinary people to read about the newly proposed laws and the debates around them and, occasionally, to add their own reflections and experiences in the cheap popular tracts and newspapers.[36] The public theatre also shaped thinking on these matters as social satire and farce became its most popular themes from the 1870s on. Scandalous court cases involving conjugal and sexual norms were attended by large numbers of people, reported and discussed in great detail in newspapers, re-enacted in popular farces and even painted in woodcuts and bazaar art.[37] And, since women's lives were at the heart of this discussion, a market emerged for women's writings, which then began to appear in print in not insignificant numbers from the 1860s.[38]

The woman as author was a completely new social category. Before the nineteenth century, not a single full text written by a woman has come down to us in Bengal. Through their publications, women now vaulted over the public–private divide, while they remained physically largely in seclusion. It was no easy matter becoming an author. When the nineteenth century opened, the illiteracy of the Hindu woman was a normative requirement, ensured by custom with the decree that the literate woman was destined to be widowed. There were a few exceptions to this general rule, but, on the whole, they were remarkably meagre.[39] Christian missionary schools failed to make a dent, for their system of tutoring married women in their female quarters of the household foundered on family fears about conversion. Mid-century Hindu reformers were faced then with overwhelming social ostracism when they prodded an indifferent state to fund a few schools for girls. A few daring husbands taught their child wives in great secrecy, and a few bold fathers sent their daughters to school. These produced an orthodox backlash of formidable proportions, including attacks on schoolbuses, obscene press campaigns, and the intimidation of families. The educated woman became a folk-devil in popular representations: immoral, lazy, selfish, a reader of romantic novels and neglectful of basic household duties, she was even depicted as having lost her breast-milk and her reproductive organs. Education was the signifier of sexual difference, the site and the justification of male power. Its appropriation by women would invert social and sexual roles and even the biological organs. Both orthodox and the cultural nationalists equally upheld the traditional Hindu woman, learned in household wisdom and rich in fidelity and tenderness, as the sign of a living culture.[40]

Women writers were nonetheless encouraged by a cheap print literature that was easy to read and portable and by the development

of prose that was easy to write, and a growing public interest in what
women had to say about themselves. Above all, they were encouraged
by the rumours that women were reading and writing in these new
times. In a remote East Bengal village, in an extremely orthodox
upper-caste household, Rashsundari, a young and timid housewife
was so stimulated by such news that she developed a double life.
Pretending still to be the docile wife, she taught herself the letters
in great and fearful secrecy in the solitude of her kitchen, where she
spent her days. When she was a mature mother of many sons, she
began to read and write openly. In 1868, she finished a narrative of
her life – *Amar Jiban* or *My Life* – which happens to be the first
autobiography in the Bengali language. In this text she welcomed the
new times, particularly the rule of the Queen, when women at last
learned to read, without which, she said, they would remain dependent on men all their lives.[41] She celebrated her literacy by coining a
magnificent new word: *jitakshara*, or the woman who has mastered
the word. The mastery did not refer to economic independence or
mobility. Rather, it suggested independence of thinking and intellectual
autonomy, which would free women's minds from male instructions.
She frequently used the metaphor of blindness and sight vis-à-vis
illiteracy and literacy, again suggesting that seeing with men's eyes
was another name for blindness. Reformers might have sought com-
panionate wives when they educated their women; women, however,
regarded their education as freedom to think independently of men.

The entitlement to reading was contrary to prescription and it was
forbidden by authoritative voices in the community. By insisting on
mastering the word, women therefore chose to defy the commands
of their culture; they moved towards a new horizon, self-acquired
and held against prescription. The stricture against education came to
figure as the source of a broad structure of injustice. In 1849, a group
of reformers met a girl of 9 at her home since they had heard that she
was learning to read and write. In order to assess her progress and test
their hypothesis that women could indeed learn when they are taught,
they asked her to compose a poem in their presence. She wrote a
verse that rhymed perfectly in Bengali:

> Women of this land are kept like animals
> They get no education, men do not respect them.
> Men treat them with contempt just because they are women.
> Since men cannot be born without women
> Why do they not accept that women have inner qualities?[42]

Older women, learning to write, publicised their bitterness against their social world, their community commands, in great profusion. They described a great wrong done to them in the name of religious prescription by men who had actually defied the will of God. Soudamini Debi wrote to the women's journal *Bamabodhini Patrika* in 1865: 'Are we not the children of the Great Father? How much longer do we stay chained at home ...?' An anonymous woman wrote in 1868: 'Our Father! Must we live in chains all our lives, even though we are your daughters? Alas, were we born in this land to perform low tasks?'[43]

These were dangerous words. In a community where life-situations are explicitly hierarchised according to caste and gender, women claimed equality in learning opportunities in the name of a common humanity. Moreover, they alleged a male conspiracy to withhold education from them. 'Ignorant and cruel men have separated us from this priceless and infinitely pleasurable jewel that is knowledge, and we foolish women still serve them like servants', wrote Kailashbashini Debi in 1863.[44] The woman, she said, did not get a fair exchange in return. Men left her reigning in a household which, contrary to their claims, was without love or pleasure. 'The Hindu household is a most terrible mountain range, infested with wild beasts.'[45]

Mastery over words was thus acquired in the name of a common humanity which, contrary to scripture or custom, was interpreted to signify equalisation of a basic competence. A poem in a women's magazine told men:

Men you have inflicted a terrible wrong
On the defenceless women of this land
And, to pay for that,
You will forever be exiles in your own land.[46]

Indeed, the fact that men had stolen women's right to education would be paid for with a loss of men's own citizenship rights. Education became the signifier for an entire order of gender, a language for speaking about rights and of their abduction by men.

In this essay I have not attempted to provide either a comprehensive or a connected history of women's rights-acquisition, since there was no such sequenced, deliberate journey. Nor have I referred to the significant landmark events in the process. Instead I have analysed disjointed events and sought out unlikely and small places where rights-like properties were claimed or displayed at a time when rights as a concept had little currency in the vocabulary of Bengali Hindus. At the most, a basic immunity was solicited for the woman's physical and sexual life, which was to be rendered unconditional. The woman herself had claimed certain entitlements for herself that strained against the commands of her family, her male guardians, and her community.

Seyla Benhabib and Jürgen Habermas have braided together the woman as a subject with her society and her lifeworld. In a sense, my study bears this out, for the nineteenth-century approaches to immunities and entitlements developed within the larger structures of new, unstable and uncertain moralities and sensibilities. But for many of the new voices that were articulated in the public sphere, the narrative unity that made them into subjects had to break away from the inherited ancestral culture that entirely framed their existence. The act of secession from culture was more significant than the fact that a new world was also in the making, which provided some sustenance. The new female autobiographies express the wrenching separation from the lifeworld. The modern female self had to narrativise itself against the grain of ancestral culture.

Modernity ruptures cultures, lifeworlds, and communities into many conflicting fragments. The public sphere, in turn, creates a dialogic relationship between them. These dialogues, however, may not always be conducive to consensus, to the invention of a new compound where all orders would find something of themselves. For consensus may also be compromise, retention of that which has always disempowered some and will continue to aim to disempower – in the name of threatened culture if no longer in the name of patriarchal discipline.

Notes

1. Martha C. Nussbaum, *Sex and Social Justice* (Oxford University Press, Oxford and New York, 1999), pp. 39–54.
2. Seyla Benhabib, *Situating the Self: Gender, Community and Postmodernism in Contemporary Ethics* (Polity Press, Cambridge, UK, 1992), pp. 14–17.
3. Jürgen Habermas, 'Struggles for Recognition in the Democratic Constitutional State', in *Multiculturalism*, ed. Amy Gutman (Princeton University Press, Princeton, NJ, 1995), pp. 107–14.
4. Charles Taylor, 'Politics of Recognition', in *Multiculturalism*, ed. Amy Gutman (Princeton University Press, Princeton, NJ, 1995), pp. 25–73.
5. Nancy Fraser, 'What's Critical about Critical Theory: The Case of Habermas and Gender', in *Feminism*, vol. 1, ed. Susan Moller Okin and Jane Mansbridge (Elgar Publishing House, Aldershot, UK, 1994), p. 87.
6. Poems written by anonymous women in *Narishiksha*, part 2 (Calcutta, 1884), pp. 210, 194.

7. See Sir William Markby, erstwhile judge in Calcultta High Court and fellow of Balliol College, *Hindu and Mohammadan Law* (Calcutta 1906), pp. 2–3.
8. Regulation IV of 1793. Cited in the Original Civil Court Ruling of 16 March, 1868 by Justice Markby, in the Secretary of State versus the Administrator-General of Bengal, *The Weekly Reporter*, Bengal, Calcutta, 1858, Supplementary Volume I, p. 57.
9. Regulation IV of 1793, p. 63.
10. See Tanika Sarkar, *Hindu Wife, Hindu Nation: Religion, Community, Cultural Nationalism* (C. Hurst, London, and Permanent Black, Delhi, 2001).
11. See Nancy Fraser, 'Rethinking Recognition', *New Left Review*, May–June 2000, pp. 112–13.
12. See *Nutan Panjika* (Serampore, 1870–1871), p. 1.
13. See Ishanchandra Vidyabagish, *Ekadashi Vyavastha* (Boalia, 1856).
14. See Mrinalini Sinha, *Colonial Masculinity: The Manly Englishman and the Effeminate Bengali in the Late Nineteenth Century* (Manchester University Press, Manchester, 1995), pp. 33–69.
15. See Lata Mani, *Contentious Traditions: The Debate on Sati in Colonial India* (University of California Press, Berkeley, 1998), pp. 11–42.
16. See Regulation XVII of 1829.
17. See S. D. Collet, *The Life of Letters of Raja Rammohun Roy*, ed. D. K. Biswas and P. C. Ganguly (Sadharan Brahmo Samaj, Calcutta, 1962).
18. See, for instance, Bankimchandra Chattopadhyaya, *Bishabriksha* (Calcutta, 1873).
19. *Chittabilashini* (Calcutta, 1856), pp. 64–6.
20. See, for instance, Ramdhan Tarkapanchanan Bhattacharyya, *Vidhabavedannishedhak,* (Dharmasabha, Boalia, 1864).
21. Mani, *Contentious Traditions.*
22. See Lucy Carroll, 'Law, Custom and Statutory Social Reform: The Hindu Widow Remarriage Act of 1856', in *Women in Colonial India: Essays on Work, Survival and the State,* ed. J. Krishnamurty (Oxford University Press, Delhi, 1989), pp. 1–27.
23. Carroll, 'Law, Custom and Statutory Social Reform', pp. 1–27.
24. Ashok Sen, *Ischwarchandra Vidyasagar and the Elusive Milestones* (Papyrus, Calcutta, 1977); also see Sumit Sarkar, 'Vidyasagar and Brahmanical Society', in *Writing Social History* (Oxford University Press, Delhi, 1998), pp. 216–82.
25. Carroll, 'Law, Custom and Statutory Social Reform', p. 3.
26. *Murshidabad Patrika*, 18 April 1873, Report on Native Newspapers (Bengal, 1873).
27. *Dacca Prakash*, 20 April 1873.
28. *Bengalee*, 17 May 1873.
29. Manmohan Basu, *Hindur Achar Vyavahar* (Calcutta, 1873).
30. See Tanika Sarkar, 'Talking about Scandals: Religion, Law and Love in Late 19th Century Bengal', *Studies in History*, 13 (1997).
31. See 'The Queen versus Madhub Chunder Giri Mohunt', Calcutta High Court, 15 December 1873, in *The Weekly Reporter,* Criminal Rulings (Calcutta, 1874).
32. *Bengalee*, 1 November 1873.
33. *Dainik O samachar Patrika*, 15 January 1891, RNP (Bengal, 1891).
34. *Bangabashi*, 21 March 1891, RNP (Bengal, 1891).
35. The history of this bill is discussed extensively in Sarkar, *Hindu Nation, Hindu Wife.*
36. By Revd Long's reckoning, as many as twenty-five new newspapers were started to discuss widow remarriage. See Benoy Ghosh, 'The Press in Bengal', in *The History of Bengal, 1757–1905*, ed. N. K. Sinha (Calcutta University Press, Calcutta, 1967), p. 227.
37. See Jatindra Jain, *Kalighat Painting: Images from a Changing World* (Mapin Publishing, Ahmadabad, 1999), pp. 16–96; also Tanika Sarkar, 'Talking about Scandals', pp. 63–97.
38. See Usha Chakravarty, *Conditions of the Bengali Women in the 19th Century* (Calcutta, 1960).

39. William Adam, 'Female Instruction', in *Second Report on the State of Education in Bengal, 1836*, ed. and reprinted by A. N. Basu (Calcutta University Press, Calcutta, 1941), pp. 187–8.

40. See Tanika Sarkar, *Words to Win: The Making of Amar Jiban, a Modern Autobiography* (Kali for Women, Delhi, 1999), pp. 67–89.

41. See Sarkar, *Words to Win*.

42. Benoy Ghosh (ed.), *Samayikpatre Banglar Samajchitra*, vol. 2 (Papyrus, Calcutta, 1970), pp. 27–8.

43. See Sarkar, *Words to Win*, pp. 71–3.

44. Kailashbashini Debi, *Hindu mahilaganer Heenabastha* (Calcutta, 1863), p. 62.

45. Debi, *Hindu mahilaganer Heenabastha*, p. 67.

46. *Narishiksha*, part 2, p. 210.

1902: Women get vote
↳ Aboriginals → considered floral or fauna

Citizenship as Non-Discrimination: Acceptance or Assimilationism? Political Logic and Emotional Investment in Campaigns for Aboriginal Rights in Australia, 1940 to 1970

Marilyn Lake

In the Australian state of New South Wales (NSW) in the 1940s and 1950s, Aboriginal people lived under a regime of confinement, segregation and discrimination. If residing on an official reserve or station, they were restricted in their movements and subject to the control and surveillance of the Aborigines Welfare Board. If living in towns or cities, they were subject to exclusion from, or segregation in, schools, hospitals, cinemas, swimming pools and hotel bars. As historian Peter Read put it: 'there was scarcely a town in the central west of New South Wales [and one could add, on the north coast] where a local Aborigine could try on clothes, sit down for a meal, get a haircut, go to secondary school, run for office, join a club, drink in the lounge bar or work in a shop'.[1] But until 1967, when a referendum made it possible for the federal government to legislate in the area, Aboriginal policy came under the jurisdiction of the states, so the legislation and regulations governing Aboriginal people's lives varied markedly across Australia.

Campaigns for reform were thus addressed to state governments or their agencies, such as the NSW Aborigines Welfare Board, which in 1949, received a protest about the exclusion of Aboriginal people from the public swimming pool at Kempsey, a town on the north coast. The letter came from the feminist organisation, the United Associations of Women (UA), formed in Sydney, by Jessie Street, some twenty years earlier. In condemning the Kempsey Council's policy of excluding Aboriginal people from the municipal swimming pool, the secretary of the UA explained that: 'This action of the Kempsey Council violates every principle of the UN Charter to which Australia contributes'. Members of the UA had

> concerned themselves with this matter because one of the Objects of our Association is the removal of discriminations which operate unjustly against individuals. In this we ally ourselves with that clause of the UN Charter which affirms 'there shall be no discrimination on account of race, colour, creed or sex'.[2]

In response, the Aborigines Welfare Board assured the UA that 'the Board in furthering its policy of assimilation was anxious that Aboriginal children should have every opportunity in association with other children and that it was felt their attendance at the baths afforded an excellent opportunity in this regard'.[3]

This is an interesting exchange and suggests some of the themes to be pursued in this paper: first, the centrality of the concept of the individual to ideas of non-discrimination and modern citizenship; second, the importance of the concept of 'inclusion' (as distinct from identity) in emancipatory discourse in the historical conditions of modernity; third, the importance of the discursive framework of non-discrimination for a feminist coalition around racism (which was, nevertheless, fraught with gendered tensions) and fourth, the 'dangerous intimacy' between the 'progressive' principle of non-discrimination and the 'repressive' policy of assimilation, between the processes of subjectification and subjection.[4]

I shall explore these themes by charting the political alliance between three women from very different backgrounds – Faith Bandler, a black Australian of Pacific Islander (later 'South Sea Islander') descent; Pearl Gibbs, an Aboriginal woman from Dubbo in outback New South Wales; and Jessie Street, a leading white feminist of upper-class

background – who worked together, and with others in their networks, in the 1950s and 1960s, in effective campaigns for Aboriginal
citizenship. They worked in two key organisations, the state-based
Aboriginal-Australian Fellowship (AAF) and the Federal Council for
the Advancement of Aborigines (FCAA), later the Federal Council
for the Advancement of Aborigines and Torres Strait Islanders
(FCAATSI). The women activists' achievements included the repeal
of remaining discriminatory legislation and the abolition of the
Aborigines Welfare Board in New South Wales, and the passage of the
1967 federal referendum, which, in removing two 'discriminatory'
clauses from the Australian Constitution, was hailed as a recognition
of Aboriginal people's full citizenship.

Finally, I want to point to the different political subjectivities
invoked in campaigns against racial discrimination, on the one hand,
and in support of [Aboriginal identity] on the other. Whereas the
outlawing of racial discrimination could be seen as the realisation of
the modern promise of a non-discriminating citizenship – and thus
was important in assuaging the past hurt of exclusion – the assertion
of Aboriginal claims to a distinctive and prior relationship to the
country now called Australia arose from a profound sense of loss –
loss of land, loss of culture, loss of people. Different political subjectivities were constituted in different kinds of 'wounded attachments'
to the past; they spoke to different, but not mutually exclusive, histories of pain.[5] Aboriginal people had suffered both the hurt of racial
discrimination and exclusion *and* the loss of their country and culture.

Historical accounts of campaigns for Aboriginal rights in Australia,
from the 1950s to the 1970s, have usually charted the changes in
orientation in terms of a radicalising shift away from claims for equal
citizenship, or civil rights, towards an assertion of self-determination
and demands for group-specific indigenous rights. There is usually
the suggestion in these accounts that the second political phase
represented a necessary advance in political enlightenment towards a
recognition of Aboriginal difference and group-specific Aboriginal
rights.[6] But there has been little exploration of the different political
subjectivities called up by campaigns for equal citizenship, on the one
hand, or indigenous rights, on the other, nor any investigation of the
emotional or psychic investments in these different mobilisations.
And with the exception of Ann Curthoys's excellent study of racial
politics in the New South Wales country towns visited by University
of Sydney students on the 1965 'Freedom Ride', the role of gender

and sexuality in campaigns for Aboriginal rights has received little attention by Australian historians.[7]

I want to suggest that any account of political subjectivities must attend to the structures of feeling that informed them – we need a sense of the interplay between psychic life and political mobilisation, the way in which emotional 'need' has translated into political 'demand'.[8] As Cora Caplan has written:

> Ignore that shifting reciprocal relationship, which constructs the particular subjectivities lived by women and men of different historical periods, classes, races and cultures and it becomes especially problematic to discuss how both individual and collective resistance to oppression is shaped and enabled. We need a perspective on history and subjectivity to understand why social movements develop and fail, what sustains the collective morale of a strike, the popularity of a peace movement, the anger of an ethnic community, the defiance of a young civil servant.[9]

Recent work on the emergence of 'recognition struggles' has pointed to the emotional dynamics – the feelings of 'damage' or 'harm' – that inform them (a point that has been lost in much of the debate about the relative claims of 'recognition' and 'redistribution' that followed). In his influential essay 'The Politics of Recognition', Canadian theorist Charles Taylor explained:

> The thesis is that our identity is partly shaped by recognition or its absence, often by the misrecognition of others, and so a person or group of people can suffer real damage, real distortion, if the people or society around them mirror back to them a confining or demeaning or contemptible picture of themselves. Nonrecognition or misrecognition can inflict harm, can be a form of oppression, imprisoning someone in a false, distorted, and reduced mode of being.[10]

Wendy Brown, in 'Wounded Attachments: Late Modern Oppositional Political Formations', interrogates the 'logics of pain' and the 'history of suffering' that animate these political movements more closely. She asks whether such 'wounded attachments' are not really barriers to an emancipatory political project.[11]

But 'wounded attachments' can have different political implications and their 'resolution' can produce paradoxical effects. To refer to the Australian context, Aboriginal people were oppressed as both black and indigenous: they were racially vilified and they were dispossessed. Thus, the triumphant passage of the 1967 referendum which symbolised the acceptance of Aboriginal people into the Australian nation as equal citizens (and thus assuaged the hurt of racial exclusion) at the same time worked to reinforce their sense of grief as indigenous people who had lost their country. In a sense, their triumphant entry into full citizenship – with its corollary of assimilation as individuals – symbolised their ultimate loss as a people. It was this sense of loss that fuelled their ongoing 'recognition struggle' – the demand for recognition of their Aboriginality – which took on a new and, arguably, gendered, dynamic in the separatist politics that gained ground in the wake of the Referendum.

The principle of non-discrimination and its corollary of a citizenship of inclusion were important in enabling women's inter-racial political alliance in the 1950s, but for Faith Bandler, the younger, black, woman, who would become a leading Aboriginal rights activist and acclaimed public figure, these commitments also grew from her emotional formation as a political subject. For Faith Bandler, equal citizenship meant the repudiation of racial distinctions. 'Let's tell the world there's only one Australian', she proclaimed, in 1967, at the height of the referendum campaign, 'and his colour doesn't matter at all'.[12] Citizenship meant acceptance by fellow Australians and the importance of such 'acceptance' to her own sense of self-esteem was conveyed in a newspaper report on her appointment as NSW Director of the 'Vote Yes' campaign: 'Poised and eloquent, she has no trouble these days of [sic] being accepted as an equal by Australians with whom she mixes'.[13]

Not surprisingly, then, the emergence at the end of the 1960s of a defiant discourse on Black Power, which in the distinctive Australian context translated into separatist claims for Aboriginal self-determination, proved personally and politically disorienting to this champion of non-discrimination, as the ideal of an inclusive citizenship began to be critiqued as a repressive politics of assimilation, and non-indigenous Australians – black or white – were made to feel increasingly unwelcome in Aboriginal rights organisations.

For Faith Bandler, now 82 years old, the definition of equal citizenship in terms of non-discrimination was formative and to this day she reserves her highest praise for those, like her adored mentor Jessie Street, who 'did not see the colour of one's skin'. Ida Faith Mussing was born in 1918 in the small town of Tumbulgum on the Tweed River in northern New South Wales, one of eight children (four boys and four girls) born to Ida and Peter Mussing. Her mother, of Scottish-Indian descent, had served as a maid in a grand mansion in Brisbane and was widowed with two small daughters, when she met and married Faith's father in 1906. He had arrived in Australia as a boy in the 1880s on a 'slave ship', having been abducted as a child from the island of Ambrym, in the New Hebrides (now Vanuatu), one of around 60,000 Pacific Islanders brought to work on the sugar cane plantations in Queensland in the nineteenth century. Her father died when she was just 6 years old and her mother took the family to the larger town of Murwillumbah, also on the northern New South Wales coast, not far from Kempsey.

Unlike Aborigines, who were deprived of the rights of citizenship unless they secured a demeaning 'certificate of citizenship' by repudiating their Aboriginal kin and community, the descendants of Kanakas or Pacific Islanders (or South Sea Islanders as they would later be called) enjoyed the political and civil rights of Australian citizens. They were, nevertheless, discriminated against in daily social relations, excluded from hotels, restaurants and cinemas, because they were black, or 'coloured', to use the contemporary term. Faith was called names at school (such as 'blackie' or 'nigger') and local hotels refused her brothers employment. Interviewed by a newspaper in the 1960s, she remembered the hurt of racism: 'as a child in a NSW North Coast town years ago, she knew the stigma of being a dark Australian – the exclusion from the picture theatre, the gibe of a white schoolchild, the barbed remark of an adult'.[14]

In 1951, Faith's older brother John, together with his wife, Agnes, had been moved to write to their local member of federal parliament, to protest against the experience of segregation at the 'Picture Houses':

> May I take the liberty on behalf of the Coloured Population of Tweed Heads to approach you regarding their status in so far as being allowed to enter the Picture Houses in Tweed Heads and Coolangatta.
>
> When entering the building the Coloured People are allowed one area and the Whites another area and the coloured people feel that it is a slight against their Freedom. Also as they are allowed to cast a vote and put their chosen representative into Parliament they feel that they should be able to enter a public building and decide where they wish to sit and not be herded into one place as they have been doing in the past.[15]

As citizens, as people 'allowed to cast a vote and put their chosen representative into Parliament', the Mussings considered that their status also entitled them to 'enter a public building' and to sit alongside other citizens, should they so wish. Citizenship meant no distinctions, being free from discrimination of any kind. But there was also in the letter a suggestion of the deeper harm caused by segregation:

the existential pain of being treated like animals, 'herded into one place', denied their humanity.

Faith recalled the debilitating personal effects of the experience of growing up in a racist society in an interview with her friend, the Communist writer Len Fox, conducted in the early 1980s for their jointly prepared book of recollections about the Aboriginal-Australian Fellowship, an organisation she and Pearl Gibbs formed in 1956. 'When you have been discriminated against,' she remembered, 'you are not conscious of other people being discriminated against on the grounds of race, because it so occupies your whole being so much, it is such a terrible experience that you can only think about yourself'. She also recalled the importance of the American experience of slavery in giving meaning to her family's experience and shaping their protest:

> we had magazines in the house about the Africans, and about the black Americans; and I knew about the slave trade, and we always sang the slave songs in the evenings. My brothers used to save up to buy a record of Paul Robeson's and we would all sing with him, as well as singing the songs of his people.[16]

Her identification with the American experience was also evident when, in 1950, Faith Mussing (as she still was) addressed a rally in Sydney, called by the Australian Peace Council, to protest against the gaoling in the United States of the writer Howard Fast, found guilty of 'un-American acivities'. Faith was an admirer of his novel *Freedom Road*.

Published in 1946, Fast's novel about the aftermath of the Civil War in the United States told of the time in the South when 'white men and black men lived together, worked together and built together ... In many, many places, they died together, in defence of what they had built.' There were just a few years of racial equality before the Ku Klux Klan destroyed this fine 'experiment'. Fast said he wrote *Freedom Road* to memorialise this special time, because when it had been destroyed by the racists 'not only were material things wiped out and people slain, but the very memory was expunged'. But for eight years, the experiment in freedom and equality had worked: 'the Negro had been given the right to exist in this nation as a free man, a man who stood on equal ground with his neighbour ... he had been given the right to work out his own destiny in conjunction with the southern poor whites'.[17]

In her speech at the Howard Fast protest rally, Faith endorsed this vision and imagined a future for the Australian nation in these terms.

'Howard Fast tells us that not only can black and white people fight and die together', she said, 'but they can also live and work together. As I read that, I thought of our Aborigines. They haven't been given a chance to show the truth of this.' The desirability of black and white living and working together became for Faith a lifelong theme of her public speaking.[18]

Along with many in the left-wing circles in which she mixed, by the early 1950s, Faith had become increasingly angry at the oppressed condition of Aboriginal people in Australia. Men on the left identified most readily with emerging struggles around pay rates and working conditions in the pastoral industry in the north of the country in Western Australia and the Northern Territory. Faith's attention was directed to the plight of Aboriginal people closer to home, by a woman who would become a close friend and political ally, Pearl Gibbs, who came from Dubbo in western New South Wales. Faith met Pearl in the short-lived Sydney branch of the Melbourne-based Council for Aboriginal Rights in 1950, when she had already spent decades fighting for her people's rights.

Pearl Gibbs was born in 1901, the year in which the Australian colonies federated to form the Commonwealth of Australia. One of the most powerful sentiments animating this new nation-state was its commitment to the ideal of White Australia, a commitment translated with indecent haste into laws to deport Pacific Islanders (the 'Kanakas') and restrict further non-white immigration. Section 127 of the Constitution, which stipulated that Aboriginal people would not be counted in the national census, made it clear that there was no place in this imagined community for indigenous Australians, who were categorised, in the evolutionary wisdom of the time, as 'a dying race'. People of mixed descent, it was assumed, would disappear by merging into the general population. Pearl Gibbs, part-Aboriginal woman, was born into a country in which there was no conceivable future for her people.

She grew up in New South Wales, in Brewarrina and Yass, where her Aboriginal mother worked as a domestic servant. She attended segregated schools in Yass and Cowra and from the 1920s became politically active, on behalf of her people, providing assistance to Aboriginal girls apprenticed out as domestic servants by the Aborigines Protection Board (forerunner to the Aborigines Welfare Board) and organising a strike of pea pickers in Nowra.

In 1937, she joined William Ferguson in organising the Aborigines' Progressive Association, to campaign for the extension of basic citizenship rights to Aboriginal people and as general secretary she wrote in the following year to the League of Nations, to draw attention 'to the ill treatment of the Aborigines throughout Australia in the past' and asking for international assistance in removing a particularly punitive judge from the Court in Darwin (wrongly believing that the League of Nations had a mandate over the Northern Territory). She wrote:

> Because he has an obvious bias against the Aborigines, and is unable to distinguish between revenge and justice, and overlooks the violation of Aboriginal women and girls by whites and Asiatics, we ask for the immediate recall of Judge Wells from the Darwin Bench.
>
> We respectfully ask the Government to adopt a more humane and scientific Aboriginal policy, and thus end Australia's present treatment of the Aborigines, which is incurring the contempt of the civilised nations of the world.

A Geneva official's cursory note read: 'I don't think any action is possible or desirable'.[19]

In the late 1930s, Gibbs extended her work for Aboriginal rights, helping to organise the 'Day of Mourning', in Sydney, in January 1938, on the occasion of the 150th anniversary of the arrival of the first British settlers, or the 'invaders', as Aborigines preferred to call them. Their manifesto, which emphasised their history of dispossession, read in part:

> The 26th of January, 1938, is not a day of rejoicing for Australia's Aborigines; it is a day of mourning. The festival of 150 years' so-called 'progress' in Australia commemorates also 150 years of misery and degradation imposed upon the original native inhabitants by the white invaders of this country ...
>
> You are the New Australians, but we are the Old Australians. We have in our arteries the blood of the Original Australians, who have lived in this land for many thousands of years. You came here only recently, and you took our land away from us by force. You have almost exterminated our people, but there are enough of us remaining to expose the humbug of your claim, as white Australians, to be called a civilised, progressive, kindly and humane nation ...[20]

The call for an equal citizenship was couched in a larger politics of grief: Aborigines were in mourning for the loss of a country which had been theirs for 'many thousands of years'.

By the early 1950s, Pearl Gibbs was determined to form a new inter-racial body to bring to an end the discriminatory regime of the New South Wales Aborigines Welfare Board, to which she had been elected as Aboriginal representative in 1954. White people had to take responsibility for ending racial discrimination, because it was white people who were the problem, not Aboriginal people, as she reminded Len Fox, who had expressed an interest in joining the new organisation:

> I first met Pearl in the early 1950s when my friend Faith Bandler persuaded me to join a small committee formed for Aboriginal Rights ... I sat opposite her thinking that her skin was no darker than mine, that she could easily have passed herself off as a white and had an easy life ... But I realised that Pearl was talking to me.
> 'You know', she was saying, 'it's all your fault'. I looked at her in surprise, and asked her what was my fault. 'The Aboriginal problem', she replied. 'It's not an Aboriginal problem. It's a white problem.'[21]

She shared her vision of a new inter-racial Aboriginal rights group, free from domination by churches or political parties, with Faith Bandler, who, although having suffered racial discrimination, mixed easily in the cosmopolitan and literary circles of postwar Sydney and had a number of influential white friends.

The first gathering of the new group was held in the Kirribilli home of Muir Holborn, poet and president of the Fellowship of Australian Writers, and the second in the Sydney flat of Lucy Woodcock, an activist with the New South Wales Teachers' Federation, member of the United Associations of Women and a friend of Pearl Gibbs and Jessie Street. Thus was the Aboriginal-Australian Fellowship born. Irene McIlwraith, like Faith's husband, Hans Bandler, a refugee from Nazism, who would become secretary, remembered the first meeting:

> there was a room full of people. Someone got up and told a horrible story about the terrible conditions the Aboriginal people lived under – they were discriminated against in the picture theatres – there were two communities, black and white. The Blacks were living in very bad housing and were not given jobs in towns.[22]

The aims of the AAF were, as another member later phrased it, to work for 'equal rights and acceptance of Aborigines in New South Wales and to implement a policy of broader economic and educational opportunities, social and cultural contacts. And of course full citizenship rights.'[23] There was some retrospective embarrassment about their initial aims, because of the AAF's express commitment to the goal of 'assimilation', which, by the 1960s, had come to be understood as a threat to Aboriginal identity.

When elections were held for office bearers, Pearl Gibbs, who had put so much effort into establishing the organisation, was passed over for the position of president in favour of a man, Bert Groves, a long-time Aboriginal activist, who had also worked with William Ferguson in the 1930s. Pearl was elected vice-president, but, according to those close to her, she was deeply upset at being overlooked and disappeared up bush to nurse her wounds. Coalition politics entailed particular challenges for women activists confronted by men's need to assert their authority. The Aboriginal-Australian Fellowship and the Federal Council for Aboriginal Advancement (later FCAATSI) would be racked by tension and conflict – over policy priorities, strategies and tactics and, importantly, the position and authority of Aboriginal and/or black members – but the conflict was also, and often at the same time, gendered.

Within a few months of his election to the presidency of the Fellowship, Bert Groves was involved in conflict with two women on the executive, both of whom were accused of flouting his authority and forced to resign. In 1957, the secretary, Irene McIlwraith had been asked by Groves to travel to the country to investigate newspaper reports of racial conflict in the town of Walgett 'as part of Fellowship policy to promote better relations between white and coloured residents'.

McIlwraith was shocked at what she found – Aborigines lived in appalling poverty and were subjected to systematic racist abuse – and she wrote a long report which she distributed to newspapers and politicians, but without Groves's authority. In a humiliating move, she was asked to type and sign a 'statement of responsibility' which read in part:

> I typed and had the report duplicated without any member of the Executive nor the Fellowship, nor Mr Groves, the President, having read it or seen it. I then posted the Report to a number of people, members of the NSW and federal governments, leaders of political parties and NSW members of parliament, trade unions etc without any authorisation by the President ...[24]

McIlwraith was forced to resign from her position.

A similar conflict arose the following year involving Faith Bandler, who also felt obliged to resign from her position as vice-president. She was censured by Groves for changing arrangements for a Fellowship birthday party (she chaired the organising committee) without his permission. In her letter of resignation, Faith pointed to her authority to speak for the 'coloured people of this country' and hinted at Groves's role of usurper (displacing Pearl Gibbs):

> My work for the advancement of the coloured people of this country dates back a number of years, and only by the experience I gained through those years was it possible together with Mrs Pearl Gibbs and several European Australians to form this organisation, the Aboriginal-Australian Fellowship. My sincere desire ... is that the Fellowship shall be guided by its members in all its decisions it makes for the betterment of the lives of Aborigines.[25]

Shortly after this stand-off, Groves himself resigned from the Fellowship to join the re-formed Aborigines' Progressive Association, Faith was reinstated as vice-president and Charles Leon, an Aboriginal man, became the next president.

The three women, who would become close friends and political allies – Jessie Street, Faith Bandler and Pearl Gibbs – met in Sydney in the context of leftist politics. Street was the oldest and wealthiest of the three and although vilified as a communist sympathiser, enjoyed the self-confidence of the white ruling class. Born in India in 1889, she grew up on a New South Wales pastoral property inherited by her mother, and received her early schooling largely from governesses. She enrolled at the University of Sydney, from which she graduated in 1910, with a Bachelor of Arts degree. There she also met her future husband, Kenneth Street, a law student at the university, and they married in 1916. By the late 1940s, her husband had become Chief Justice of New South Wales, while Jessie, the mother of four children, had become one of Australia's leading feminists. As an outspoken supporter of the Soviet Union during the war, she was also subject to increasing public criticism and placed under surveillance by the Australian Security Intelligence Organisation (ASIO), until finally pressured to leave the country. About these accusations, Street commented: 'I am not a Communist, but I have no political inhibitions and am prepared to work with anyone, be they Communist or not, for those things I believe to be right'.[26]

Jessie Street was a founding member of the Feminist Club, established in Sydney in 1914, which merged in 1929 with two other women's groups to become the United Associations of Women, of which Street became president. She was a fearless advocate of women's rights – independent, assertive, hard-working, generous and determined. She championed equal pay and opportunities, an independent income for mothers, an equal moral standard, and, during World War

Two, launched the Sheepskins for Russia campaign. As Faith Bandler recalled recently, Jessie had guts:

> she couldn't care less what people said about her – didn't worry her. If she believed in something, she went at it like a bull at a red rag and nothing would stop her ... she more than any other person on this earth influenced my life. And she said to me one day, 'I'll tell you what Faith, if one puts their mind to what they want, they'll get it'. And she was thinking more of preventing another world war and ... of feeding hungry people. And doing things about women's rights and blacks' rights. Well my life with Jessie wasn't dull I can tell you.[27]

In 1945, Street was one of those honoured to represent her country at the foundation conference of the United Nations Organisation (UNO) in San Francisco, where she lobbied tirelessly, working with Bertha Lutz from Brazil, for recognition of the principle of equal rights for men and women in the Charter and then the establishment of a Commission on the Status of Women. As the Commission's first vice-president, Jessie Street was also active in promoting, with varying success, feminist amendments to the Draft Declaration of Human Rights. Together with Chairman Bodil Begtrup from Denmark, Street was caught in the classic feminist paradox of attempting to secure recognition of sexual difference (for example, the rights of mothers), while outlawing sexual discrimination.[28]

The repudiation of discrimination or distinctions between human beings was the animating ideal of the Charter and the Universal Declaration of Human Rights, as enunciated in Article 2:

> Everyone is entitled to all the rights and freedoms set forth in this Declaration, without distinction of any kind, such as race, colour, sex, language, religion, political or other opinion, national or social origin, property, birth or other status.

This became the guiding principle for the progressive politics of coalition after World War Two – informing understandings of modern citizenship as inclusive and assimilationist. It was these understandings that were invoked by the United Associations of Women, when they protested against the exclusion of Aborigines from the Kempsey swimming pool.

Jessie Street and Faith Bandler met each other through the activities of the Australian Peace Council, formed in Sydney in 1949. It was a Communist-front organisation whose goal was to prevent another war by fostering closer ties between East and West and a more sympathetic attitude to the Soviet Union and its allies. As a public speaker for the New South Wales branch of the Peace Council, Faith Bandler, in promoting peace, usually alluded to her people's history of oppression as 'slaves', their experience of being abducted from their Island homes and worked (often to death) on sugar plantations in Queensland in the late nineteenth century.

Although in her early years, Faith had gained a strong sense from her father and brothers of her identity as a South Sea Islander, by the mid 1950s she had fashioned herself into a thoroughly modern woman. And to be modern was to be assimilated. In the late 1930s, she had travelled south with her sisters to the dazzling metropolis of Sydney, where she secured work as a companion to a family friend in Clifton Hills, a benefactor who also paid for Faith's piano and singing lessons. Faith, like her mother, was blessed with a fine soprano voice, which she put to good use during World War Two, entertaining the troops and rural communities, while enlisted in the Australian Women's Land Army. On her discharge in November 1945, she took work as a dressmaker, and, to live in greater freedom, rented a room in the inner-city, cosmopolitan centre of King's Cross, the gathering place of artists, Communists, Jewish refugees and self-styled bohemians of many nationalities.

In 1951, Faith travelled for the first time to Europe, one of more than ninety young people who comprised the Australian delegation to the Communist-inspired Berlin Youth Festival. This was a large cultural event and as a member of the Margaret Walker dance group, her role was to dance the part of 'The Little Aboriginal Girl' in a programme that presented aspects of Australian history and politics. (Significantly,'The Little Aboriginal Girl' was not about Aboriginality, but rather was a US-inspired depiction of the pain of a child subjected to racial exclusions in the playground.) On her return to Australia, Faith renewed her friendship with Hans Bandler, a Jewish refugee from Austria, whom she had met briefly before embarking for Europe. In the late 1930s, Hans had been incarcerated in Buchenwald and Dachau, sites of horror which Faith confronted at first hand when in Europe in 1951.

Trained in Vienna as a civil engineer, Hans Bandler was a keen bush-walker, a film enthusiast and, like Faith, passionate about classical music; both were subscribers to Sydney Symphony Orchestra concerts. They were married in 1952 and their daughter Lilon was born in 1953. At French's Forrest, on the outskirts of Sydney, they built a house together and established a home that became a meeting place for the leftist, cultured, often European-born middle classes, whom they gathered around them. As Faith recalled many years later, 'New Year's Eve we would have as many as fifty–sixty people. And they were people from the New Theatre and the Labor party – the Communist party, from the Schubert Society, from the Bartok Society and ... I would do *all* the preparation'.[29] In the modern way, Faith had to combine her political activism with the demanding duties of a wife, mother and hostess. Her boundless energy, capacity for organisation and social skills impressed those with whom she worked, including Jessie Street, who couldn't believe that a woman could accomplish so much without domestic help.

Jessie Street had campaigned for Aboriginal rights since the 1940s, when, influenced by her old friends Ada Bromham and Mary Montgomerie Bennett, she had incorporated a range of recommendations relating to 'Aboriginal and coloured people' into the Australian Women's Charter, a document drawn up following the large feminist conferences held in Sydney in 1943 and 1946.[30] Forced into exile in England, between 1950 and 1956, by Cold War politics in Australia, Street had joined the executive committee of the Anti-Slavery Society in 1954 and worked on a submission about the position of Aboriginal people, which she hoped to place before the Human Rights Commission of the Economic and Social Council of the United Nations, showing the ways in which Australia's Indigenous people were denied fundamental human rights.

Street was, in the event, unable to go to New York, because as a suspected Communist, she was refused a visa by the United States government, which infuriated her, but in any case, she had become convinced that it would be better for an Australian body to present the case. In preparation for her return to Australia, she wrote to her many contacts in Australia (including Pearl Gibbs and Faith Bandler) urging the necessity of a national Aboriginal rights organisation, which could seek accreditation with the Economic and Social Council. Writing to H. G. Clements, secretary of the Western Australian branch of the Australian Peace Council, in early 1956, Street urged the need to hold a conference to establish a federal organisation: 'If the subject of the Australian Aboriginals is to be brought before the UN, I believe it would help considerably if you had an all Australian Organization'.[31] She also wrote to her feminist friend Ada Bromham, then living in Queensland. 'When I come out to Australia next year', Street wrote, 'I would like to have the opportunity of getting in touch with as many people as possible who are interested in improving the conditions of the Aborigines to ask them whether it is possible or advisable to form some sort of federal body. I shall value your advice on these subjects.'[32]

When Shirley Andrews, a scientist, folklorist, member of the Communist party and secretary of the Council for Aboriginal Rights in Melbourne, heard of these developments, she wrote to Jessie, full of enthusiasm:

> We understand that you are interested in this project and have considered coming out to Australia to set up a federal body to deal with the approach to the UNO. My committee have asked me to write to you conveying our enthusiasm and support for this idea. We have long felt the need for a federal organisation ... the trade unions and Labor party are showing increasing activity in support of better conditions for Aborigines and in both many people seem to be conscious of the fact that it has been one of their weak spots in the past ... It would be of great value in getting general support to have an Australia-wide body to handle the UNO approach because many people who heartily agree that the matter should go to the UNO are a little unwilling for it to be raised by an organisation outside Australia.[33]

Meanwhile, another friend, Ann Waters, who had also worked for the Anti-Slavery Society in England, replied from Sydney that:

> A group of people has met on a couple of evenings recently and decided to proceed with the organisation of a formal committee. The moving force is Mrs Pearl Gibbs, herself a quarter-caste, who is the Aboriginal representative on the Aborigines Welfare Board. People actively interested at this stage include Muir Holborn the writer, Johnny Walker the architect, Faith Bandler of Fijian descent [sic] and various others whom you probably wouldn't know.[34]

The Aboriginal-Australian Fellowship would be central to realising Street's second reform strategy – the launching of a petition calling on the government to hold a referendum to secure the constitutional amendment necessary to enable the federal government to assume responsibility for Aboriginal affairs. Her two proposals were complementary: a federal organisation could make representations to the UNO and exercise pressure on the federal government; and with the enactment of a constitutional amendment, the federal government would be empowered to make 'special laws' with regard to Aboriginal people and thus could be held accountable for their welfare.

The guiding ideal for these reforms was the UNO principle of non-discrimination: the purpose of the referendum was said to be to delete 'discriminatory clauses' from the Australian Constitution, first, by amending Section 51 to enable the Australian government to make 'special laws' in the area of Aboriginal welfare and second, by repealing Section 127, to allow Aboriginal people to be counted in the national census. It was the definition of the campaign as one against 'discrimination' which was crucial to its success and allowed a wide range of people to identify with it. For Faith Bandler, its purpose was to signify the nation's acceptance of all Australians as equal citizens, regardless of their colour; for Pearl Gibbs, the referendum was important in ending nearly two centuries of discrimination against her people; for Jessie Street, the referendum was crucial in winning equal rights for Aborigines and in signifying to the world that Australia adhered to international principles of human rights.

Emotional investments shaped these political commitments for whites as well as blacks. A sense of national shame was the crucial dynamic for many white campaigners for Aboriginal rights such as Street. Recent work by John Chesterman has demonstrated the importance of the threat of ongoing international embarrassment to policy change relating to enfranchisement and social security in the 1960s, and sensitivity to international censure also explains the widespread support of white Australians for the campaign to amend the Constitution, which ultimately resulted in a 'Yes' vote of more than ninety per cent in 1967.[35] To address the oppressed condition of indigenous people, Street invoked the international principle of non-discrimination. The first petition for the referendum, written in Street's hand, read in part:

> believing that many of the difficulties encountered today by Aborigines arise from the discrimination against them in two sections of the Commonwealth Constitution, which specifically exclude Aborigines from the enjoyment of their rights and privileges enjoyed by all other Australians ... [36]

Street asked Faith Bandler to take the petition to the executive of the AAF and to secure their endorsement.

The petition calling for a constitutional referendum was launched at a large public meeting in Sydney Town Hall, in April 1957, organised by the AAF. It was said to be the first public meeting in Australia with an Aboriginal chairman, Pastor Doug Nicholls, who proved reluctant at the last minute, however, to share the platform with 'that Communist Jessie Street'. The huge audience of some 1,500 people included hundreds of Aboriginal people, thanks to Pearl Gibbs's extensive contacts in New South Wales. A specially chartered bus brought a large number from the reserve at LaPerouse. Faith's social arrangements, including entertaining interstate visitors and local organisers in her home, ensured good will and consolidated interstate networks.

A letter to Faith from Rosine Guitermann, a member of the executive of the Aboriginal-Australian Fellowship, a Jewish Australian, a Communist and an old friend of Jessie Street, paid tribute to her organisational abilities:

> My most hearty congratulations on the magnificent meeting ... Not only was it so informative and interesting, But I feel that the emotional, moral and spiritual appeal and that vast audience was tremendous. I felt to misquote very slightly from English history 'on that day, you lighted such a candle in Australia, as, by God's grace, shall never be put out. Surely the majority of those present will never again be tempted to be smug and complacent in regard to events in Australia since 1788.[37]

The petition was launched, hundreds of signatures were collected that evening, thousands more copies of the petition were distributed to trade unions, women's groups and church groups, and within a fortnight the first batch was presented to the federal parliament. The following year, Faith Bandler took the petition to the postwar feminist organisation, established by Street, the Australian Women's Charter Conference. The minutes recorded:

> Mrs Faith Bandler of the Aboriginal-Australian Fellowship spoke of the hardships of the Aborigines especially in regard to human rights, which, she claimed, was every man's right. She said that even in the taking of the Census they are not counted with human beings, but classed with animals. The Fellowship has a Petition which they hope to present to the Federal Government for alterations to the Constitution by means of a Referendum, which will delete clauses that place the Aboriginal people apart from the rest of the community.

The Conference endorsed the Petition, and the following year recommended that governments provide better housing for Aborigines and urged communities in which Aboriginal people lived to provide 'neighbourly assistance and social acceptance, so that these Old Australians may take their place in the Australian Nation'.[38]

From the early 1960s, the petition campaign was taken over by the Federal Council for Aboriginal Advancement, which had been formed, following Street's assiduous networking, in Adelaide, in 1958. To maintain the momentum, a redrafted second petition, titled 'Towards Equal Citizenship for Aborigines', was launched by the

Federal Council at another large public meeting, in Sydney, in 1962. In her book about her involvement in the Federal Council's campaign for the referendum, *Turning the Tide,* Faith drew an explicit link between the personal and political, between her father's people's experience of national exclusion, when the new Commonwealth government had tried to deport them and her own political commitment:

> We faced the almost impossible task of turning the tide against years of a flow towards segregation of Aboriginal people. Vivid in my own mind was the deportation of the Pacific Islanders from the shores of North Queensland, after they had given fifty years of their labour to the development of the Australian sugar industry.[39]

Much of the public speaking, lobbying and coordination of the campaign for constitutional reform was carried out by three women – Kath Walker, an Aboriginal poet and orator, who was appointed Queensland secretary to FCAATSI in 1962; Faith Bandler, who was appointed NSW secretary to FCAATSI in the same year, and Shirley Andrews, secretary of the affiliated Victorian group, the Council for Aboriginal Rights.

In the course of the campaign, Faith Bandler and Kath Walker became star media performers and were in great demand as public speakers. Although they did so much of the work of publicity and organisation for FCAATSI, the top three positions on the federal executive were, from the beginning, held by men – from the 1960s, Joe McGinness, an Aboriginal man from Cairns, was president; and, of two non-Aboriginal men, Gordon Bryant, a Labor politician from Victoria was senior vice-president and Stan Davey, a minister in the Church of Christ, also from Victoria, was general secretary.

The male domination of coalition politics appalled long-time feminist Jessie Street, who urged Shirley Andrews to stand for general secretary: 'Would you be prepared to take on the secretaryship of the Commonwealth body? You know I always hoped that you would do this when we were discussing its formation.'[40] And Street wanted Faith to become president: 'She seems to be more on the ball than anyone else I know of except you,' she wrote to Andrews.[41] She wrote to Joe McGinness asking if he would nominate Bandler as his successor, as 'she was doing such a good job in New South Wales', but nothing came of these discussions and the male triumvirate of McGinness, Bryant and Davey remained firmly in control until the end of the sixties.

The men were also opposed to Street taking a case on behalf of FCAATSI to the United Nations, as she had always intended. There was a long tradition in Australia of feminists seeking international support for their causes, and an equally long tradition of masculinist opposition to any challenge to the authority of the sovereign nation state.[42] When Street asked Shirley Andrews about the feasibility of approaching the United Nations in the early 1960s, the forthright Andrews replied:

> Your idea of going to New York yourself is an excellent one. Our only problem is getting your credentials from the Federal Council's executive. One would need to be a fully trained psychiatrist to work out the odd motives of some of the male members of this body. I find them completely incomprehensible myself. Stan Davey is the main snag as he is such an undemocratic person, that if he is opposed to a thing it is difficult to get it through the executive.[43]

Andrews also knew about the importance of men's networking to maintaining their hold on power.

Men consolidated connections made through political parties and the churches. Stan Davey's position as Church of Christ mentor to Aboriginal activist Pastor Doug Nicholls was the basis of a crucial anti-Communist alliance, which Shirley Andrews no doubt found provoking. She commented to a friend: 'I put my foot in it the other day by attacking Doug who has been particularly opportunistic lately, and I was really fed up with him. However, as Doug is Stan's special protege I should have kept quiet'.[44] Political antagonisms were also gendered – as Faith Bandler would find when confronted with a realignment of political forces after the passage of the referendum in 1967.

Although, as Bain Attwood and Andrew Markus have made clear in their recent book *The 1967 Referendum, Or When Aborigines Didn't Get the Vote*, the referendum did nothing in and of itself to extend legal or civil rights to Aborigines (they already had the vote) it was understood as granting them full citizenship, because henceforth Aborigines would be counted in the national census.[45] Australians were persuaded that the passage of the referendum signified recognition of Aboriginal people's status as equal citizens in the sense that they would now be part of the Australian nation. The more emphasis there was on becoming part of the nation, however, the more Aboriginal people themselves began to express their doubts about the meaning of such acceptance. 'We want to be part and parcel of the community,' said Bert Groves in 1967, 'but we want to do this without losing our identity as Aborigines.' He emphasised that Aborigines wanted integration, not assimilation, which he defined as 'a modified method of extermination over a long time'. 'Once assimilation was complete the Aboriginal race would cease to exist, and the Aboriginal problem would cease with it.'[46]

Groves had first critiqued the assimilationist assumptions of citizenship when reading a paper on behalf of the AAF at the founding conference of the Federal Council of Aboriginal Advancement, in Adelaide, in 1958. The critique of assimilation was strongly influenced by Rosine Guitermann, who drew, in turn, on Jessie Street's work with the Anti-Slavery Society and the Sub-Commission for the Protection and Prevention of Discrimination against Minorities at the United Nations. Groves's paper read:

> The question as to the use of the word 'assimilation' has been discussed by the Executive of our Association and it has been decided that it is not a correct term to be used in the constitution of any Aboriginal organisation. Assimilation is the official policy of all the Australian governments – it is welcomed by most missionaries and humanitarians and also by most socialists.
>
> But what does it imply? Certainly, citizenship and equal status – so far, so good; also the disappearance of the Aborigines as a separate cultural group and ultimately their physical absorption by the European part of the population. It is assumed that if the Aborigines are going to lead the same life as other Australians, then they must disappear as a culturally distinct group. We feel that the word 'integration' implies a truer definition of our aims and objects.
>
> Our policy of assimilation, in fact, is simply a kindly form of white chauvinism; an expression of our belief that there is nothing worth preserving in Aboriginal culture and of our dislike of accepting a permanent national minority in Australia.

In the 1950s and 1960s, Australians from diverse backgrounds came together in campaigns for Aboriginal rights. Central to these campaigns in New South Wales was the coalition established by Jessie Street, Faith Bandler and Pearl Gibbs, joined in friendship and in their shared commitment to the goal of ending discrimination against black Australians. But the meanings attributed to 'blackness' varied, and political positions and expectations were shaped by subjective investments. For some the issue was racial discrimination; for others it referred to the status of indigenous peoples in Australia and their loss of land. Faith Bandler identified strongly with the symbolic politics of the referendum; for her it signified equal citizenship. Ken Brindle, an Aboriginal member of the Aboriginal-Australian Fellowship recalled:

> You, Faith, were all tizzed up about the referendum every time you opened your mouth. You went on about the referendum all the time ... I couldn't see how it would benefit us ... I couldn't buy your referendum. I was more

informed than the average Aboriginal, but I couldn't understand it ... I just thought you had a thing about the bloody referendum ... a bug in your bonnet.[47]

And similarly, Aboriginal activist Shirley Smith remembered:

Faith had been telling me about the Referendum ... but it didn't make much sense to me. Well, it is true that we Aboriginal people had never been allowed to vote, but ... most of us had never thought about it much, or talked about it ... As far as being a citizen, it wasn't even a word I thought about.[48]

Yet it was a key word for Faith, because equal citizenship spoke to her yearning for a world in which 'colour doesn't matter at all'.

For many Aboriginal campaigners, however, the issue was not so much 'colour', but 'country'. From the mid 1960s, in northern Australia, different Aboriginal groups had mobilised to defend their lands from the incursions of mining companies. The struggle waged by the Gurindji had attacted nation-wide support. In the southern states, Aboriginal people were also struggling to remain on reserve lands. For activists such as Pearl Gibbs, Kath Walker (soon to rename herself Oodgeroo Noonucal) and Bert Groves, it was their collective rights as a people, rather than their individual rights as modern citizens, that were most important to their sense of identity. During the 1960s, their 'recognition struggle' for rights as a dispossessed people began to be re-activated.

In its first years, the AAF frequently spoke of its aims in terms of 'the assimilation of the Aboriginal people into the community', but it is clear that the Aboriginal members were increasingly unhappy with this definition of their aspirations. They didn't want to blend into the broader society as individuals; rather they wanted society to accept and support the continuing existence of Aboriginal communities, culture and identity. Moreover, they wanted to determine their political goals themselves.

Pearl Gibbs began to put her efforts into enabling Aboriginal people to organise and speak for themselves. In October 1965, she helped arrange an all-Aboriginal conference in Sydney, with participants from all parts of New South Wales. It was an opportunity to hear from Aborigines themselves about 'policies formulated for them, but never by them, or in consultation with them'. There were sessions on housing, employment, education, land rights and cooperatives and 'A Bigger Say for Aboriginal People'. In the 1970s, Gibbs was an active contributor to the meetings which established an independent

New South Wales Land Council, which pressured the NSW government to pass land rights legislation.[49]

After the triumphant passage of the referendum, allowing the federal government to make 'special laws' for Aborigines, the question immediately arose: who should say what Aborigines wanted, who had the right to speak? The politics of advocacy gave way to the politics of representation and indigenous men moved to exclude non-indigenous supporters, notably the prominent black leader Faith Bandler, from meetings and positions of authority. In October 1967, Charles Perkins and Pastor Doug Nicholls called an Aborigines-only meeting in Sydney to form a new organisation, the National Aboriginal Affairs Association, to allow Aboriginal people 'national expression'. The meeting condemned FCAATSI for failing to represent Aboriginal people or Aboriginal opinion and for electing Faith Bandler to an executive position without the permission of the Aboriginal people.

The antagonism between Perkins and Bandler erupted into public view the following month in a bitter confrontation on television, on Bob Sanders's *People* show, screened on Channel Seven, during which Perkins named names of alleged Communists in FCAATSI and Bandler retorted that he had never been shy in accepting money and other resources from FCAATSI, when it suited him. The *Sun* newspaper called the encounter 'one of the most vicious barneys [brawls] seen on Australian television'.[50] Prominent women, especially those like Faith Bandler, who was elegant and eloquent, challenging and beguiling, who was fêted by the white media and basked in the limelight, encountered considerable hostility from those who envied her prominence and resented her power.

When Aboriginal poet and activist Kath Walker addressed a meeting of the Committee for Aboriginal Unity, in March 1970, in Adelaide, where she was a guest at the local Writers' Festival, she urged the women present to allow Aboriginal men to take over the leadership of their struggle. 'Stand back and let your men come forward,' she told the women at the meeting. 'Women had been leaders in Aboriginal affairs for too long … We must give our men back their manhood and their authority'.[51] Walker then reported on the progress of a new all-Aboriginal organisation, the Tribal Council, in her home state of Queensland, where the young men had taken over, with her blessing. Her son Denis had persuaded her that she had been wrong in her previous approach to securing equality. The new idea was for Aboriginal people to withdraw from coalition politics and consolidate their power.

The movement was led by young men and the new Tribal Councillors in Queensland included: Denis Walker, financial coordinator and housing; John Whittaker, health; Len Watson, education; Fred Gesha, employment, and Pastor Don Brady, legal aid.[52] They had been inspired in part by the visit to Australia in 1969 by the West Indian exponent of Black Power, Dr Roosevelt Brown, accepting an invitation from Melbourne activist Bruce McGuiness, who advised a nervous public: 'The white Australian has done his bit. He has established organisations for us; he has fought our battles; he has raised his voice for us; but now it is time for the black man to emerge as his own advocate.'[53]

At the annual conference of FCAATSI, in 1970, the tension around the issue of Aboriginal authority and power led finally to a formal split, but not all Aboriginal people left the organisation. Joe McGinness remained president and a young man from Queensland, John Newfong, was elected secretary and would shortly become involved in a bitter and symbolic dispute with Faith Bandler, who had declined to participate in the wreath-laying protest at the Bi-Centennial celebrations of Captain Cook's 'discovery' of Australia.

For Aboriginal activists, the occasion was another reminder of their historic loss, and they organised a ritual of mourning in Sydney. As a non-indigenous Australian, Faith felt that it was inappropriate for her to join in the grieving, but her decision was condemned by Newfong as evidence that she had become a bourgeois sell-out. She felt too much at home, he alleged, with the well-heeled ladies who lived in the leafy suburbs of Sydney's North Shore, a milieu he knew well, because he had helped Bandler raise money for Land Rights there. Criticised for spending too much time on the Captain Cook protest, Newfong resigned from his position as general secretary of FCAATSI and was replaced by Bandler, the first time a woman had held the post. In that capacity, she again attracted the attention of the national media when she defended the Aboriginal Tent Embassy, which had been erected by Aboriginal activists in front of the federal parliament in Canberra, to protest against their loss of country and the fact that indigenous people had become aliens in their own land.

Bandler's success on national television did little to appease her detractors. By 1973, as the politics of Aboriginal self-determination gained ascendancy, Bandler was marginalised in the coalition she had done so much to nurture. As she prepared to depart the scene, she received a tribute from the reconstituted Queensland branch of

FCAATSI (its Aboriginal members having followed Kath Walker into the National Tribal Council):

> We realise how successful you have been in attracting the support of other organisations to the cause, and in using your tact and resourcefulness to maintain the contacts and friendships that are already established. You have set a good example, in your devotion to FCAATSI as a multi-racial organisation which opposes racialism in any shape or form, and from any source whatsoever ...
>
> Above all we remember the way you held the organisation together, at a time when racialism was rearing its head, within its own ranks. We admire you for the wise and determined stand that you took at that time. You have made a great contribution to the Advancement of Aborigines and Islanders in the way you have encouraged people to work together and co-operate with one another, quite irrespective of the colour of their skin and their traditional background ...[54]

It was a fitting tribute to someone who had first spoken of the importance of blacks and whites living together and working together at the Howard Fast rally over twenty years earlier.

The divergence that opened up in campaigns for Aboriginal rights, between those who yearned for inclusion as equal citizens and those who favoured autonomy and self-determination reflected important ideological shifts, and different subjective investments, but the divisions were also shaped by gendered antagonisms. For Faith Bandler, painful childhood experiences of exclusion and her father's stories about the deportation of his people had sown the seeds of a desire for personal acceptance and a longing for a world which didn't see the colour of one's skin. During and after the referendum campaign, she found such acceptance in full measure, but the greater her public recognition, the greater the resentment of some of her erstwhile political colleagues, especially men who themselves aspired to leadership. Their sense of historic loss was exacerbated by the threat to their manhood posed by the ascendancy of women and whites in their political struggle. It has been widely recognised that the movement towards self-determination reflected an important development in the history of campaigns for Aboriginal rights, but the political dissension that erupted between Bandler and some of the Aboriginal men with whom she had worked also reflected different subjective investments and thus different needs. Bandler's need for acceptance arose from the family memory of exclusion; Aboriginal men's bid for autonomy and power arose out of a history of dispossession, a loss experienced in specific contexts as a loss of manhood. Self-determination – or Black Power – promised its restoration.

Notes

1. Peter Read, *Charles Perkins: A Biography* (Viking, Ringwood, 1990), p. 97. See also Heather Goodall, *Invasion to Embassy: Land in Aboriginal Politics in New South Wales, 1770–1972* (Allen and Unwin, Sydney, 1996), Parts IV and V; and Anna Haebich, *Broken Circles: Fragmenting Indigenous Families 1800–2000* (Fremantle Arts Press, Fremantle, 2000), pp. 501–11.

2. Caroline Scrimgeour to Minister for Interior, 6 September, and to Aboriginal Welfare Board, 4 October 1949, quoted in Marilyn Lake, *Getting Equal: The History of Feminism in Australia* (Allen and Unwin, Sydney, 1999), p. 208.

3. Lake, *Getting Equal*, p. 208.

4. I owe the phrase and the idea of 'dangerous intimacy' (between subjectification and subjection) to Denise Riley, *'Am I That Name?': Feminism and the Category of Women in History* (Macmillan, London, 1988).

5. Wendy Brown, 'Wounded Attachments: Late Modern Oppositional Political Formations', in *Feminism: The Public and the Private*, ed. Joan B. Landes (Oxford University Press, Oxford, 1998).

6. See, for example, Ann Curthoys, 'Citizenship, Race and Gender: Changing Debates Over the Rights of Indigenous Peoples and the Rights of Women', in *Suffrage and Beyond: International Feminist Perspectives*, ed. Caroline Daley and Melanie Nolan (Auckland University Press, Auckland, 1994); Bain Attwood and Andrew Markus (eds), *The Struggle for Aboriginal Rights: A Documentary History* (Allen and Unwin, Sydney, 1999); and John Chesterton, 'Taking Civil Rights Seriously', *Australian Journal of Politics and History*, 46 (2000), p. 4.

7. Ann Curthoys, 'Sex and racism: Australia in the 1960s', in *Forging Identities: Bodies, Gender and Feminist History*, ed. Jane Long, Jan Gothard and Helen Brasch (University of Western Australia Press, Nedlands, 1997).

8. Marilyn Lake, 'The Constitution of Political Subjectivity and the Writing of Labour History', in *Challenges to Labour History*, ed. Terry Irving (University of New South Wales Press, Sydney, 1994), pp. 81–6.

9. Cora Kaplan, *Sea Changes: Culture and Feminism* (Verso, London, 1986), p. 5.

10. Charles Taylor, 'The Politics of Recognition', in *Multiculturalism*, ed. Amy Gutmann (Princeton University Press, Princeton, 1994), p. 25; see also Nancy Fraser, 'From Redistribution to Recognition? Dilemmas of Justice in a Post-Socialist Age', *New Left Review*, vol. 212; Iris Young, 'Identity versus Social Justice?', *New Left Review*, vol. 222; Anne Phillips, 'Inequality and Difference', *New Left Review*, vol. 224.

11. Brown, 'Wounded Attachments', p. 451.

12. Kay Keavney, 'Let's Tell the World ...', *Australian Women's Weekly*, 10 May 1967, reprinted in Bain Attwood and Andrew Markus, *The 1967 Referendum, Or When Aborigines Didn't Get the Vote* (Aboriginal Studies Press, Canberra, 1997), p. 107.

13. Wallace Crouch, 'Say "Yes" to Human Dignity', *Daily Telegraph*, 20 April 1967.

14. Crouch, 'Say "Yes" to Human Dignity'.

15. John and Agnes Mussing to Mr Anthony, MHR, 1 July 1951; Bandler papers, Mitchell Library, ML MSS 6243, Add-on 2196/1.

16. Faith Bandler and Len Fox, *The Time Was Ripe: The Story of the Aboriginal-Australian Fellowship, 1956–69* (Alternative Publishing Co-operative Ltd, Chippendale, 1983), p. 1.

17. Howard Fast, *Freedom Road* (Bodley Head, London, 1946), pp. 255–6.

18. National Archives of Australia, Series 6119/90, extract from *Tribune*, 5 July 1950.

19. League of Nations Archives, Pearl Gibbs to President, League of Nations, 'Political', 1/34895.

20. Reprinted in Bandler and Fox, *The Time Was Ripe*, pp. 54–5.

21. Bandler and Fox, *The Time Was Ripe*, p. 41.

22. Bandler and Fox, *The Time Was Ripe*, p. 62

23. Aboriginal-Australian Fellowship papers, Statement about Past Work, 1962, ML MSS 4057/1.

24. Aboriginal-Australian Fellowship papers, Minutes, Mitchell Library, ML MSS 4057/1.
25. Bandler to Executive, 20 August 1958, Aboriginal-Australian Fellowship papers, ML MSS 4076/6.
26. Street to Florence Rutter, 21 March 1953, NLA MS 2683/10/19.
27. Interview with Faith Bandler conducted with Carolyn Craig, 27 June 1997.
28. Lake, *Getting Equal*, pp. 191–3.
29. Interview with Faith Bandler conducted with Carolyn Craig, 27 June 1997.
30. Lake, *Getting Equal*, pp. 194–6.
31. Street to H. G. Clements, 29 October 1955, Street papers, National Library of Australia (NLA), MS 2683/10/50.
32. Street to Bromham, 28 July 1956, Street papers, NLA, MS 2683/10/109.
33. Andrews to Street, 27 August 1956, Street papers, NLA, MS 2683/10/124.
34. Waters to Street, 28 March 1956, NLA, MS 2683/10/69.
35. John Chesterman, 'Defending Australia's Reputation: How Indigenous Australians Won Civil Rights, Part One', *Australian Historical Studies*, 116 (2001), pp. 20–40.
36. Quoted in Peter Sekuless, *Jessie Street* (University of Queensland Press, St Lucia, 1978), pp. 174–6.
37. Guitermann to Bandler, 14 May 1957, Aboriginal Australian Fellowship papers, ML MSS 4057/11.
38. Australian Women's Charter conferences, Minutes, Aboriginal Australian Fellowship papers, ML MSS 4507/1.
39. Faith Bandler, *Turning the Tide: A Personal History of the Federal Council for the Advancement of Aborigines and Torres Strait Islanders* (Aboriginal Studies Press, Canberra, 1989), p. 94.
40. Street to Andrews, 8 October 1961, Council for Aboriginal Rights papers, State Library of Victoria, MS 12913, box 9/7.
41. Street to Andrews, 2 October 1961, CAR papers, box 9/7.
42. See, for example, Lake, *Getting Equal*, ch. 5.
43. Andrews to Street, 14 July 1964, CAR papers, MS 12913, box 9/9.
44. Andrews to Joyce, undated letter [1963], CAR papers, MS 12913, box 9/8.
45. This issue is discussed extensively in Attwood and Markus, *The 1967 Referendum*.
46. 'Appeal for Yes vote to Realise Dream', *Sydney Morning Herald*, 13 May 1967, reprinted in Attwood and Markus, *The 1967 Referendum*.
47. Faith Bandler, *Turning the Tide*, p. 135.
48. Quoted in Attwood and Markus, *The 1967 Referendum,* p. 53.
49. See Heather Goodall, 'Pearl Gibbs', in *200 Australian Women: a Redress Anthology*, ed. Heather Radi (Women's Redress Press, Sydney, 1989), pp. 211–13.
50. *Sun* Newspaper, 16 November 1967.
51. 'Queensland People Find Their Roots', *Origin,* 19 March 1970.
52. *Origin*, 19 March 1970.
53. *Origin*, 18 September 1969.
54. Assistant-Secretary, Queensland Council AATSI to Faith Bandler, 8 May 1973, Bandler papers, ML MSS 2196/1/2.

Producing Citizens, Reproducing the 'French Race': Immigration, Demography, and Pronatalism in Early Twentieth-Century France

Elisa Camiscioli

The 'immigrant question' of early twentieth-century France was formulated with reference to both the labour power and reproductive value of potential foreigners. Politicians, industrialists, social scientists, and racial theorists agreed that the 'demographic crisis' had created a shortage of citizens as well as workers, and thus immigrants who came to work in France must also be assimilable, and able to produce indisputably French offspring. The new emphasis on assimilability was a reflection of the widespread panic created by depopulation, as social critics with pronatalist convictions lamented the steady drop in French births, and the 'individualistic' nature of French men and women which had, in their view, encouraged Malthusian reproductive practices.[1] They argued that depopulation had social as well as economic consequences, evidenced by the lack of husbands for French women, young men for the army, and children for the future labour force. Despite the pronounced nationalism of the pronatalist movement, its leaders therefore conceded that in order to mitigate the effects of the demographic crisis on the labour market and the French family, the importation of foreign workers was a necessary, though temporary, solution.[2]

In late nineteenth- and early twentieth-century Europe, populationist discourse equating demographic strength with international prominence had become increasingly prevalent.[3] As competition among nations no longer centred on their productive capacity alone, the formerly private, female sphere of reproduction assumed a more prominent role in the political life of the nation.[4] With the reproductive potential of citizens transformed into an object of social inquiry, hygienists and other 'experts' focused their attention on the health and well-being of the general population, and of the nation's children and its mothers.[5] Degeneration theory also flourished in several European nations, pointing to the prominence of depopulation, high infant mortality rates, venereal disease, and alcoholism among their citizen bodies.[6] In France, where the rhetoric of demographic decline assumed a particularly strident pitch, a wide range of individuals joined in the national quest to improve the quality and quantity of the population. Immigrants would also be enmeshed in this discursive web linking fecundity, racial hygiene, and a traditional vision of the family.

No European nation experienced demographic decline more acutely than France, and the casualties of the First World War, added to an already low birthrate, exacerbated French anxieties. From 1911 to 1938, the French population increased by only two million inhabitants, despite the addition of 1.7 million people from Alsace and Lorraine.[7] On the eve of the Great War, the average French family was composed of two children, and, in 1926, only three families out of ten could claim three or more.[8] In fact, French demographic growth in this period was largely due to immigration. The 1931 census counted 808,000 Italians, 508,000 Poles, and 352,000 Spaniards, to name the most numerous groups.[9] In the interwar period, nearly three million foreigners resided in France, and three-fourths of all demographic growth could be attributed to immigration.[10]

This essay will explore how members of the pronatalist movement, in their efforts to combat the demographic crisis, debated the possibility of foreign immigration to France. Because depopulation provided a unique opportunity to remake the citizen body, pronatalist discourse on the immigrant question reveals how gender, race, and reproduction structured national identity in early twentieth-century France. The movement's belief that reproduction was an obligation of citizenship determined its support for immigration from 'demographically prolific' nations such as Italy, Spain, and Poland.[11] Its members claimed that in less modern states, 'preindustrial' values promoted high birth-rates among selfless parents who, unlike their French counterparts, honoured their national obligation to procreate. Thus the culturally conservative rhetoric of pronatalism, which heralded patriarchal authority, maternal virtue, fecundity, and traditionalism, was employed to assess the assimilability of potential foreigners. That is, the very values pronatalists wished to revive among the French were projected onto foreign populations as well.

The debate on fecundity and assimilability, however, was carried out in a particular racial order. Although family immigration also occurred in this period, foreigners to France in the early twentieth century were overwhelmingly young and unmarried men. Male foreigners were, in many regards, particularly welcome: the catastrophic loss of French men in the Great War had created a shortage of husbands for French women while exacerbating the effects of depopulation.[12] The demographic crisis thereby forced hybridity upon the nation; intermarriage with 'racially' appropriate foreign men was encouraged, as it was necessary for the rebuilding of the national body.[13] Participants in the immigration debate conceived of the 'French race' as a dynamic construct with the ability to incorporate select elements into its fold. In consequence, the dominant racial metaphor of this period was one of judicious mixing, rather than an appeal to 'racial purity'. The sanctioning of prescribed forms of racial mixing, however, did not refute the logic of biological essentialism. Only 'compatible' blood was to be combined with that of the French, in order to sustain, or even regenerate, the race.

Moreover, the surplus population of Africa and Asia, and, specifically, the potential labour source of the French colonies, had to be dismissed as a possible remedy for depopulation in the metropole. Although Africans and Asians had immigrated to France before, during, and after the First World War, the pressing need to reconstitute French families in the interwar years reframed the immigrant question. As assimilability and the ability to reproduce French offspring became the most salient criteria by which foreigners were to be judged, the evaluation of simple labour power no longer sufficed. Pronatalists therefore cautioned against the importation of non-white workers, arguing instead that the Italians, Poles, and Spaniards were the most viable candidates for naturalisation. This amounted to a repudiation of the universalist vision of the Enlightenment and the Revolution which, in its purest form, viewed all bodies, whether white or of colour, as essentially the same.[14] Instead, within the historically specific political economy of mass immigration and colonialism, the possibility of assimilation – and hence citizenship – was closed to those whose difference was deemed immutable.

By examining the relationship between fecundity and civilisation in demographic discourse, this essay underscores how the perceived consequences of modernity, expressed most starkly by the decline in fertility rates, were conceived in racialised and gendered terms. It does so by exploring how, in their discussion of foreign immigration, various members of the pronatalist movement invoked race, gender, and reproduction in order to construct the ideal citizen body. The essay focuses in particular on three significant contributors to the debate on immigration and repopulation: the *Alliance National pour l'Accroissement de la Population Française* (National Alliance for the Increase of the French Population), France's largest and most influential pronatalist movement, which by 1939 could claim 25,335 members; the *Conseil Supérieur de la Natalité* (CSN) (Superior Council on the Birthrate), a pronatalist advisory committee created in 1920 from within the Ministry of Hygiene, Social Assistance, and Prevention in order to 'research all measures likely to fight depopulation, to raise the birthrate ... and to protect and honour large families'; and journalist Ludovic Naudeau's popular account of French depopulation, first appearing in the newspaper *L'Illustration*.

In several important demographic studies of the late nineteenth and early twentieth century, depopulation was theorised in terms of the relationship between civilisation and birthrate.[15] For example, liberal economist Paul Leroy-Beaulieu of the Collège de France juxtaposed the depopulation of northern Europe and North America with escalating birthrates in the African and Asian world, and argued that as a nation modernised, achieving a higher standard of living and increased industrial production, its birthrate necessarily fell.[16] This was, of course, a dramatic refutation of Malthusian doctrine, which prophesied an exponential increase in human populations and thus a depletion of global resources. After approximately 1860, Malthusianism fell out of favour, and demographers focused instead on the trend toward fertility decline or, in the words of Leroy-Beaulieu, the 'true law of population among civilised people'.[17] Hoping to attain a greater level of material comfort, even the 'humblest of citizens' began to postpone marriage, limit births, and opt for an 'individualistic' existence which, according to the pronatalist position, blatantly ignored the collective concerns of the nation.[18]

A society's birthrate could therefore be expressed as inversely proportional to its level of 'civilisation'. According to Leroy-Beaulieu, civilisation was an urbanised society with a democratic government and a developed middle class, in which education, affluence, and leisure had been extended to the majority of the population.[19] Despite the virtues of the civilised state, depopulation was the necessary outcome: 'In recent and present times, the diminution of fecundity among the civilized nations ... can be considered a general, if not universal fact.'[20] Demographers explained that while the state of civilisation facilitated global predominance and justified European expansion overseas, it was a double-edged sword, bringing degeneration and depopulation in its wake. Ironically, the march of progress ultimately compromised the power of 'civilised' nations, now confronted with the demographic superiority of less developed societies.

In Africa and Asia, where the colonial project was to transport civilisation to 'savage' and 'barbarous' lands, birthrates were high despite substantial mortality rates. Demographer and physician Jacques Bertillon succinctly explained: 'the most ignorant countries are also the most fecund ones'.[21] The anticlerical and socialist-leaning demographer Arsène Dumont echoed the conservative Bertillon's position, claiming 'Those who absorb no part of civilisation, like the poor in France and barbarians worldwide, conserve their high birthrates, while those who absorb much of civilisation ultimately die as a result'.[22] Demographers hypothesised that as African and Asian societies modernised, embracing industrialisation, hygienic practices, and democratic values, they too would begin to limit their births. But in the meantime, with African and Asian populations growing unchecked while birthrates in most European nations dwindled, the fertility of non-white people was perceived as a threat to white hegemony worldwide.[23]

Opponents of non-white immigration therefore insisted that it was the duty of the entire Occidental world to form a united front against immigrants of colour.[24] According to this view, Malthusianism among Europeans was nothing short of race suicide, a myopic practice that amounted to an abdication of the white mission to civilise the globe.

If strength was in numbers, as pronatalists argued, Europeans and North Americans must not remain passive while non-whites propagated at their expense. In the words of Auguste Isaac, the Catholic deputy named Minister of Commerce in 1919, father of eleven children and founder of the pro-family lobbying group *La Plus Grande Famille* (The Largest Family):

> If the white race restrains [its births], who will guarantee us that the yellow race will follow its example? Who will assure us that the black race will sacrifice the fecundity which, to cite but one example, is a cause of anxiety for whites in the United States?[25]

Depopulation was thus characterised as a 'general phenomenon ... which one could note among all people of the white race', now menaced by the fecundity of the Asian and African world.[26] Around the turn of the century, high Asian birthrates in addition to several important examples of Asians asserting themselves against white nations – such as the Boxer Rebellion, the Russo-Japanese War, and the founding of the Congress Party – aided in the construction of the phantasmic 'Yellow Peril'.[27] The possibility of Chinese or Japanese expansion heightened Europe's wariness with regard to population increases outside of the western world. Prominent pronatalist Fernand Boverat explained: 'Among the coloured races, and the yellow race in particular, birthrates remain formidable. Japan will see its population rise by one million people per year. For a country like France, which has a great colonial empire ... this demographic disequilibrium is particularly serious.'[28]

Pronatalists, colonialists, and economists viewed the 'Yellow Peril' in terms of the possible economic threat a densely populated Japan or China would pose to the West.[29] Because they believed demographic strength correlated with the desire for territorial expansion, it was feared that the fecundity of East Asians would reverse the accustomed relationship between coloniser and colonised, endangering western markets and challenging European imperial hegemony.[30] Both Paul Haury, a history professor whose plan for teaching demography (and hence depopulation) in primary and secondary schools was sanctioned by the Minister of Public Instruction in 1929, and Leroy-Beaulieu argued that western surplus population was necessary for the construction of empire, as it afforded excess Europeans the possibility of settling in the colonies. As a consequence, demographic decline in the metropole, by reversing normative population dynamics, endangered the colonial legacy and threatened to 'destroy the equilibrium of the human races'.[31]

Thus in France, pronatalist concerns were not galvanised by German demographic strength alone. Instead, a vision of colonial imperialism and a 'Europe submerged' by non-whites intensified French anxiety.[32] Only white immigration could provide assimilable labour power while counteracting the demographic might of Africans and Asians. While it met French requirements for foreigners to serve as both workers and citizens, it also allowed members of a transnational white polity to secure themselves against the fertility of the non-western world. Foreign labour would therefore have to be recruited among European countries with surplus populations. The partially modernised and demographically prolific nations of southern and central Europe constituted an intermediate category between the depopulation of northern Europe, and the fecundity of Africa and Asia (see Figures 1 and 2).[33]

Because the economic development of nations like Italy, Spain, and Poland could not accommodate the size of their populations, many

Type de familles espagnoles (Côte Basque) misérables et prolifiques.

Figure 1: 'From the Basque Region: Destitute and Prolific Type of Spanish Family'. In Georges Mauco, *Les Etrangers en France: Etude géographique sur leur rôle dans l'activité économique* (Armand Colin, Paris, 1932).

Une belle famille italienne immigrée dans l'Isère. Types d'Italiens du Nord, robustes et travailleurs.

Figure 2: 'A Handsome Italian Family, Immigrated to the Isère Region: Northern Italian Type, Robust and Hardworking'.
In Georges Mauco, *Les Etrangers en France: Etude géographique sur leur rôle dans l'activité économique* (Armand Colin, Paris, 1932).

Women are tools of the state

workers opted to immigrate to depopulated and industrialised states. Not only could the Italians, Spaniards, and Poles fill shortages in the fields and factories; they could also reproduce with native women without substantially changing the 'racial composition' of the French people. According to demographer Arsène Dumont, it was best to seek out immigrants like the Italians who had not yet 'broken their ties with their native land', as they retained high fertility rates and the values that promoted large families.[34] For jurist René Le Comte, Italian fecundity was a means to combat the 'Yellow Peril' by providing white, assimilable labour power to industrialised and depopulated nations:

> The rapid growth of Italian emigration in the past twenty years is one of the most fortunate occurrences from the point of view of the future of the white races. As the yellow races have started to breach European hegemony, it is high time to reinforce the white element in both Americas, the North of Asia, Australia, South Africa, and the Mediterranean basin.[35]

But as Karen Offen's seminal article has shown, one cannot separate arguments regarding fertility decline from the greater debate on the role of women in French society.[36] Demographers agreed that the state of civilisation brought with it many consequences, and that nations like Italy, Spain, and Poland had retained the best of the pre-industrial world: prolific birthrates, a commitment to hard work, a strong sense of family and, a value praised by some but not all pronatalists, a more pious Catholicism. In turn, these traits were reinforced by traditional conceptions of masculinity and femininity which, by preserving the 'innate' distinction between the sexes, promoted fertility and a devotion to family life. In contrast, social critics like Leroy-Beaulieu noted that in modernised nations like France, the boundaries between women and men had been blurred, and the feminist movement, which sought to make women identical to men, was largely responsible for depopulation. He wrote: 'The masculinisation of women is, from all points of view, one of the grave dangers facing contemporary civilisation. It is a *facteur desséchant et stérilisant* (desiccating and sterilising factor).'[37]

By the turn of the century, the connection between depopulation and feminism had been firmly established, and as one further manifestation of the 'individualist virus', feminism was said to have encouraged French women to abandon their prescribed role as mothers and homemakers. Similarly, pronatalists called into question the virility of the nation and its male citizenry, conflating the frailty of a depopulated France with the effeminacy of French men. In this context Fernand Boverat, the most prominent figure of the pronatalist movement, warned that for nations as well as men, to be 'afflicted with a pernicious anaemia' rendered them vulnerable to outside attack.[38] Immigration was to reinvigorate the national body by introducing young and robust male elements from Europe into an anaemic population further debilitated by the casualties of the Great War. In the context of a biological understanding of degeneration and revivification, then, foreigners were frequently described as the 'blood transfusion' necessary to curtail or even reverse the effects of national decline. Albert Troullier of the Alliance argued that the nation should select its immigrants like a physician preparing for a transfusion, '[choosing] an individual without physiological flaws, with blood *compatible* to that of the person requiring the transfusion ... There exist actual blood types and one cannot, without great danger, mix the blood of different and *incompatible* groups'.[39]

[Unmarried foreign men, however, were widely considered to be promiscuous, dissolute, and unstable.[40] Social commentators claimed that foreign bachelors were more prone to alcoholism, criminality, and venereal disease, and without wives to persuade them to settle in one place, they wandered France in search of work, or returned to their native land, thus mitigating their contribution to the national economy. The 'excess virility' of male immigrants was therefore to be tempered by marriage, with their sexuality channelled through the conjugal union in the interests of repopulating the French nation. For this reason, pronatalists encouraged both family immigration, and the marriage of male immigrant workers shortly after their arrival in France. Thus, once again, the pronatalist position on immigration mirrored its entreaty to the French nation as a whole, exalting marriage, fecundity, and procreative sex enacted within the confines of traditional gender roles.

Linking the problem of reproduction to the racial order of the early twentieth century, pronatalists conveyed white demographic panic while condemning the existing gender order. In reconstituting the citizen body, both the labour power and reproductive value of potential foreigners would be considered. On each count, the contribution of white Europeans was deemed far superior to that of Africans and Asians. Specifically, pronatalists held that an immigration of Latin and Slavic elements could supply qualified labour without recourse to Chinese and colonial workers. According to the Alliance's monthly journal:

> After having been flooded during the war with Kabyle street sweepers, Annamese stokers, Negro dockers, and Chinese labourers, whom we had to import because it was the best we could get, we were forced to send the majority of these worthless immigrants back to their faraway homelands. They were more disposed to pillage and thievery than serious labour. The re-establishment of the peace has permitted us to replace these 'undesirables' with our usual immigrants, the Italians and the Spaniards.[41]

Pronatalists did not believe that immigration was the ideal means to combat depopulation: they feared that foreigners would form unassimilated pockets within the nation, and that, without careful mixing, the racial integrity of the French people would be compromised. They agreed that, in order to raise the native birthrate, their utmost priority was to encourage a change in French values; nevertheless, they conceded that immigration could, in the meantime, serve to revivify French demographics. According to Alliance member Albert Troullier:

> It is indispensable that, starting now, we replace all the dead and the sick by assimilation and naturalisation, while waiting for the normal creation of future households. Let it suffice to say that immigration cannot be the primary means of fighting the national danger of depopulation. It is only a temporary remedy, and a perilous one at that. Immigration should only allow us to wait for the re-establishment of French demographic power, without modifying the special characteristics of the race.[42]

The Alliance's presence in the depopulation debate was enduring, determined, and obstreperous. Founded in May 1896 by demographer Jacques Bertillon, Drs Charles Richet and Emile Javal, civil servant Auguste Honnorat, and Catholic statistician Emile Cheysson, the Alliance was initially comprised of secular and socially conservative patriots, most of them bourgeois businessmen, industrialists, doctors, and lawyers. However, its blend of anti-individualism, anti-feminism, and nationalism permitted ties with Catholics as well as those sympathetic to the populationist policies of Nazi Germany and fascist Italy.[43] The Alliance led a widespread propaganda campaign that included the publication of pronatalist brochures, periodicals, films, demographic statistics, and proposals for legislative action, and its lobbying efforts had a direct effect on postwar legislation such as the 1920 law repressing propaganda for contraceptives, the 1923 law aimed at increasing prosecutions for abortions, and the granting of family allowances for dependent children. Its members held that depopulation was largely the fault of the Third Republic's institutions and policies, as they promoted individual rights at the expense of collective duties. According to Susan Pederson, Alliance members viewed depopulation as the result of a 'liberal and individualistic political and economic order that disproportionately rewarded the childless'. Demographic decline, they claimed, could only be reversed if liberal institutions like the tax system, military, civil service, and perhaps even the wage system were reworked to favour prolific fathers.[44]

At annual congresses and in its journal, members of the Alliance frequently debated questions of assimilation and naturalisation. They held that the stability of the family was the key to social peace, but, paradoxically, found among foreigners some of the best examples of strong and unified households. For Fernand Boverat, father of four, veteran of the Great War, and president of the Alliance in the interwar period, fulfilling the demand for labour power and repopulation went hand in hand: 'It is not a question of importing any workers to France, but good workers, and assimilable workers.'[45] The government, Boverat explained, must implement a tripartite plan which sought to increase native births while encouraging immigration and naturalisation.[46] First and foremost, depopulation had to be rectified internally, by French men and women, with the support of the state. In the meantime, however, immigration would serve as a stopgap measure replenishing the anaemic French population. While the Alliance claimed that unassimilated, non-naturalised foreigners were a potential danger to the 'French race', its members had little sympathy for the harshest French critics of immigration. Auguste Isaac explained:

> Those who complain the most about the intrusion of foreigners are generally not those who make the most personal efforts or sacrifices to change the state of affairs. The same pens warning of social ills are often used to propagate the very ideas that foster them: the love of material well-being, the right to happiness, the glorification of pleasure, and distaste for the family.[47]

Naturalisation was, of course, the bona fide emblem of citizenship, and because the Alliance wished to see a clear increase in French population statistics, it demanded that assimilable foreigners be naturalised quickly, without complications or delays. It also called for the simplification of naturalisation procedures, and that its cost be substantially reduced. Because 'those families with the most mouths to feed will have the least disposable income', Boverat argued that extraneous taxes like the *droit de sceau* and the *droit de chancellerie* (taxes of the Seal and the Chancellery) be eliminated.[48] Moreover, he claimed that the 1,000-franc naturalisation fee was too high for 'Belgian, Swiss, Italian, and Polish workers, who comprise the majority of those suitable for naturalisation'.[49] Albert Troullier went further still, insisting that because immigrants from Belgium, Italy, Poland, and Spain were the most likely to assimilate, and in the shortest amount of time, the French state should facilitate their naturalisation.[50]

The Alliance also framed the problem of immigration and depopulation in terms of white demographic panic. In its official publications, references to the 'Yellow Peril' were abundant, depopulation was repeatedly described as the 'plague of the white race', and low European birthrates were explained through recourse to the rhetoric of degeneration. In numerous articles and speeches, president Fernand Boverat hierarchised foreigners according to their assimilability and potential for citizenship. He explained that although Belgium and Switzerland had furnished assimilable workers in the nineteenth century, shrinking birthrates in those nations made it necessary to evaluate other sources. Boverat insisted that the only countries able to supply France with both labour power and assimilable immigrants were Italy, Spain, Czechoslovakia, Poland, and Romania. As for the Greeks, 'Levantines', and Kabyles of North Africa, he continued, these populations were, 'with some exceptions … second-rate immigrants that no country is actively seeking out, and which we have no interest in attracting to France'.[51] While this group was not classified among the assimilable, and in all likelihood was not recognised as fully white, its difference was less weighted than that of Asians and other Africans who, according to Boverat, should under no circumstances be permitted to enter France in large numbers.[52] He wrote: 'Despite the dangers of depopulation we must carefully avoid the mass immigration of men of colour, at the risk of witnessing the development of racial conflicts on French soil, the disastrous consequences of which we have already seen in the United States.'[53]

A demographic study of foreigners in the departments proposed by the *Commissions départementales de la Natalité* (Departmental Commissions on the Birthrate), a federation of local pronatalist associations reporting directly to the CSN, reaffirmed Boverat's position. It concluded that after the Italians, the Spaniards assimilated most rapidly, and as for the Poles, although the cohesiveness of their communities slowed their insertion into French society, they nevertheless had the potential to assimilate. On the other hand, because the Armenians, Levantines, and the Jews of central Europe were said to possess a 'mentality very different from that of the French population', assimilation was considerably more difficult, usually requiring the passage of several generations. Finally, the inquiry stated that the assimilation of North Africans was a 'nearly impossible' endeavour. Linking them with disease and degeneration in a tendentious social logic, researchers documented a high incidence of syphilis and tuberculosis among North African immigrants, in addition to a crime rate exceeding that of any other group. The study then reaffirmed that French vitality was dependent on its status as a white nation, concluding that the 'introduction or maintenance of North African workers on our metropolitan territory, and of all other workers who do not belong to the white race, or who have a mentality different from our own, appears detrimental to both the physical and moral health of our race'.[54]

Similarly, Social Catholic Louis Duval-Arnould, vice-president of the CSN and president of the pro-family league *La Plus Grande Famille* (The Largest Family), agreed that only European immigrants could provide France with both labour power and reproductive value. He explained that because foreign blood would eventually mix with that of the French, 'it would not suffice to import good workers' – immigrants who were also assimilable were needed. Small additions of Latin and Slavic blood, he claimed, would not substantially modify the 'essential characteristics' of the French people.[55] His stance on colonial immigration, however, was far more censorious. Duval-Arnould employed the racialised and gendered idiom that had been established during the First World War, when work scientists, heads of industry, and envoys of the Labour Ministry held that colonial (and particularly Indochinese) workers, because of their 'docility' and lack of physical strength, constituted a 'feminised' labour force whose industrial output was thereby compromised.[56] He wrote:

> The recruitment of European workers is more valuable than that of colonials, which was attempted at the end of the war, and now seems to have been abandoned. The quality of [colonial] labour was revealed to be feminine, no doubt the result of profound differences of mores and climate. Here we have nothing to regret from the ethnic point of view.[57]

Fellow Social Catholic Monsignor Gaston Vanneufville also affirmed that importing colonial labour in the context of the demographic crisis had far-reaching consequences. He claimed that to advocate the employment of Asian and African immigrants was to view them as nothing more than 'human material', or to neglect the obvious fact that male foreigners, 'when bringing us their labour, also bring us their personalities'. He wrote: 'They are or will become heads of households [in France], and just as they were members of civil society in their native country, they will constitute an integral part of ours'. Vanneufville therefore called upon Social Catholics and other members of the pro-family lobby to consider both the public and private life of foreigners when gauging their assimilability, as a concern for labour power alone reduced the worker to little more than 'human material'. But for Vanneufville, to envision male workers as 'heads of household' meant reascribing them with difference: because the vast majority of Africans and Asians were 'pagans' with 'tastes', 'sentiments', and 'passions' contradicting those of French civilisation, their assimilation was impossible.[58]

For Social Catholics and other Catholic-identified members of the crusade against depopulation, the common Catholicism of Spanish, Italian, and Polish immigrants heightened their prospects for assimilation. However, members of the Alliance were overwhelmingly secular Republicans, and, as a consequence, they rarely employed religious discourse to justify particular exclusions. Although the French public sphere still bore the imprint of pre-Revolutionary Catholic culture, the vehemently anti-clerical Third Republic had transformed it into a secular and universalist space. Indeed, diehard Republicans feared that the piety of Poles and Italians would prevent them from properly assimilating, and noted with relief that these populations generally de-Christianised shortly after their arrival in France. It is striking, however, how easily those steeped in the universalist tradition invoked racialised language instead, claiming that Italians and Spaniards were not more assimilable because they were Catholic, but rather, because they were Latin and white.

While the Alliance conducted a parliamentary and legislative assault on behalf of the pronatalist cause, one of its most successful popularisers was author Ludovic Naudeau. As an international correspondent for the Paris newspaper *Le Temps*, Naudeau had earned his journalistic reputation with his eyewitness accounts of the Russo-Japanese war and the Bolshevik revolution, having been detained in Japanese and later Bolshevik prison camps for his efforts. Returning to Paris after the First World War, he was employed by the popular weekly review *L'Illustration*, publishing accounts of his travels to various European countries as well as books on modern Japan and Russia, both of which were awarded prizes by the French Academy. In addition to his acclaimed exposés of the rise of fascism and Nazism, Naudeau turned his flair for travel writing infused with political analysis upon his native France. After a two-year journey through twenty French departments to document the gravity of depopulation, in 1929 and 1930, his findings were printed as a serial in *L'Illustration*. This dense, meticulous, and highly subjective work is indicative of the shift in the 1930s toward an increased public awareness of the populationist platform: its publication generated passionate responses from readers, including a barrage of letters to the author, debates in provincial newspapers, and the undertaking of several local monographs further investigating the depopulation problem.[59] In 1931, Naudeau's study was reprinted as a bestselling book entitled *La France se regarde: le problème de la natalité*.[60]

Naudeau also held that despite the potential dangers of immigration, it was the necessary first step in combating depopulation. Following the demographic arguments of Bertillon, Leroy-Beaulieu, and Dumont closely, he concurred that French depopulation was a reflection of the relationship between fertility and civilisation.[61] Moreover, he agreed that the pernicious 'individualism' of the French had produced a population more interested in pursuing pleasure than fulfilling its collective duties to the nation. French women, in particular, were guilty of this charge, as Naudeau claimed that the female gender was most easily seduced by the desire for luxury and material comfort.[62] Even before the First World War, it was widely accepted by Republicans, Catholics, and socialists alike that French women, in their quest for economic independence and sexual freedom, had abandoned the obligations of social citizenship, namely motherhood and care of the domestic sphere.[63] The charge that 'female individualism' engendered depopulation and other social ills had become, by the interwar years, a ubiquitous critique of the perceived gender order.[64]

Naudeau began his study with the uncompromising stance that France had always been, and must remain, a white nation. Despite the magnitude of French demographic decline, he explained, the 'integrity of the white race' was a value he planned to uphold. Employing contemporary metaphors that invoked the unity of metropolitan France and its colonial empire, Naudeau expressed disdain for those who envisioned a 'greater France', composed of 'one-hundred million Frenchmen'. In his view, colonial immigration would blur the boundaries between the ruler and the ruled, compromising the safety of French possessions, and promoting hazardous forms of racial mixing. He wrote: 'I affirm that we will not sustain our place in the world if we do not remain what we have always been: a white nation. Our colonial empire is guaranteed by the strength of the metropole'.[65]

Naudeau therefore called for the immigration of the transition populations of Europe. At the end of his long tour of the French departments, he concluded, without hesitation, that no immigrants were better candidates for assimilation than the Italians. He described them as diligent, fertile, and simple people who flourished in the countryside, and maintained a strong commitment to family life. Because the Italians had not yet fallen victim to the potential ills of modernity, Naudeau portrayed their immigrant communities as idyllic havens brimming with the most wholesome of pre-industrial values. In contrast, the French family, which had once possessed such admirable traits, was currently falling into a state of degeneration. Thus, when relaying his visit to the Lot-et-Garonne, Naudeau praised the Italians as passionately as he excoriated the French. He began his cautionary tale by explaining that throughout this department, there were numerous cases of impoverished Italian families arriving with no money, but many children. While sons were hired out as agricultural labourers, and daughters sent to work as maids in neighbouring villages, the family, as a unit, cultivated their land. Because family members were 'numerous, hardworking, frugal, and humble in their desires', the land was paid for in the course of a few years. Meanwhile, the former proprietor of the land, an 'old, solitary, hunched up Malthusian', has retired to the city to 'sadly vegetate' while paying an enormous rent. Naudeau concluded:

> The simple power of fecundity and labour produced the buying power sufficient for [the Frenchman] to be evicted and effaced. Having all his life sought out too many material pleasures, too many egotistical satisfactions, this Frenchman, at the end of his life, is nothing but a lugubrious island, a *déraciné* [uprooted individual], and ... a vanquished man.[66]

Naudeau's trenchant observations illustrate how strongly he believed civilisation was a double-edged sword which, while ushering in progress, had also undermined paternal authority, work discipline, and a sense of civic duty. Because the French placed material comfort and a higher standard of living before the good of the national community, the birthrate was rapidly declining, the countryside had been left fallow, and society was becoming dangerously atomised. Although Naudeau echoed the familiar conviction that the state of 'primitive life' conformed best to high fertility rates, he too called for a reconciliation of fecundity and civilisation. Because all societies would eventually undergo the shift to modernity, the state must correct the social ills this transition had engendered: 'When, through the inevitable workings of civilisation, [the state of primitive life] is dispelled, it is necessary to substitute powerful social and sanitary organisations, as we must not leave uprooted proletarians to fend for themselves. In short, civilisation must remedy the ills that it causes.'[67] Thus like other pronatalists, Naudeau called for government-sponsored social reform to counteract the dangers of too much civilisation.

Because the Italians lived 'close to nature' and subordinated all other desires in order to acquire property for cultivation, they reminded Naudeau of a France that had disappeared several decades ago. He repeatedly called for the French to imitate their diligence and sobriety, and the simplicity of their lives. Moreover, he invoked the probity of Italian women in an effort to further vilify *la femme moderne*, whose selfish and pleasure-seeking nature was evidenced by her refusal to produce children for the nation. So monstrous were French women who abandoned their maternal role that Naudeau was forced to look abroad for examples of feminine virtue. Faced with the high fertility rates of Italian families, he demanded: 'Is it not because [Italian women], known for the simplicity of their attire ... and paying little mind to fashion, content themselves with being mothers, as did our French women, one hundred years ago?'[68]

Naudeau saw in the Italians those rooted, conservative, family-oriented values the French once possessed. However, he understood all too well that if the French had something to learn from the Italians, this greatly complicated the assimilation process. If the pronatalist crusade was primarily about changing the mores and values of the degenerate French, it follows that little was to be gained in making the Italians resemble the French too closely. His greatest fear was one that was echoed in a number of pronatalist circles: what if the Italians, as they assimilated, developed the same Malthusian practices so dear to the French? How could social critics argue for the need to turn immigrants into French men and women if, at the same time, they were insisting that French mores had to change? Could the fecundity of less 'civilised' people be harnessed without their constituting dangerous, unassimilated pockets of foreigners in the midst of French territory? It was possible, Naudeau hypothesised, that first-generation Italians would remain prolific because they brought with them from Italy a strong work ethic, a commitment to family life, a disdain for luxuries, and a disposition that allowed them to be content with little. However, the need to assimilate the Italians, while simultaneously benefiting from their particular national character, led him to fear the worst. He asked: 'will they remain fecund once they have assimilated our mores? Will the second and third generation be even more prolific, or will they conform to the milieu that surrounds them? If we are to assimilate them, is that not because we want to make them resemble us?'[69]

Several demographic investigations evaluating the fertility of marriages with one or two spouses of foreign origin confirmed Naudeau's worst fears. According to the CSN, while the birthrates of immigrant households were superior to those of the French, they were also considerably higher in marriages between foreigners than in those with one French partner. Moreover, Boverat claimed that a number of statistical studies demonstrated the ease with which foreign women adopted pernicious French habits. His colleague M. Beth corroborated this point, maintaining that in certain Polish households, after six years of marriage and the birth of only one child, the wife had already undergone six consecutive abortions.[70] These findings were also confirmed by a study of foreigners in the departments proposed by the *Commissions départementales de la Natalité*. It found that fertility rates for mixed marriages were substantially lower than those for immigrant couples, especially when the wife was French. Franco-Italian households had hardly more children than French ones, and, beginning with the second generation, the birthrates of foreigners were almost as feeble as those of their French neighbours.[71] Auguste Isaac had reported the same pattern nearly a decade earlier: 'By the second generation, foreign elements from prolific countries frequently assume the habit of "voluntary sterility" which prevails here [in France].'[72]

More evidence was provided by demographer Georges Mauco's monumental study of immigration to France, the authoritative work on foreign labour in this period, combining fieldwork, statistical analysis, and geography. Mauco found that the number of children in foreign households was substantially higher than those of the French (see Figures 3 and 4). For example, while the average French family had only 1.9 children per household, Spanish immigrants topped the list with 2.6, followed by the Poles with 2.5, and the Italians with 2.3. Nevertheless, he claimed that because neo-Malthusian ideas and contraceptive practices spread rapidly among immigrants, their high fertility rates would begin to drop as the length of their stay in France increased. He affirmed that while the newly-arrived retained the high birthrates of their native lands, they rapidly yielded to French influence, consciously limiting births and striving instead for small families. Then, in a language common to the most sensationalist of pronatalist texts, Mauco claimed that among some immigrant groups, women had abortions in a 'casual manner that verged on recklessness', while the Poles and the Spaniards, the 'most uncultivated and simple' of all, even resorted to infanticide.[73]

The notion that mixed households were less fertile than those composed of two foreign spouses was, however, a completely logical outcome of Republican assimilationist theory, according to which immigrants could be rendered culturally similar to the French by the power of the soil, the French language and school system, and

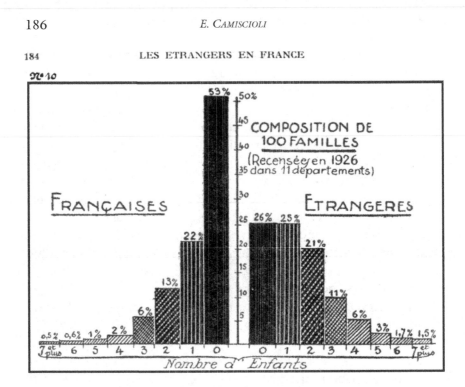

Figure 3: 'Number of Children in French and Foreign
Households, According to the 1926 Census'. In Georges Mauco,
*Les Etrangers en France: Etude géographique sur leur rôle dans
l'activité économique* (Armand Colin, Paris, 1932).

its women. That is, in the era of depopulation and mass immigration,
it was commonly held that French women were responsible for
assimilating foreign husbands and half-foreign children. This was an
extension of the gendered duties of social citizenship that had been
set in place during the Revolutionary era, according to which French
women, as 'guardians of tradition', were to execute their civic role
from the confines of domestic space.[74] All participants in the immigration debate conceded that the best way to assimilate foreigners was
through marriage to a French woman. For example, Mauco claimed
that intermarriage was more effective than naturalisation in integrating
foreigners into the national body.[75] And Ludovic Naudeau, despite
his distaste for the individualism of French women, recognised their
assimilative power. He wrote:

> The woman is the great protector of the native language, mores, traditions, and
> even of national prejudices. It is the woman who transmits them to future

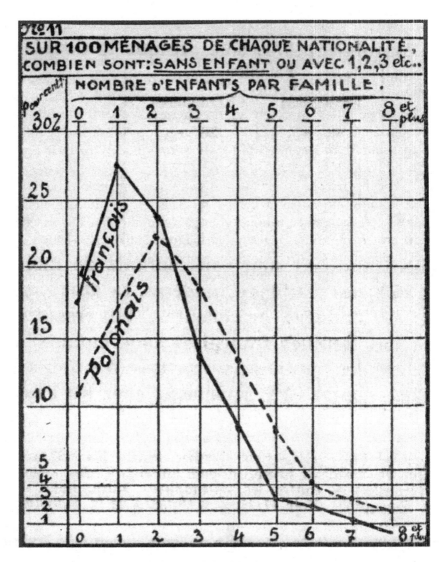

Figure 4: 'For One Hundred French and One Hundred Polish Households, the Number of Children Per Family'. In Georges Mauco, *Les Etrangers en France: Etude géographique sur leur rôle dans l'activité économique* (Armand Colin, Paris, 1932).

generations. And it is the woman who, in a few years, assimilates to her race the heterogeneous elements. A child born in France of a French woman will feel French, nothing but French, and besides, according to law, he will be French.[76]

In consequence, pronatalists were forced to acknowledge the incompatibility of their dual image of French women as both corrupters and saviours of the nation. According to such a logic, if native-born women had the power to assimilate foreign men, they could also corrupt them with Malthusian practices. And if the soil, capitalist work discipline, and secondary education were to render the second generation indistinguishable from the native population, it was unlikely that immigrant families could serve as role models for their French neighbours.

For this reason, pronatalists insisted that immigration could serve as nothing more than a 'temporary palliative' to the demographic crisis.[77] If the French nation were to survive, the state had to extend its protection to the family, rather than the individual, while revising its definition of citizenship to encourage reproduction. This was to culminate in the government sponsorship of pronatalist reforms by decree-law in 1938 and 1939, and was enshrined in the 1939 *Code de la Famille* (Family Code), drafted by the newly formed *Haut Comité de la Population* (High Committee on Population), whose members included Boverat; demographer, politician, and Alliance member Adolphe Landry; and Georges Pernot, president of the *Fédération des Associations de Familles Nombreuses de France* (Federation of Associations of Large Families of France). Included was the extension of the existing family allowance system which, although funded by private initiatives like the *caisses de compensation* (welfare funds) established by industrialists, had been regulated by the state since 1932; a birth premium paid for a first child born within the first two years of marriage; the mandatory teaching of demography in schools; and an amplification of repressive measures designed to combat abortion. The family allowance system mandated equal assistance to households regardless of their social class, favouring those with three or more children. That is, rather than redistributing income to poorer families, the allowances privileged 'fecund' French citizens over those who chose to remain childless.[78]

Thus pronatalism, immigration, and assimilation were three inseparable components of the early twentieth century's demographic calculus, with the integration of appropriate foreigners as one part of a broader project seeking to remake the French family. Meanwhile, because countless French men and women had ignored their civic obligation to procreate, 'assimilable' foreigners could gain access to the nation by displaying the qualities pronatalists believed to have once been intrinsically French: a love for the countryside, a commitment to family, and a collectivist vision of civic life. The CSN's stance on foreign fathers of large families provides an important example. The CSN met regularly to discuss problems related to depopulation, prenatal and infant care, and the protection of children and mothers. Its thirty members – generally leaders of the Alliance and pro-family groups, along with its vice-president, the indefatigable Boverat – were charged with drafting bills, decrees, and circulars on issues pertaining to the French family.[79] Because the government had assigned the CSN the task of researching methods to combat depopulation, the immigrant question was also debated at its meetings. Its positions were surprisingly generous toward 'assimilable' and prolific foreigners, calling for their naturalisation and the granting of various privileges that citizenship alone can bestow. Pronatalists had long advocated that, in exchange for their patriotism, large French families be rewarded with family suffrage, monetary allocations, a reduction in military service, and the like. The extent to which they were willing to extend these privileges to foreign families that fulfilled their reproductive obligation to the state greatly complicates our understanding of the movement's nationalism.

The CSN called for the naturalisation of members of the 'assimilable races': primarily Latins and, to a lesser degree, Slavs. Italians and Spaniards were considered elements of first choice, although the CSN also supported the recruitment of Portuguese and Swiss workers in smaller numbers.[80] Moreover, it advised that immigrant populations be selected according to their birthrates, as the civic duty of reproduction was one of several 'services' immigrants could offer the French nation. Boverat wrote: 'Of course, [a foreigner's] professional skills must, in most cases, be taken into consideration. But in our opinion, the ability to found on our soil a line of descendants able to become French must prevail over all other considerations.'[81]

At the onset of the Depression, the CSN took the unexpected stance of defending the right of select immigrants to continue working in France, dismissing the widespread call to halt all immigration and send foreigners back to their native countries as a 'simplistic solution'. Although French workers should be shielded from unemployment as much as possible, the CSN held that it was a 'vital necessity' to retain immigrants who had given birth to 'assimilable children' on French soil, in addition to those who were capable of doing so in the future. Moreover, the nation must continue to attract assimilable foreigners, as the dangers of depopulation far outweighed those stemming from

an economic depression: 'A nation does not die from an unemployment crisis, even one that lasts twelve or eighteen months. However,
if a nation resigns itself to a feeble birthrate, it is fatally condemned
to disappear.'[82]

If immigrants were to be expelled from France, the CSN claimed
that those who were unmarried, married but childless, or over the
age of 40 should be the first to leave. In contrast, every effort was to
be made to retain immigrants who had brought large families with
them to France, or who had given birth to several children since their
arrival. Foreign fathers of large families were to be shielded from
unemployment to avoid their repatriation, along with their children,
whom the CSN viewed as future citizens, and thus crucial elements
in its strategy for repopulation. Specifically, Boverat called for accom-
modating the 'young people of the prolific races': the Italians, Spaniards,
and Poles. He maintained that men from these nations, whether
married to French women or those of their own nationality, had the
greatest potential for assimilation. Boverat even argued that, instead
of repatriating immigrants to alleviate unemployment, the circumstances of the Depression should be exploited to French advantage.
He wrote:

> Let us make use of the unemployment problem in other countries to attract
> to France foreigners who are easily assimilable, and who already have young
> children ... In order to make room for them, do not hesitate to get rid of those
> without children. Right now we have an unusual opportunity to select our
> immigrants. In a few years, this moment will have passed, as the majority of
> European countries will be too conscious of the value of human capital to allow
> us to take their young children from them.[83]

The CSN also urged individual industrialists and employers to
refrain from firing foreign fathers of large families, and called upon
the government, through the Ministries of Labour and Agriculture,
to take an active interest in the problem. Because reproduction was
construed as a civic duty worthy of compensation from the state, the
CSN asked that work inspectors representing the Ministry of Labour
compel employers to retain both French fathers, and foreign fathers
with children living in France. The CSN concluded its list of demands
with the plea that foreign men heading large families be treated
'as Frenchmen' for as long as their applications for naturalisation
were still pending, and, more generally, that the Ministries of Labour
and Agriculture refrain from adopting any measures with regard to
foreigners that might have an adverse effect on the French birthrate.[84]

In their effort to reinvent the French family and redefine the practice of citizenship, pronatalists invoked the categories of gender, race, and reproduction to define the stakes of the immigrant question. The language in which they discussed degeneration and national renewal was to be echoed in the political and social hygienic discourse of the Vichy state, whose impulse to regulate reproduction, marriage, and domestic life had its roots in the populationist politics of the Third Republic.[85] Under Pétain, prominent pronatalists like Boverat, Haury, Duval-Arnould, and Mauco would continue their efforts to revive the traditional family, along with its high birthrates, cultural conservatism, and gender dimorphism. With the Occupation serving as further evidence of the wounded virility of French men, the selfishness of French women, and the perils of depopulation, the Vichy state was to both amplify and institutionalise the natalist-familialism of the interwar years.

Pronatalist ideology was a vital part of the political culture of the French Third Republic, and for this reason, any study of immigration to France must reckon with its position on foreigners, citizenship, and nationhood. Ultimately, the impulse to hierarchise immigrants according to their productive and reproductive value was a rejection of the Revolutionary doctrine of universal humanism which, in its capacious understanding of community, heralded the abstract sameness of all beings. Similarly, pronatalist discourse on immigration severely undermined the Republican and assimilationist model of nationhood, according to which any foreigner willing to assume the French cultural patrimony would be granted access to the citizen body. Instead, the abstract egalitarianism of the 'French citizen' was repeatedly confronted with the intractable problem of difference, an unsurprising consequence of the grounding of citizenship rights in patriarchy, bourgeois individualism, and hierarchical racial difference. In this manner, the nation's hopes and anxieties were deflected onto those who had come from beyond its borders, as the Italians, Poles, and Spaniards were to assist in restoring the racial and gender order.

Notes

Illustrations: Every effort has been made by the author to trace a copyright holder for the illustrations, but none has been found.

1. Secondary literature on the demographic crisis includes Angus McLaren, *Sexuality and Social Order: The Debate over the Fertility of Women and Workers in France, 1770–1920* (Holmes and Meier, New York, 1983), pp. 1–27, 169–83; Robert A. Nye, *Crime,*

Madness, and Politics in Modern France: The Medical Concept of National Decline (Princeton University Press, Princeton, 1985), especially pp. 121–70; Robert A. Nye, *Masculinity and Male Codes of Honor in Modern France* (Oxford University Press, New York, 1993), pp. 72–97; Karen Offen, 'Depopulation, Nationalism, and Feminism in Fin-de-siècle France', *American Historical Review*, 89 (1984), pp. 648–76; Susan Pederson, *Family, Dependence, and the Origins of the Welfare State, Britain and France, 1914–1945* (Cambridge University Press, Cambridge, 1994), especially pp. 25–78; Mary Louise Roberts, *Civilization without Sexes: Reconstructing Gender in Postwar France, 1917–1927* (University of Chicago Press, Chicago, 1994), especially pp. 89–151; and Joseph J. Spengler, *France Faces Depopulation* (1942; repr. Duke University Press, Durham, NC, 1979).

2. In contradistinction to the claims of Mary Louise Roberts and Andrés Horacio Reggiani. See Roberts, *Civilization without Sexes*, p. 103; and Reggiani, 'Procreating France: The Politics of Demography, 1919–1945', *French Historical Studies*, 19 (1996), p. 752. Françoise Thébaud notes that the *Alliance National pour l'Accroissement de la Population Française* assumed an 'ambiguous' stance with regard to foreigners, but does not explore its policy on immigration. See 'Le Mouvement nataliste dans la France de l'entre-deux-guerres: l'Alliance National pour l'Accroissement de la Population Française', *Revue de l'histoire moderne et contemporaine*, 32 (1985), pp. 276–301.

3. Joshua H. Cole, *The Power of Large Numbers: Population, Politics, and Gender in Nineteenth-Century France* (Cornell University Press, Ithaca, NY, 2000); Carl Ipsen, *Dictating Demography: The Power of Population in Fascist Italy* (Cambridge University Press, Cambridge, 1997); William H. Schneider, *Quality and Quantity: The Quest for Biological Regeneration in Twentieth-Century France* (Cambridge University Press, Cambridge, 1990); Richard A. Soloway, *Demography and Degeneration: Eugenics and the Declining Birthrate in Twentieth-Century Britain* (University of North Carolina Press, Chapel Hill, 1990).

4. Elisabeth Domansky, 'Militarization and Reproduction in World War One Germany', in *Society, Culture, and the State in Germany, 1870–1930*, ed. Geoff Eley (University of Michigan Press, Ann Arbor, 1996), pp. 427–63.

5. Anna Davin, 'Imperialism and Motherhood', in *Tensions of Empire: Colonial Cultures in a Bourgeois World*, ed. Frederick Cooper and Ann Laura Stoler (University of California Press, Berkeley, 1997), pp. 87–151; Jacques Donzelot, *The Policing of Families* (Pantheon, New York, 1979); Sylvia Schafer, *Children in Moral Danger and the Problem of Government in Third Republic France* (Princeton University Press, Princeton, 1997).

6. Robert Pick, *Faces of Degeneration: A European Disorder, c.1848–c.1918* (Cambridge University Press, Cambridge, 1989).

7. Thébaud, 'Le Mouvement nataliste en France', p. 276.

8. Jean-Marie Mayeur and Madeleine Rebérieux, *The Third Republic from its Origins to the Great War, 1871–1914* (Cambridge University Press, Cambridge, 1984), p. 330.

9. Marianne Amar and Pierre Milza, *L'Immigration en France au XXe siècle* (Armand Colin, Paris, 1990), p. 271.

10. Gérard Noiriel, *Population, immigration, et identité nationale en France, 19e–20e siècle* (Hachette, Paris, 1992), p. 53.

11. On the 'civic duty of reproduction', see Pederson, *Family, Dependence, and the Origins of the Welfare State*.

12. For implications of the 'man shortage', see Elisa Camiscioli, 'Intermarriage, Independent Nationality, and the Individual Rights of French Women: The Law of 10 August 1927', *French Culture, Politics, and Society*, 17 (1999), pp. 52–74; Siân Reynolds, *France Between the Wars: Gender and Politics* (Routledge, London, 1996), pp. 25–6.

13. Camiscioli, 'Intermarriage, Independent Nationality, and the Individual Rights of French Women'.

14. Maxim Silverman, *Deconstructing the Nation: Immigration, Racism, and Citizenship in Modern France* (Routledge, London, 1996), pp. 19–27.

15. On 'civilisation theory' and its proponents, see Spengler, *France Faces Depopulation*, pp. 162–8.

16. Paul Leroy-Beaulieu, *La Question de la population* (Félix Alcan, Paris, 1913).

17. Leroy-Beaulieu, *La Question de la population*, p. 237. On the shift away from Malthusianism, see Yves Charbit, *Du Malthusianisme au populationnisme: Les Economistes français et la population, 1840–1870* (Presses Universitaires de France, Paris, 1981).

18. Mario Gianturco, 'Le Problème international de la population', *Revue politique et parlementaire*, 426 (1930), pp. 225–6.

19. Leroy-Beaulieu, *La Question de la population*, p. 184. While providing a negative appraisal of democracy, Arsène Dumont also linked its emergence with the state of civilisation. See *Dépopulation et civilisation: Etude démographique* (Lecrosnier et Babé, Paris, 1890), pp. 145–55.

20. Paul Leroy-Beaulieu, 'La Question de la population et la civilisation', *Revue des Deux Mondes*, 15 October 1897, p. 871; Dumont, *Dépopulation et civilisation*, pp. 106, 130, 238–51.

21. Dr Jacques Bertillon, *La Dépopulation de la France: Ses conséquences, ses causes: Mesures à prendre pour la combattre* (Alcan, Paris, 1911), pp. 130, 128–37; Dumont, *Dépopulation et civilisation*, pp. 80–88; René Martial, *Traité de l'immigration et de la greffe interraciale* (Imprimerie Fédérale, Cuesmes-lez-Mons, Belgium, 1931), pp. 176–82; Frédéric Sipperstein, *La Grève des naissances en Europe et ses problèmes* (Librairie Sociale et Economique, Paris, 1939), pp. 101–28.

22. Dumont, *Dépopulation et civilisation*, p. 241.

23. Passing mention is made of this point in Philip E. Ogden and Marie-Monique Huss, 'Demography and Pronatalism in France in the Nineteenth and Twentieth Centuries', *Journal of Historical Demography*, 8 (1982), p. 293.

24. Jean Pluyette, *La Doctrine des races et la sélection de l'immigration en France* (Pierre Bossuet, Paris, 1930), p. 140; Martial, *Traité de l'immigration*, pp. 240–41.

25. Auguste Isaac, 'Discours', Congrès National de la Natalité, *Compte rendu*, 1922, p. 19.

26. Tournaire, *La Plaie française* (Librairie-Bibliothèque Auguste Comte, 1922), p. 231.

27. John Laffey, 'Racism and Imperialism: French Views of the "Yellow Peril", 1894–1914', *Third Republic*, 1 (1976), pp. 1–52; Benoît Massin, 'Lutte des classes, lutte des races', in *Des Sciences contre l'homme*, ed. Claude Blanckaert (2 vols, Editions Autrement, Paris, 1993), vol. 1, *Classer, hiérarchiser, exclure*, p. 137.

28. Fernand Boverat, 'La Dénatalité, ses causes et les mesures à prendre pour l'enrayer', *Le Musée social*, 1 (1936), p. 4. See also Tournaire, *La Plaie française*, p. 247.

29. Laffey, 'Racism and Imperialism'.

30. On the possibility of Asian imperialism, see Leroy-Beaulieu, *Question de la population*, pp. 153–70, 487; René Maunier, *The Sociology of Colonies: Introduction to the Study of Race Contact*, trans. E. O. Lorimer (2 vols, 1936; repr. Routledge, London, 1949), vol. 1, pp. 35–6, 387; Tournaire, *La Plaie française*, p. 246; Louis Varlez, 'Les Problèmes de migration à la Conférence de la Havane de 1918', *Revue international du travail*, 19 (1919), p. 11.

31. Leroy-Beaulieu, *Question de la population*, p. 487; Paul Haury, *La Vie ou la mort de la France* (Vuibert, Paris, 1923), p. 12.

32. Hervé Le Bras, 'The Demographic Argument in France', in *Population and Social Policy in France*, ed. Máire Cross and Sheila Perry (Pinter, London, 1997), pp. 26–7.

33. Leroy-Beaulieu, *Question de la population*, p. 287.

34. Dumont, 'Démographie des étrangers habitant en France', *Bulletin de la Société d'anthropologie de France*, 1894, p. 425.

35. René le Conte, *Etude sur l'émigration italienne* (A. Michalon, Paris, 1908), pp. 388–99. In the United States, where the racial stock of Italian immigrants was less valued, the Dillingham Commission's Report on Immigration warned of the 'immense capacity of the Italian race to populate other parts of the earth', such as Argentina and Brazil, where Italians now outnumbered the Spanish and Portuguese. See Matthew Frye Jacobson,

Whiteness of a Different Color: European Immigrants and the Alchemy of Race (Harvard University Press, Cambridge, MA, 1998), p. 80.

36. Offen, 'Depopulation, Nationalism, and Feminism'.
37. Leroy-Beaulieu, *Question de la Population*, pp. 270–3.
38. Fernand Boverat, 'La Dénatalité, ses dangers et les mesures à prendre pour l'enrayer', *Le Musée social*, January 1936, pp. 4–5.
39. Albert Troullier, 'Immigration-Démographie', *L'Economie nouvelle*, June 1928, p. 314. Emphasis in the original.
40. See, for example, Alix Duquesnoy, 'Les Mineurs polonais dans le bassin houiller du Nord', *Correspondance de l'Ecole Normale Sociale*, June–July–August 1939, in Archives Nationales 6AS 36, Fonds Max Lazard; Paul Guériot, 'Une Politique de l'immigration', *Revue politique et parlementaire*, June 1924, p. 433; Georges Mauco, *Les Etrangers en France: Etude géographique sur leur rôle dans l'activité économique* (Armand Colin, Paris, 1932), p. 524.
41. 'Immigration et naturalisation', *Revue de l'Alliance Nationale pour l'Accroissement de la Population Française* (hereafter *Revue*), 134 (1923), p. 279.
42. Trouillier, 'Immigration-Démographie', p. 299. See also 'Rapport de Charles Lambert, député du Rhône, sur la naturalisation des étrangers', Congrès National de la Natalité, *Compte rendu*, 1927, p. 73.
43. On the Alliance, see Cheryl A. Koos, 'Gender, Anti-individualism, and Nationalism: The Alliance Nationale and the Pronatalist Backlash against the *Femme Moderne*, 1933–1940', *French Historical Studies*, 19 (1996), pp. 699–723; Thébaud, 'Le Mouvement nataliste en France'.
44. Pederson, *Family, Dependence, and the Origins of the Welfare State*, p. 61.
45. Boverat, 'Il faut à la France une politique d'immigration', *Revue*, 129 (1923), p. 119. On Boverat, see Robert Talmy, *Histoire du mouvement familiale en France, 1896–1939* (2 vols, Union Nationale des Caisses d'Allocations Familiales, Paris, 1962), vol. 2, pp. 222–3.
46. Boverat, 'Une Politique de naturalisation', *Revue*, 138 (1924), p. 49.
47. Isaac, 'Discours', Congrès National de la Natalité, *Compte rendu*, 1926, p. 13.
48. Boverat, 'Comment faciliter la naturalisation de bons éléments français', Congrès National de la Natalité, *Compte rendu* (1925), p. 53.
49. Boverat, 'Rapport sur la naturalisation', Congrès National de la Natalité, *Compte rendu*, 1922, p. 58.
50. Troullier, '42 millions d'Italiens', *Revue*, 165 (1926), p. 102. See also Isaac, 'Discours', Congrès National de la Natalité, *Compte rendu*, 1925, p. 20; Isaac, 'Discours', Congrès National de la Natalité, *Compte rendu*, 1926, p. 13.
51. Boverat, 'Il faut à la France une politique d'immigration', p. 119.
52. There is a long French tradition of 'whitening' the Kabyles, hence distinguishing Berber-speaking North Africans from Arabs. See Patricia M. E. Lorcin, *Imperial Identities: Stereotyping, Prejudice and Race in Colonial Algeria* (I. B. Tauris Publishers, London, 1995).
53. Boverat, 'Il faut à la France une politique d'immigration', pp. 119–20.
54. Boverat, 'Rapport générale sur l'immigration et l'émigration étrangères dans le département: Ses effets sur la nuptialité et la natalité', Conseil Superieur de la Natalité (hereafter CSN), *Rapports et vœux*, 1936, p. 43.
55. Louis Duval-Arnould, 'Les Problèmes de l'immigration étrangère en France', Semaines Sociales de France, *Compte rendu*, 1926, p. 626.
56. See Elisa Camiscioli, 'Rebuilding the French Race: Immigration, Reproduction, and National Identity in France, 1900–1939' (PhD dissertation, University of Chicago, 2000), ch. 2.
57. Duval-Arnould, 'Les Problèmes de l'immigration', p. 627.
58. Mgr. Vanneufville, 'La main-d'œuvre étrangère et les migrations ouvrières', Semaines Sociales de la France, *Compte rendu*, 1920, p. 345.
59. Talmy, *Histoire du mouvement familiale*, vol. 2, p. 220.
60. Ludovic Naudeau, *La France se regarde: Le Problème de la natalité* (Hachette, Paris, 1931).

61. Naudeau, *La France se regarde*, pp. 11, 116. For his appreciation of Bertillon, Leroy-Beaulieu, and Dumont, see pp. 442–3, 448–50.
62. Here especially, Naudeau follows Dumont. See Cole, *The Power of Large Numbers*, p. 207.
63. Cole, *The Power of Large Numbers*, p. 197.
64. See Roberts, *Civilization without Sexes.*
65. Naudeau, *La France se regarde*, p. 8.
66. Naudeau, *La France se regarde*, p. 68; see also pp. 39, 66.
67. Naudeau, *La France se regarde*, p. 116.
68. Naudeau, *La France se regarde*, p. 66; see also p. 186.
69. Naudeau, *La France se regarde*, pp. 54, 154–5, 333–4.
70. 'Rapport sur l'immigration et l'émigration étrangères', CSN, *Rapports et vœux*, 6 (1936), p. 10.
71. Boverat, 'Rapport générale sur l'immigration', p. 42.
72. Isaac, 'Discours', Congrès National de la Natalité, *Compte rendu*, 1926, p. 13.
73. Mauco, *Les Etrangers en France*, pp. 184, 186.
74. Camiscioli, 'Intermarriage, Independent Nationality, and the Individual Rights of French-women', pp. 61–2. On Republican motherhood, see Joan Landes, *Women and the Public Sphere in the Age of the French Revolution* (Cornell University Press, Ithaca, NY, 1987).
75. Mauco, *Les Etrangers en France*, p. 532.
76. Naudeau, 'Les Dangers et les ressources de l'immigration', *L'Illustration*, 1 (1924), p. 392.
77. Boverat, 'Rapport générale sur l'immigration', p. 42.
78. Pederson, *Family, Dependence, and the Origins of the Welfare State.*
79. Talmy, *Histoire du mouvement familial*, vol. 1, pp. 211–17.
80. 'Rapport sur l'immigration et l'émigration étrangères', p. 12.
81. Boverat, 'Le Chômage et les immigrés', rapport présenté à la section permanente du CSN, 19 January 1931, Supplément au fascicule no. 1, 1931, p. 3.
82. Boverat, 'Le Chômage et les immigrés', pp. 1–2. See also Boverat, 'Le Chômage et les immigrés: Ne refoulons pas les chefs de famille', *Revue*, 223 (1931), pp. 402–5.
83. Boverat, 'Le Chômage et les immigrés', pp. 3–4.
84. Boverat, 'Le Chômage et les immigrés', pp. 4–5.
85. Miranda Pollard, *Reign of Virtue: Mobilizing Gender in Vichy France* (University of Chicago Press, Chicago, 1998), pp. 33, 40.

Citizenship as Contingent National Belonging: Married Women and Foreigners in Twentieth-Century Switzerland

Brigitte Studer (translated by Kate Sturge)

'As marriage is of all human actions that in which society is most interested, it became proper that this should be regulated by the civil laws.'

Montesquieu, *The Spirit of Laws*, Book XXVI, chapter 13[1]

In 1937 Dr Max Ruth, high-ranking police department official at the Swiss Ministry of Justice and Police, published his influential treatise 'Das Schweizerbürgerrecht' ('Swiss Citizenship'). In it he wrote:

> Citizenship is something whole, indivisible, absolute, something that one has or does not have, but which one cannot have in part or conditionally or in an altered form. Thus everyone has or fails to have it in the same degree. Here in Switzerland there are no classes of citizens, nor any distinctions in citizenship based on how it is acquired or how long it has been held.[2]

The concept of citizenship has a dual dimension, which the Swiss term '*Bürgerrecht*' underlines. It emcompasses both citizenship rights – the individual's integration into a juridical and political space, a territorial integration that in the democratic state is attended by universal rights and obligations – and the status of nationality itself, which marks inclusion in and exclusion from the national community.[3] Contrary to Max Ruth's account of Swiss citizenship, the modern, constitutional state breached the principle of universality in both respects: women and men received unequal treatment firstly in the internal relation of state to citizens, and secondly in the external relation of state to non-nationals.

Of the two aspects of citizenship outlined above, this paper will focus on the second, nationality. Historical research, and especially research in gender history, has long demonstrated that citizenship is a dynamic concept and that not all citizens enjoyed citizenship rights in equal measure.[4] But as regards nationality, too, in many states an exception existed until well into the twentieth century. Nationality was far from being something whole, indivisible or absolute that could only be lost through voluntary renunciation: if a woman married a foreign national, she was deprived of her own nationality.

This arrangement, known as the 'marriage rule', often had harsh consequences. For example, during the Second World War the Swiss Irma Bornheim became stateless upon marrying a German Jew. In late August 1942, when the Swiss borders were sealed, she wrote from Paris to the Swiss President, asking to be allowed to regain her Swiss nationality: 'I really am a true Swiss; I went to school in Switzerland and my parents and forebears all served the country.' She asked for her reintegration into nationality to be 'granted by special grace, the normal course of law being closed to me'.[5] After a year of administrative formalities Bornheim was finally allowed to enter Switzerland as a refugee, but not to apply for reintegration into Swiss nationality. Because her husband, who had been deported by the Nazis, was classed as 'missing', she could not satisfy the condition for reintegration that her marriage first be dissolved. Some women's cases took an even more tragic course. The mentally ill Frieda Rech, married to a German, was sent back to her village of residence in the Third Reich, where she appears to have fallen victim to Nazi euthanasia policies.[6]

Not until 1957 was the United Nations' Convention on the Nationality of Married Women ratified, requiring signatory states to disregard women's marital status in their nationality legislation. Neither marriage or divorce nor changes in the husband's nationality were to have automatic consequences for the nationality of the wife. For many countries this was a novelty, and in fact Switzerland did not fulfil the Convention's requirement until the amended nationality law was passed on 23 March 1990, coming into force on 1 January 1992.[7]

In the following paper, the practices and controversies surrounding the special legal treatment of women according to their marital status will be examined for the case of Switzerland – a country whose high migrant population throughout the century meant that a large number of Swiss women who remained in their own country after marriage came to be classed as 'aliens'.[8]

Unlike most states in Europe and North and South America, in Switzerland these discriminatory measures remained in effect for most of the twentieth century, although international shifts in the codification of female nationality had an impact on Swiss deliberations of the issue of marriage and citizenship. The Swiss case in particular seems to support the view of French ethnologist Marcel Mauss: while there is a tendency for different societies' legal institutions to move into line with each other, juridical phenomena shape fundamental structures and values of a society that prove particularly resistant to reform.[9]

For women who married foreign nationals, one of the most important principles of the modern nation state was violated – the principle that there can be no involuntary loss of nationality. This fact will serve as a magnifying lens to examine the gendered construction of the national. The marriage rule is particularly revealing in that it marks the intersection of population policies, including those towards foreigners, with the politics of marriage and the body. In the discourses and practices around deprivation of and reintegration into nationality for Swiss women marrying foreign husbands, divergent interpretations of the social and gender order were both expressed and constituted: the notions articulated at any one point were always in flux, and adapted or 'modernised' themselves as Swiss society was transformed.

In particular, these conceptions of social relations were closely interlocked with attitudes toward self and other, with notions of the 'Swiss' and the 'un-Swiss'. Excluding women who had married foreigners also meant drawing normative boundaries internally. The use of certain 'gender technologies'[10] in the construction of the national, by which knowledges of gender were deployed to regulate the political, served to specify the rights and duties of the Swiss citizen, and especially the female Swiss citizen. They served to delimit the 'imagined political community', as Benedict Anderson has defined the nation,[11] and to determine who was outside it.

Indeed the modern nation state introduced legal regulation and hence defined the boundaries of nationality.[12] The wife's adoption of her husband's nationality was an invention of the administrative state in the late eighteenth and the nineteenth century. In France the system was codified in the Code Civil of 1804; in the USA not until 1855, culminating in 1907, when women's loss of nationality was laid down explicitly in law.[13] Switzerland waited until 1940 to introduce such a law. Why did this discrimination persisit when the trend otherwise pointed towards a reduction of legal disparities? This question is especially interesting because the modern nation state considered standardisation essential, for reasons not only of principle (lawfulness, equality) but also of practicality (efficient administration) and politics (stabilising the social order).

One answer may be found by separating the dual strands that pervade the tradition of modern citizenship. J. G. A. Pocock's influential study identifies these as republicanism, based on civic duties and virtues, and the more recent universalist liberalism.[14] The former is corporative in orientation, focusing on the family or small, manageable communities and stressing the tasks of the citizen within such communities; the latter privileges the individual's equality of rights. Recent research shows that Pocock's interpretation of different but parallel 'languages' can very fruitfully be applied to Swiss history.[15] For a country characterised by its plethora of particularist interests, the concept of nation offered by civic republicanism – one based on active political participation – provided a shared point of reference that could also accommodate the liberals. The federal state of 1848 was a product of liberalism, yet from the very start it included important elements of the republican tradition. Clear traces of this fact can be seen in the locally organised structure of Swiss nationality: in Switzerland, nationality can still only be conferred through membership of a municipality. Furthermore, for the whole nineteenth and twentieth century Swiss nationality was not contractualist but genealogical, normally transmitted by the principle of *jus sanguinis* (citizenship conveyed through blood lines/heredity). Up to the present day, no *jus soli* (citizenship dependent upon place of birth/parents' residency) has existed.

Inclusion in nationality is thus seen as a matter of destiny, independent of the individual will and of personal interests. Since, on the other hand, 'naturalisation' – voluntary entry into the nation – is also possible, the Swiss example here illustrates the contradiction, highlighted by Benedict Anderson, within the modern nation, which is at once both open and closed. Even if an individual can be integrated via naturalisation, discursively the modern nation draws its strength from equating itself with a community. To belong to this community, what counts is not free will but 'natural' ties (such as skin colour, gender, family relationships or place of birth).[16] Other historians, such as Eric Hobsbawm, have also emphasised that various and conflicting projects are at work in every nation-building process.[17]

This coexistence of different political traditions often gives rise to disputes over the definition of citizenship and hence of national belonging, and these are ultimately negotiated and decided on the national political plane. For this reason, the following investigation will focus on the bureaucratic administration, which, as Max Weber has shown, is the defining agency of the legal and rational rule of modern societies.[18] Here, one occupational group in the state's sphere plays a key role, namely the juridical experts. The 'juridical field', to follow Pierre Bourdieu, is a highly differentiated one, comprising divergent political and personal positions, conflicts of competence and competitive relations. The state-recognised experts in law and justice also held different amounts of symbolic capital. Yet, in a certain sense, they owned the monopoly on the definition of the area.[19] The field was largely cordoned off against non-authorised actors from outside.

Of course, the juridical field was not the only one to participate in the process of defining national belonging. However, it was a central site of the formation of this discourse. In addition, the implied actors – councillors, officials, politicians, and law professors, even the politically committed women's representatives – all had to articulate their positions within the logic of state authority and juridical patterns of thought. That this rationalised language concealed not only political strategies but also very particular conceptions of social order is something we have learned from the work of both Pierre Bourdieu and Michel Foucault.[20]

Over and above the immediate determination of nationality, the discourses and practices I shall investigate here reflected and regulated the organisation of gender relations within marriage. In particular, they inscribed their norms on the gendered body and its functions in reproduction.

As the twentieth century began, this issue acquired a new social and political relevance. In many European countries, declining birth rates and increasing hostility to immigration combined to form an explosive mixture of anxiety and aggression in population policy. The tension between the irreconcilable principles of the nation's openness and its closedness[21] initially remained unresolved. The First World War provided the first decisive impetus towards a bounded or closed nation, followed by the effects of the Depression and the Second World War. This article aims to show that the process of 'closing' the nation would not only redefine the categories of aliens and refugees, but would also profoundly affect the political status of Swiss women who allied themselves to 'the other'. In part, the debate around inclusion and exclusion was articulated through the definition of patterns of female belonging.

While the impact of these events was Europe-wide, Switzerland shows a certain time-lag. In terms of society and mentality, in Switzerland the 'war culture', the system of socially mediated values, symbols and norms that specifically prevailed in wartime, persisted well into the years after the Second World War.[22] I have divided my analysis of this process into several phases in order to highlight those historical moments in which controversies accumulated and converged, often galvanising a legislative resolution. Analysis of these moments illuminates the close interweaving of discursive gender construction, nation state, legal system and politics.

The first phase covers the second half of the First World War, from 1917, and the interwar period up to the mid 1930s, when questions of citizenship and migration gained in significance and led to a concentration of international legislation. During this period jurists and state bureaucrats contended with the problematic contradictions between internationalisation of law and the discourse of '*Überfremdung*', a term perhaps best translated as 'swamping' by the alien.

The creation in 1917 of the Swiss *Fremdenpolizei*, which oversaw the policing of foreigners in Switzerland, marked an incisive shift in state policy towards immigration and aliens. It marked the emergence of a central administrative apparatus for monitoring settlement and residence, also impelling a radical shift from liberal to restrictive discourses of naturalisation and more restrictive naturalisation practices. Assimilation was no longer considered the desired outcome of naturalisation but rather its precondition.[23] Underlying this shift was a new perception of threat to the nation, officially articulated in the notion of *Überfremdung*, which was to dominate Switzerland's public discourse right into the 1950s and 1960s.[24]

In the interwar period, criticism of the 'marriage rule' was beginning to mount both in Switzerland and internationally. Previously barely questioned, the rule meant that in the cases of marriage between partners of different nationalities, the woman immediately acquired her husband's nationality and lost her own. Three reasons may be identified for the shifting perceptions of this rule that seem to apply to the majority of countries involved. Firstly, the experience of the First World War showed that the arrangement could have serious consequences for many women, who might become stateless or, as relatives of a citizen of an enemy state, face retaliatory measures in their own country. Secondly, the war was followed by a speedy rise in general support for universal suffrage and the women's vote, leading to increased reservations about the automatic naturalisation granted to the wives of nationals. Finally, numerous international women's organisations – such as the International Alliance of Women (IAW), the International Council of Women (ICW) or the Women's International League for Peace and Freedom (WILPF) – called for a nationality law that disregarded marital status. 'That a married woman should have the same right to retain or change her nationality as a man' was the demand addressed to the Versailles Conference in 1919.[25]

Swiss women's organisations, which were closely connected to international networks, had become increasingly aware of the growing significance of this issue since the war. In 1916 the Swiss women's suffrage association (Schweizerischer Verband für Frauenstimmrecht or SVF) convened a committee to study the question, followed in 1917 by the convening of a similar committee by the umbrella organisation of the Swiss women's associations, the Bund Schweizerischer Frauenvereine (BSF).

Espousing the principle of individuality, the women's associations introduced a 'new' conception of nationality that would become generally known in legal and political circles as the 'modern' one.[26] In contrast to the 'classical' or 'traditional' understandings of nationality and citizenship, it posited an incontrovertible individualisation of all citizens of a state, irrespective of gender and marital status.[27] The demands of the women's organisations thus focused attention on the question of coherence among theories of state, constitutional principles, legal dogmas and judicial practices. They cast new light on the long extant tension between corporatist and individual notions of citizenship, between the close attention the modern state should pay to its individual citizens and the subsumption of individual women into the family.[28]

In Switzerland the principle of the individual equality of all citizens was written into the 1848 constitution (art. 4: 'All Swiss are equal before the law') and the modified constitution of 1874. The interpretation of this clause long remained almost unchallenged, but towards the end of the nineteenth century questions began to arise, first from individual women, then from women's organisations, as to whether the term 'Swiss' did not actually include the female sex as well.[29] Jurists thus faced increasing calls to provide a theoretical legitimation for the inequality that existed. The same applied to the marriage rule.

The practice of depriving women of their nationality upon marriage to an alien, nowhere enshrined in positive statutory form during the nineteenth century (or beyond that, up to 1941), was said to be based on customary law. According to article 54, paragraph 4 of the modified Swiss constitution of 1874, the married woman would acquire the nationality of her husband, or, if marrying within Switzerland, she would be admitted to full membership in her husband's *Heimatgemeinde* (community of origin), a status which children inherited from fathers and which men could also pass to their wives.[30] The point of this provision, as numerous jurists later explained, was to force the municipalities to accept wives of community members (Bürger) and thus entitle them to the social benefits this status accrued, including social assistance and welfare.[31] Controversies persisted over the issue of whether these provisions meant a corresponding loss of citizenship in her home municipality for the Swiss woman marrying a Swiss man from a different area or the loss of nationality for the Swiss woman marrying an alien. At the beginning of the century, however, the tendency seemed to be towards abolishing the rule. In 1903, while Swiss immigration policy was still in its liberal phase, the legislature initially made it possible for widowed, separated and divorced women to regain their nationality without cost.[32]

There was yet another reason why jurists disagreed on the legality of the marriage rule. Since 1848, Swiss nationality legislation had followed the maxim that the application of the Swiss norm must not cause statelessness.[33] Yet this was exactly what the marriage rule did cause, if the husband's country did not automatically grant nationality to women who 'married in'. In the interwar period, the countries applying this type of rule were still a minority, but a growing one. In 1933 there were twenty-two of them, including the Soviet Union, the USA, Belgium, France, Canada, China and several South American countries, as against forty-two states which continued to maintain the principle of unified family nationality.[34] The Swiss federal court had decided in 1910, citing a 1798 precedent, that in cases of potential stateless-ness the woman should be allowed to retain her Swiss nationality.[35]

One legislative shift towards the 'modern' principle lent particular energy to the international and Swiss debate between the wars. In 1922 the USA's Cable Act secured the principle of independent nationality for married women. The guarantee was partial: it applied only as long as the woman remained in the USA, and not if she had lived in her husband's country for over two years or for over five years in any foreign country. The Cable Act also abolished the husband's right to automatically obtain nationality for his wife.[36] After Soviet Russia in 1918, the USA now became the first western country to adopt the 'modern', equality-based perspective in nationality matters. Latin American and Caribbean states soon followed.[37]

Aside from numerous campaigns by the large international women's organisations, ICW, IAW and WILPF, as well as the International Federation of University Women (IFUW), the period following the Cable Act saw a male-dominated group, the Gesellschaft für Inter-nationales Recht (Society for International Law), publicly supporting international regulation of the issue for the first time. At its 1922 conference, the Society passed a resolution calling for 'the question of nationality of married women to be regulated uniformly by treaty', which gave married women the right to decide.[38] An initial step in this direction was expected in 1930 from the third League of Nations conference on legal codification, in The Hague. However, the confer-ence was a disappointment. The delegates could only manage to agree on a declaration of principle, restricted to recommending the forty-seven participating states to modify their nationality legislation so as to prevent a woman from losing her nationality against her will and solely due to marriage.[39]

In Switzerland, the Cable Act paved the way for a government resolution of November 1922 which provided new legal backing to the federal court's practice of allowing Swiss women to retain their nationality of descent where necessary.[40] This did not, of course, settle the question of principle, and the SVF therefore reopened the issue at its 1923 general meeting. The association passed a resolution favouring a right of option for Swiss women 'marrying out' which would have enabled her to hold dual nationality.[41] The federal admin-istration rejected the proposal without further comment.

This unceremonious rejection illustrates the uneasy position of the Swiss women's organisations. Swiss women had no right to vote or to stand for election until 1971, and until 1923 the federal court had not even granted women throughout Switzerland the right to practise law, on the grounds of their lack of political rights.[42] After the First World War the occasional representative of the women's organisations was appointed to extra-parliamentary commissions or to the federal consultation process, but this practice depended on who was politically responsible at any one time.[43] For the most part, the organisations had to be content with intervening from the outside, often with the help of supportive reports from respected male jurists, or with finding male representatives to work on their behalf. In short, until the last quarter of the twentieth century women were only marginally present at the sites where competing concepts of nationality were negotiated and ultimately defined.

A further obstacle to women's demands was an increase in the strength of the federal administration, which underwent rapid expansion in the 1920s, particularly in the areas of immigration policy and the policing of aliens.[44] Power was also shifting within the administration, from the *Fremdenpolizei* to the police service department of the Swiss Ministry of Police and Justice (EJPD), marking a political change in immigration practices that now sought to intensify the monitoring of foreigners within the country rather than merely seeking to fend off 'undesirable aliens' at the Swiss border. Reflecting this new emphasis on the domestic aspect of immigration policy, in 1926 the police department of the EJPD became the agency responsible for deliberating the requests of Swiss women to regain their nationality, which had previously been in the jurisdiction of a section of the Ministry of Foreign Affairs, or as it was then known, the Political Ministry.[45]

One of the driving forces behind the construction of a set of restrictive legal instruments and an equally restrictive administrative practice in immigration policy was the head of the police department, Dr Ernst Delaquis (1878–1951).[46] Born in Alexandria, Egypt, Delaquis was a doctor of law who had studied in Heidelberg, Munich and Berlin, and, before his appointment as section head in the Swiss federal administration, had held a professorship of criminal law in Frankfurt. Until he left the administration in 1929,[47] he worked to centralise competence in matters of immigration law in the hands of the Confederation, as well as to create selective conditions for foreign nationals wishing to reside or settle in Switzerland. Delaquis believed that the state ought to be able to choose immigrants according to their 'quality' and 'usefulness'. He advocated the introduction of a checking procedure for candidates applying to settle in Switzerland, covering health, capacity to work and potential for assimilation.[48] Foreigners who were 'undesirable' or classed as potentially dangerous were to be expelled. From the perspective of the functionary Delaquis, the state was entitled to protect itself legally from abuse of its social provisions, especially welfare benefits, by certain aliens, and thus to secure its own material interests.[49] To this end he also proposed improved international regulation of the welfare obligations owed to foreign nationals.[50] In his opinion Switzerland was supporting needy foreigners generously while Swiss nationals abroad received little or no aid from their states of domicile – the reciprocity of the treaties on this matter being, he claimed, 'purely theoretical'.[51]

The arguments Delaquis brought forward to support his policy of defending the state's interests and expanding the repertoire of legal instruments of control were not merely pragmatic, administrative ones. Alongside the functional criterion that foreigners must not pose a financial burden to the state, he also drew on criteria much less easy to objectivise. Thus, among Delaquis's proposed selection conditions were the country's 'capacity for absorption' and the foreigner's 'capacity for assimilation'. As he wrote in his 1921 draft for a federal law on the rights of aliens to reside and settle, the 'number of foreigners coming in to settle permanently must not exceed what is reconcilable with the country's interests'. The chief concern of the admission procedure must, he continued, be the issue of *'Überfremdung'*.[52] By deploying this concept, which remained vaguely defined but became ever more prevalent in the 1920s, Delaquis situated himself within the framework of a discourse of national belonging that considered everything designated 'foreign' to be a threat to 'Swissness', however this was defined.

As Delaquis explained in his speeches and writings, to 'combat *Überfremdung'* was also to strengthen homogeneity and cohesion from the inside. In contrast to later interpretations of the 'danger of *Überfremdung'*, however, Delaquis's strategy did still include the integration of people who had already settled in Switzerland. One means to this was naturalisation. In 1928, before Delaquis left office, a modification of the article on nationality in the Swiss constitution had been completed. The Confederation had been granted the authority to combat *'Überfremdung'* with legislation on nationality. The goal of naturalisation, or even 'compulsory naturalisation', as the *jus soli* was sometimes known, was to bind new citizens to Switzerland, so that in cases of external threat they would be willing to fight for the country.[53] Here it becomes clear that Delaquis, while sharing in the then dominant discourse of a 'unified Swiss *Wesen* [nature, character]', defined national belonging at least partially through cultural factors.[54] For him, the decisive issue was loyalty to the country. Though such loyalty derived primarily from descent, under certain circumstances it could be assimilated or learned. Loyalty was thus to some degree a dynamic and mutable characteristic, rather than exclusively an essential or inherited quality.

The constitutional article passed in 1928 under Delaquis's aegis also gave authority to the government to pass a law which allowed the children of mothers of Swiss descent to obtain Swiss nationality via the *jus soli*, provided the parents were resident in Switzerland when the children were born. Citizenship was to be granted at the mother's inherited community of origin. Although no corresponding legal instruments were created in the subsequent years, the decision of principle had fundamental importance. Firstly, the new ruling meant that a child's membership in the nation could be inherited not only from the father but also from the mother. And for the question of married women's nationality, it implied that women's nationality was not wholly extinguished on marriage to a foreigner, as the BSF legal committee noted with approval.[55]

This did not, however, mean that Delaquis advocated a nationality independent of marital status. When in 1926 the SVF approached him on the matter, he responded with concerns encompassing civil law as well as constitutional and international questions.[56] Delaquis's negative stance reflects the ambiguity within his – and in general the Swiss – culturalist conception of the nation. Since the country's unusual ethnic and cultural heterogeneity ruled out monothetic classifications from the start, the definition of what was Swiss relied on negative differentiation, as not-French, not-German, not-Italian.[57] After the turn of the century, and particularly after the First World War, notions of ethnicity increasingly began to crowd into this definitional space. The agents of the new semantics of nation were various organisations of civil society. In Switzerland they were traditionally closely connected with the state administration, such as the Neue Helvetische Gesellschaft (New Helvetic Society), the Schweizerischer Juristenverein (Swiss Jurists' Association), the Schweizer Städteverband (Association of Swiss Towns) or the Schweizerische Gemeinnützige Gesellschaft (Swiss Charitable Society).[58] The political and citizenship-oriented view of national belonging began to give way to notions of

a culturally homogenous group that must be preserved. This homogeneity, and the national loyalty derived from it, rested first and
foremost upon descent – it was inherited. Here the argumentation
bordered on biologist theories. But at the same time it also contained
elements of an environmental theory, since under certain circumstances
Swiss nationality might constitute itself through the influence of the
family and general social milieu. The latter case found expression in
the 1928 constitutional article: integration was possible for children
born in Switzerland to mothers who had been Swiss before their
marriage.

However, it seems the constitutional article was merely one last,
ambiguous, manifestation of a liberal understanding of citizenship. As
the interwar period progressed, the dominant view of citizenship
gradually retreated from even this minimal version of a *jus soli*, and
the article was never applied. The development gained momentum
through the appointment of Heinrich Rothmund (1888–1961) to
succeed Delaquis as head of the central police service. Rothmund, a
jurist, had headed the Swiss aliens police since 1919, and from 1929
united both functions until his retirement in 1954. Like Delaquis, he
was interested in centralising immigration and nationality policy, but
he set slightly different priorities in the admission criteria for would-
be residents. As both his practice and his writings show, he placed an
even stronger emphasis on moral and ethnic criteria, without abandoning the economic and financial components of the battle against
'*Überfremdung*'. In Rothmund's view, the proposed admission checks
should chiefly address the personality and origin of the applicant: 'If
he is irreproachable, and if his race and origin allow us to assume he
will be able to enter into our way of life and our *Wesen*, in other words
that he is very likely to be capable of assimilation, then we can begin
to ask about the purpose of his stay and the occupation he wishes to
pursue.'[59] On this basis Rothmund derived a hierarchy of capacity for
integration. From the start it bore anti-Semitic traits, though their
full force emerged only after 1933 in the context of refugee policy.[60]

In view of this hardening of immigration policy and of conceptions
of national belonging, it is hardly surprising that the 1930s brought
no progress for women's demands regarding the individual right
to nationality. The women's organisations began to cooperate more
closely on the issue, and in October 1932 a joint petition was submitted
to the government by the BSF, the SVF, the WILPF, the Schweizerischer Akademikerinnenverband (Swiss Association of University

Women), and the Social Democratic party's women's group.[61] This too remained without effect. Not only did the women's organisations lack any bridgehead to the relevant offices in the federal administration, but liberalisation was also hampered by the headway made by conservative positions on family policy right up to government level.[62]

Even so, criticism of the marriage rule at home and abroad made a debate among legal scholars inevitable. The Schweizerische Vereinigung für Internationales Recht (Swiss Organisation for International Law), for example, devoted a February 1933 conference to the issue of married women's nationality. To be sure, the two keynote speakers both argued in favour of retaining the status quo, and the oppositional opinion of Antoinette Quinche, the first female lawyer in Lausanne, remained clearly a minority view.[63] The argumentation is revealing. While the second speaker, Dr Emil Beck, professor of law at the University of Berne, was content to argue historically that the Swiss marriage rule was simply a matter of customary law[64], Georges Sauser-Hall, a respected professor of law at the Universities of Geneva and Neuchâtel and member of the Institut de Droit International, tried much harder to present a plausible justification. His reasoning made it clear that the legal regulations were underlaid by social perceptions of national belonging. Differing interests, he noted, had to be weighed against one another: despite his sympathy with the individualist view held by the women's organisations, he still felt that 'perfect equality between man and woman' must be 'sacrificed to higher interests'. For reasons of 'social cohesion', family unity must take precedence.[65] He explained the need to subordinate women's interests by citing the Swiss conception of nationality, which differed both from the Soviet idea of a purely economic tie between state and citizen, and from the American notion of a territorial bond where settling in a country was decisive. In Switzerland, there was a moral and spiritual tie that depended neither on political convictions nor on residence in the country. Only nationality could form the 'cement that safeguards the cohesion of the people', and it was a 'powerful factor in the cohesion of the family'. That was why this conception had 'become tradition' in the majority of European states.[66]

Sauser-Hall was thus defending a legal practice which, as he himself admitted, sacrificed the principle of equality, but which he considered vindicated by the higher interests of the state and the community. In a country like Switzerland, with its many centrifugal forces, only a homogenous mentality could secure social stability or, as Sauser-Hall put it, could effect 'cohesion'. For this, the 'unity of the family' was an essential factor. Sauser-Hall thus once again publicly underscored the 'traditional' meaning of nationality, gender and marriage, based on a corporatist, as opposed to a liberal and individualist, view of the social order. The central structuring principle of this community – in both large (the state) and small (the family or marriage) – was a hierarchical gender relationship in which the man was the decision-maker. From the second half of the 1930s onwards and into the war, the conservative and patriarchal semantics of nation was to intensify radically. In fact, the representatives of the 'traditional' principle would even succeed for the first time in inscribing what had previously been a common-law practice into a positive statute, albeit within the temporary wartime *Vollmachtenrecht*, or special mandate law.[67] This codification arose within the discursive construction of what might be called a 'nation of descent'.

The architect of this construct was Dr jur. Max Ruth (1877–1967). From 1920 he was deputy director of the police department, and after Delaquis's retirement he took on responsibility for questions of naturalisation and nationality. In 1943 Ruth also became head of the newly created appeals department of the EJPD. Ruth was a consistent upholder of the 'classical' principle, which he justified using social Darwinist, genealogical arguments. He gave the position here termed 'nation of descent' a broad conceptual frame in the lengthy 1937 treatise mentioned above, 'Das Schweizerbürgerrecht'.[68] His theses seem to have had some public resonance, for according to Annie Leuch (1880–1978), the leading SVF proponent of nationality reform, his text was well received among contemporary jurists, both male and female.[69]

Ruth's ideas rested on a 'nationality of lineage'. This, he explained, implied a 'collective family nationality', since, according to Swiss law, 'one is not a citizen as a private person, not by virtue of one's will, but as a momentary, transient link connecting past and future generations of a lineage which is represented by the family living at any one time and which belongs to the state'.[70] Ruth's 'lineage' was the agnatic family of Roman law. His colleague and successor Jean Meyer defined this in his doctoral thesis as 'encompassing all the members descended from a common male ancestor'.[71]

When Ruth spoke of the family, he was actually referring to the legal institution of marriage. 'If marriage becomes meaningless for the acquisition and loss of nationality, the collective family nationality that rests upon it will be shattered into its constituent atoms, leaving a nationality that is entirely individual. That would mean a complete break with our historical development.'[72] Ruth was concerned not to let his account appear antiquated. On the contrary, he presented it as progress: the emergence of the 'patriarchal marriage (and family)' was a 'turning point in cultural history' which 'the women's rightists' were trying to reverse – a 'tremendous atavism, a relapse into the pre-historic time before marriage existed'. For Ruth the reasoning behind Swiss citizenship, which tightly interwove marriage or family with nationality, also made it impossible for Switzerland ever to follow the American model, let alone the Soviet one. The American case was not comparable because nationality there was based not on descent and the family community but on the 'community of settlement'; in the Soviet case because in the absence of veneration for marriage and family, nationality itself was held in slight regard.[73]

Ruth's vindication of the marriage rule, inscribing it into an apparently natural order, did not exclude rational and bureaucratic considerations. The modern social-welfare state provided for its citizens and thus needed clear criteria to ascertain who was entitled to such benefits. 'In the case of impoverishment, however, a Swiss woman who has been married to a foreigner has lost her claim to welfare provision from her previous home municipality. This may mean a situation where she has to be sent home with her husband. Certainly, that is often a harsh measure. But is it less harsh to separate the woman from her family, keep her here and send the husband and children home? Or are we expected to look after the husband and children too, who are not even Swiss?'[74]

In response to the objection that in wartime a woman could be treated as belonging to an enemy state, Ruth permitted himself the following comment: 'Let us not be presumptuous enough to make the cheap – and unfair – remark that Swiss women should generally refrain from marrying foreigners.' However, 'If a Swiss woman does decide to tie her fate to that of a foreigner, it must be said that in times of crisis we can no longer completely count on her.' When she married, remarked Ruth, a woman switched her familial lineage.[75] The allusion here is to the supposed uncertainty of female loyalty towards the national community, the 'community of destiny', upon marriage to a foreign national. After all, a woman's marriage could 'easily be stronger than her nationality'.[76] This view flowed from Ruth's conception of the family as rooted in a gender-hierarchical internal order. As Ruth put it, as long as a marriage lasted, 'the woman belongs to the man'. For the woman, marriage was not just a community, rather a 'community of destiny'. Just as the man's destiny was his fatherland, the woman's was marriage.[77]

In view of Ruth's remarks on the heredity of nationality through the agnatic family, it might seem paradoxical that he simultaneously pleaded for an increase in naturalisations. Yet on closer inspection, his call to unify federal law on the naturalisation of the 'paper foreigners' whose '*Wesen*' was 'rooted here with us' – in other words who were excellently assimilated – was less a liberalisation than an improvement in the efficiency of control. He himself considered his proposals a contribution to the 'problem of *Überfremdung*'. Very likely it was the same intention that prompted his call for the implementation of the 1928 constitutional article with its restricted *jus soli* for the Swiss-born children of a Swiss mother.[78] The 'compulsory naturalisation' he recommended for such children, or as he called it their 'incorporation', seemed to him to be a 'patriotic deed'. He saw in it a means of 'sustaining a stable *Staatsvolk* (people bound to the state) that is master in its own house'. Despite the fundamental unpredictability of female allegiance, in this case Ruth thought the state would nonetheless be able to count on a new generation of young citizens with the desired 'feeling for the fatherland' and 'convictions towards the state'.[79]

Ruth's explicitly genealogical, even *völkisch* derivation of citizenship from 'blood' illuminates a significant aspect of the marriage rule more generally. Sociologist Theresa Wobbe has, in a somewhat different context, referred to women's physical and symbolic 'vulnerability' in the construction of community.[80] The regenerative tasks allocated to women, she writes, are crucial for the maintenance of social and cultural continuity across generations; women thus constitute a vulnerable point for this continuity. To control the dissolution and formation of community and thus to preserve continuity, societies establish appropriate instruments, for example the regulation of marriage. Ruth emphasised this relationship between the control of women's bodies and control over the political body. As he wrote: 'The woman belongs to the man because marriage exists to enable the establishment of a new generation and because only the succession of generations can ensure immortality for the *Staatsvolk*.'[81]

From this point of view, depriving women of their nationality upon marriage with a foreigner may be interpreted as a radical exclusion of those women seen as being at risk of 'infringement' by another nation. For a woman who remained in Switzerland, this risk was apparently felt to be less pressing. At any rate, her offspring could be integrated without too much difficulty into the Volkskörper ('ethnic body') – or in Ruth's republican terminology, whereby the citizens themselves are the state, into the '*Staatsvolk*'. Pursuing this thinking a little further, it becomes apparent that the female body's reproductive significance had a crucial role in shaping its symbolic significance for the construction of the nation. In the organic argumentation of many (not all) proponents of the 'traditional' principle, the unity of the family was firmly intertwined with the unity of the nation to form the precondition for a stable social order.

But Ruth was also interested in population policy in the sense of an optimal management of membership of and exclusion from nationality. Representing a powerful and in some sectors highly centralised administration, he sought to establish a clear dividing line through the country's inhabitants. On one side of this line would be those whose unconditional loyalty to the state could be assumed, who could be directly counted on as belonging to the body of the state and who would be rewarded by the state with certain benefits; on the other side were those who could not be included in this unity.

From this perspective, two aspects of nationality were of particular concern to the federal authorities from the mid 1930s on: fictitious marriages, and exceptions to the marriage rule. International developments led to fears among the authorities responsible for Swiss immigration policy that increased numbers of 'undesirable' aliens would arrive and seek to gain permission to stay or settle through marriage. However, official suspicion now also extended to non-Swiss women who had been automatically naturalised via marriage to a Swiss man. In 1935 the head of the EJPD police department, Heinrich Rothmund, wrote to the head of the department of foreign affairs in the Political Ministry: 'In practice, marriages between German Jews and Swiss women are hardly in our interest, since in such cases the family will do everything it can to stay put in Switzerland. When German Jewesses marry Swiss men there is a danger of fictitious marriage, a danger that has often enough become reality.'[82]

In the years that followed, the question of fictitious marriages worried both the public and many jurists, as well as the federal court and the women's organisations.[83] The legal committee of the BSF had, with some difficulty, reached a cautious position in 1937. On the one

hand the committee, whose arguments always followed a strictly legal-
istic rationale, wished to avoid losing credibility with the authorities,
but on the other it regarded the problem of fictitious marriages as a
logical consequence of the prevailing nationality legislation.[84] As a compromise, they recommended a probationary period for the marriage of
a non-Swiss woman to a Swiss man, during which the woman would
retain her nationality of descent. After this period she would receive
facilitated access to Swiss nationality.[85] A ruling like this, argued the committee, would move Switzerland closer to the international norm,
where it was increasingly rare for marriage to bear directly on citizenship.[86] However, the committee's proposal met with no success. The
federal court moved to a more restrictive practice in 1939 which was
codified in a government decree of 20 December 1940. The suspicion
that the marriage was fictitious became grounds for annulling it.[87]

The government decree concluded a decades-long dispute over
nationality competencies and interpretation between the judiciary
and the executive – in the government authorities' favour, at least
for the time being. They removed competence for the examination of
nationality questions from the federal court, and transferred it to the
EJPD. Unlike the jurists at the top level of the EJPD, many of those
in the federal court supported the 'modern' principle in married
women's nationality. In fact, in 1928 federal judge Wilhelm Stauffer
had been the first Swiss jurist to publicly call for nationality to be
independent of marital status.[88]

The federal court also tended to apply the marriage rule in a rather
liberal way, something that had attracted criticism from Max Ruth and
others, such as the respected constitutional lawyer Walter Burckhardt.[89]
In 1938 the disagreement escalated when France further modified
its nationality legislation.[90] In the future France would no longer take
foreign legislation into account when ruling on the acquisition and
loss of French nationality.[91] The EJPD, and subsequently the Political
Ministry, instructed the Swiss Embassy in Paris and the Swiss cantonal
authorities supervising the registration of marriages that they must
uphold the previous position, whereby a married woman's nationality
could not be subject to her own free will.[92] In practice, this meant that
a Swiss woman became stateless on marrying a French man unless she
had successfully petitioned for French citizenship. The federal court
flatly contradicted this stance. In two decisions it concluded that until
her petition for French citizenship had received a response, the Swiss
woman remained Swiss, and she continued to do so if her petition was

refused.[93] Above all – and this was the crucial point for the dispute with the federal administration – she retained Swiss nationality even if she failed to submit a petition.[94]

In 1940, the government decree provided a twofold anchor for women's unconditional loss of nationality upon marriage to a foreigner: firstly by making the loss of nationality automatic for Swiss women marrying foreign nationals, and secondly by transferring competence for this issue to the EJPD. The move was strongly criticised by the federal commission monitoring the constitutionality of government practices in wartime, and Parliament held off approval of the decree. There were legal problems both on the procedural side, regarding the exclusion of the federal court, and with the lack of possibilities for appeal.[95] The latter point was corrected in the government decree of 11 November 1941: although the EJPD still retained competence on nationality issues, judicial appeal was now possible.[96]

The new decree contained detailed provisions on the 'loss of nationality through marriage' (art. 5), explicitly noting that 'when a Swiss woman concludes a marriage, valid in Switzerland, with a foreigner, she loses Swiss nationality'. For the first time, the loss of female nationality due to marriage was established in positive law.[97] Moreover, this rule was to apply in all cases, irrespective of the foreign legislation involved.

The decree bore the unmistakable signature of Max Ruth, and contemporaries confirmed that he was the driving force behind it.[98] Ruth's 1937 treatise had already expressed his disapproval of the federal court's practice of waiving the marriage rule where there was a risk of statelessness. He felt this could only be condoned for reasons of 'expediency' or 'compassion', warning that under no circumstances should any inferences of principle be drawn. 'Compassion for the woman who would become stateless must not become a general compassion for the Swiss woman who loses her nationality through marriage and exchanges it for her husband's.'[99] After the government resolution of 1941, he gave his views even more forceful expression. He rejoiced that Swiss law would no longer yield to foreign legislation; now a simple, easily comprehensible law had been established that could be 'automatically' implemented with 'logical consistency'.[100]

During the war, the federal administration translated these principles into administrative practice – with the 'logical consistency' Ruth so admired.[101] Just a few days after the decree was passed, the EJPD approached the cantons to describe its application. In part, Ruth's exact wording was used to explain the rectification of hardships arising from the marriage rule: 'Before concluding a marriage like this, the woman must consider the consequences, and subsequently she must bear those consequences. She must know that according to Swiss law the woman belongs to her husband and that as long as her marriage exists she is obliged to share his destiny.' This was no empty doctrine. As a memorandum circulated to the cantons noted, the remarks referred specifically to those Swiss women married to German Jews still living in Nazi Germany. Shortly before this time, Nazi citizenship law had collectively deprived these women of their nationality. In this case, Swiss women became 'stateless' on the basis of a foreign law, not a Swiss one, and hence it was not permissible to 'restore Swiss nationality to such women'.[102]

For many formerly Swiss women made stateless by the Nazi authorities, the consequences of this view were disastrous.[103] Not until late December 1942 were these Swiss-born women recognised as cases of hardship and allowed privileged refugee status at the Swiss border. And only in July 1944 did formerly Swiss women who had 'become foreign nationals through marriage' receive express permission to enter the country, with their children up to age 18.[104] The number of applications for reintegration into nationality provides a glimpse of the scale of the problem: between 1930 and 1950 14,340 such applications were lodged with the EJPD, of which 11,877 were approved. Of these, 99.5 per cent were from women who had married a foreign national.[105]

After the war, the changes so long desired by the women's organisations seemed possible at last. The signs included awareness of the wartime sufferings of Swiss women and the emergence of a new international conception of law based on human rights. It must have come as a disappointment when, in 1946, the government mandated Max Ruth to draw up the new nationality law.[106] Already in retirement, Ruth published his report in late 1949, proposing that the controversial government decree of 1941 be largely adopted into regular legislation. Ruth's proposal was not accepted in this form. Instead, in 1952 a compromise was agreed upon, allowing women a right of option to retain their nationality of descent, and it remained in force until the end of 1991.[107] The postwar decision, reached in the context of debate on abolishing the marriage rule, can only be described as having normalised an incoherency in the policy of the Swiss government on this issue.

The continuity in the Swiss conception of nationality was, to be sure, not the work of Max Ruth alone. His successor, Dr jur. Jean Meyer, whose doctoral thesis dealt with the loss of nationality through marriage, vigorously supported the unconditional unity of the family in nationality law.[108] At a meeting with a women's delegation on 27 September 1947, Meyer clarified his distaste for any breach of this principle – a view shared by the head of the EJPD, Eduard von Steiger, and the deputy head of its police department, Dr Robert Jezler.[109]

By now, however, the opposition had begun to mobilise. In 1951 a government-appointed commission of experts, including representatives of the women's organisations, produced a proposal that deviated from the 'classical' principle and managed to gather backing from the majority of the cantons.[110] When compared to the consultation process on Ruth's report in 1949, this development marked a shift of opinion that reflected both women's lobbying at cantonal level and the impact an official report could have on perceptions of a political issue. In fact, the draft law that was presented did not wholly decouple nationality from marital status; instead, a clause was included that gave a woman the option of making a special declaration if she wished to retain her Swiss nationality. To the chagrin of the women's associations, the idea had come from one of their own representatives.[111] The advocates of the marriage rules eagerly embraced this 'right of option' as a way of forestalling more far-reaching solutions. Although the proposal satisfied neither the women's associations nor Max Ruth, it obtained the assent of the commission's majority and was adopted in the draft legislation.[112]

The parliamentary debate that followed in 1951 and 1952 is noteworthy less because of the outcome of the vote itself than because, for the first time, the issue was being discussed by politicians, and no longer almost exclusively by civil servants and legal experts. Yet even among the legislators, it was the legally trained who made their views most clearly known. Their lines of argument were not solely legal, however: they voiced controversies around the relationship of gender, marital status and nationality that had been running for half a century.[113] The proponents of the 'modern' principle focused on the injustices arising from the marriage rule, such as the possible loss of employment for women in public service. They also deplored dependence on foreign law and, more fundamentally, cast general doubt on the legality of a loss of nationality.

In the face of such liberal and individualist reasoning, their opponents invoked topoi grounded in classical republicanism and conceptions of community. Their primary concern was the threat that seemed posed to the unity of the family. In addition, they repeatedly referred to the interests of the municipality, cast as a community that should not be burdened with financial responsibilities for people it barely knew, namely those 'Swiss women who have moved away'. They rejected the obligation to support 'countless people who have lost all connection to the municipality where they were born and are completely unknown there'.[114]

In the debate, the suspicion of deficient loyalty among women who had married a foreigner made its appearance in various guises. Two parliamentary representatives indicated the risk to the country if these women continued to be teachers, doctors or lawyers and hence held positions buttressing the state. Another painted a frightening picture of the dangers of espionage. Finally, many anti-reform arguments articulated a normative image of femininity that assigned women strict moral duties. One parliamentarian expressed his concern that unscrupulous women would exploit the right of option in order to retain their Swiss citizenship, while the others would bow to the good of the family, which was self-evidently served by the wife's adopting her husband's nationality.[115]

Extensive lobbying by women's associations, including petitions and ministerial meetings, assured that the right of option was finally ratified with a comfortable majority. Another factor shaping politicians' perceptions of the legal status quo was the injustice endured in the many 'cases of hardship' during the war, which prompted new ways of thinking about this problem, according to the speaker of one government commission.[116] More pragmatic was the concern that it was becoming increasingly difficult to apply the marriage rule without entailing statelessness, because most countries had ceased to automatically grant women their husband's nationality upon marriage in the postwar period. However, the idea that a woman ultimately had to choose between fatherland and husband had not yet been laid to rest, as the following example makes clear. The period of reflection, proposed in the draft law, would have granted women one year to apply for their retention of Swiss nationality, but the compromise procedure between the two legislative chambers led to the elimination of this period of reflection. As a Catholic-conservative deputy declared, 'Anyone entering the state of marriage must be aware of the consequences in every respect, and that includes reflecting on the question of nationality status. [...] A woman who marries a foreigner should think the matter over very carefully.'[117]

These words confirmed a prediction made by one participant at the start of the debate, that the strongest opposition to reform would be neither political nor legal, but social and moral in nature. 'Many advocates of the traditional solution', he had noted, 'fear that the demands of the women's associations express this individualism which, as a French lawyer has said, reduces marriage to a contract that must be renewed every day, and fails to comprehend the institutional character of the marriage bond effected by that contract.'[118]

As a result of the 1952 compromise, until 1 January 1992 a woman had to declare at the moment of marriage that she wished to retain her nationality. As a parliamentary supporter of the right of option explained, 'If the Swiss woman marrying out wishes to renew her faith towards the Swiss Confederation (and not just towards her husband), she may remain within the Confederate bond of loyalty.'[119]

Thus the opinions voiced in the parliamentary debate allow us to trace the conflicting representations of the Swiss citizen. For the opponents of reform, the citizen was closely bound to the local community; his relationship to the communal good was marked by readiness for self-sacrifice. Such conditions did not seem to be fulfilled by women who chose a foreign national as their life companion. The crux of this notion of the Swiss 'political body' was the republican, non-contractualist view of marriage (or family) and state. As Ruth put it, 'Marriage is destiny and fatherland is also destiny'.[120] Neither the one nor the other was subject to the free will of the individual. Moreover, one flowed from the other. For in Switzerland, the family was considered a generative element of nationality and based, in Ruth's words, on the 'male lineage'. It was not possible to escape the patrilineal and patriarchal principle: 'The more resolutely the wife binds her destiny to that of her husband, the greater chance there is of a good marriage'.[121] The woman's relationship to the state was thus only indirect, mediated by the man, and only this family constellation could guarantee loyal citizens.

In the twentieth century this conception came under increasing attack. After all, it belied the claim that citizenship entitled its bearers to legal rights, a claim which now became ever more significant. The marriage rule supposedly rested on customary law, yet leading jurists in Switzerland held that no such law had ever existed.[122] What was at stake, then, was an invented tradition – invented by administrative practice itself. The codification of this practice required elaborate strategies of justification from the juridical and administrative field, making explicit the logic which allowed parallel versions of nationality to coexist according to gender and marital status. By its very nature, this task fell to the legal profession as a group. Their monopoly as authorised experts in questions of law meant they alone were entitled to address the subject and to make competent, 'transcendent' statements.[123] Yet the members of the profession by no means shared the same interests, whether politically or professionally, as was shown by the wartime disputes between the judiciary and the federal administration. Not until the war, and indeed for positive law not until after it, did the proponents of the marriage rule succeed in codifying the construction of a conditional nationality status for women. Paradoxically, the revised nationality law of 1952 was represented as progress.[124] In reality, it legally secured the distinct position of the female citizen for the first time.

The special treatment of female citizens prescribed by the marriage rule was initially a matter of practice. Its rise to theoretical prominence coincided with the 'nationalisation' of the Swiss people. In the interwar period this process involved more than the drawing of discursive and legal boundaries between Swiss citizens and foreigners. Everything 'alien' acquired the significance of a threat to the particularity of 'Swissness'. In the more deeply incised matrix of belonging and exclusion, the female 'gendered body' presented a factor of uncertainty for the taxonomy of citizenship. For the patrilineal succession and the patriarchal family structure that shaped the view of the 'classical' principle's advocates, women marrying foreigners represented a danger to the unity of the nation in both biological and moral terms – biological because their children belonged to a 'different' nation, and moral because they owed loyalty to their foreign husband.

The position of woman within nationality can thus be regarded as analogous to the 'stranger' discussed by sociologist Georg Simmel.[125] Rather than standing outside a particular social group, this 'stranger' is to a large degree part of it, yet is not fully integrated and thus never quite considered to be loyal. Women, too, were part of the Swiss nation, but in contrast to male citizens their membership was a contingent one. If they married a foreigner, they were assumed to have taken up a position outside the community of national solidarity. Gender acted as a marker in the process of setting internal boundaries between 'self' and 'other' that was initiated in Switzerland by the First World War. It provided a symbolic boundary between a nationality that was stable and permanent, thus grounded in loyalty, and one that was inherently unstable. The resultant norm had tangible effects on the agency and actions of citizens, depending on their gender. As marriage statistics show, the marriage rule indirectly acted as a ban specifically on marriage between Swiss women and non-Swiss men. Throughout the twentieth century, there were significantly fewer such marriages than between Swiss men and non-Swiss women. In the 1950s, only one Swiss woman in twenty-one married a foreign man, as against one Swiss man in seven marrying a foreign woman,[126] and the disparity was even greater in times of crisis and war. The loss of nationality was not a peripheral matter for women, as the enthusiastic embrace of the right of option shows: in certain cantons in 1953, every single Swiss woman marrying a foreigner signed the declaration to retain or re-attain her nationality of descent.[127] Only from 1992 on did Swiss women 'marrying out' remain an unconditional part of the Swiss Confederate 'bond of loyalty' without having to make an explicit declaration. Until then they were 'borderline cases' whose membership in the Swiss nation was merely contingent.

Notes

My thanks to Gérald Arlettaz and Patrick Kury, and to the anonymous reviewers whose stimulating commentaries and criticism greatly enriched the present text.

1. The Swiss federal judge Dr Wilhelm Stauffer, in 1928 the first Swiss jurist to publicly call for nationality to be independent of marital status, quoted this passage at the start of his essay 'Ehe und Heimat', *Schweizerische Juristen-Zeitung*, 39 (1943), pp. 269–79.

2. Max Ruth, 'Das Schweizerbürgerrecht', *Zeitschrift für Schweizerisches Recht. Neue Folge*, 56 (1937), pp. 1a–156a, here pp. 5a–6a.

3. On the legal definition of nationality see, for example, Susanne Schmidheiny, *Die privatrechtlichen Folgen der selbständigen Staatsangehörigkeit der Ehefrau* (Juris-Verlag, Zurich, 1958), p. 28.

4. A typology of citizenship is provided by T. H. Marshall, *Citizenship and Social Class and other essays* (Cambridge University Press, Cambridge, 1950). For Switzerland, see Brigitte Studer, Regina Wecker and Béatrice Ziegler (eds), *Geschlecht und Staat/Femmes et citoyenneté: Schweizerische Zeitschrift für Geschichte/Revue suisse d'histoire*, 3 (1996), and *Frauen und Staat: Berichte des Schweizerischen Historikertages in Bern, Oktober 1996/Les Femmes et l'Etat: Journée nationale des Historiens suisses à Berne, octobre 1996* (Schwabe, Basle, 1998) (Itinera 20).

5. See her dossier in the Swiss federal archive, Schweizerisches Bundesarchiv E 4265 1985/57, M 2609. Cited in Ka Schuppisser, '"Denn im Herzen bin ich eine 'Schweizerin' im wahrsten Sinne des Wortes" : Wiedereinbürgerungsverfahren 1937–1947. Die ehemalige Schweizerin im Diskurs der nationalen Identität der Frau' (unpublished Master's thesis, Berne, 1998), p. 98.

6. André Lasserre et al., *La Politique vaudoise envers les réfugiés victimes du nazisme, 1933 à 1945: Rapport présenté en juin 2000 au Conseil d'Etat du canton de Vaud en exécution de son mandat du 18 juin 1997* (circulated, Lausanne 2000), p. 47.

7. Georg Kreis and Patrick Kury, *Die schweizerischen Einbürgerungsnormen im Wandel der Zeiten* (Nationale Schweizerischen UNESCO-Kommission, Berne, 1996); May B. Broda, 'Auslandschweizerinnen, ehemalige Schweizerinnen – ihre Rückwanderung aus Deutschland 1939–1948', in *Auf den Spuren weiblicher Vergangenheit (2): Beiträge der 4. Schweizerischen Historikerinnentagung*, ed. Arbeitsgruppe Frauengeschichte Basel (Chronos, Zurich, 1988), pp. 251–61; Brigitte Studer, 'Von der Legitimations- zur Relevanzproblematik. Zum Stand der Geschlechtergeschichte', in *Geschlecht hat Methode: Ansätze und Perspektiven in der Frauen- und Geschlechtergeschichte. Beiträge der 9. Schweizerischen Historikerinnentagung 1998*, ed. Veronika Aegerter et al. (Chronos, Zurich, 1999), pp. 19–30; Brigitte Studer, 'Nationalität auf Widerruf', *'98 – Die Zeitung*, 2 (1998), pp. 30–1; Regina Wecker, '"Ehe ist Schicksal, Vaterland ist auch Schicksal und dagegen ist kein Kraut gewachsen": Gemeindebürgerrecht und Staatsangehörigkeit von Frauen in der Schweiz 1798–1998', *L'Homme ZFG*, 10 (1999), pp. 13–37.

8. In 1914 the proportion of foreign nationals among residents of Switzerland was over 15 per cent. Later the number fell, rising again after 1945. In 1975 it had reached more than 16 per cent. In border cantons like Geneva and Basle the proportion around 1900 was as high as 40 per cent, in the city of Zurich 17 per cent.

9. Marcel Mauss, 'Nation, nationalité et internationalisme', in *Oeuvres* (Minuit, Paris, 1969), vol. 3, p. 618.

10. See Ruth Roach Pierson, 'Nations: Gendered, Racialized, Crossed with Empire', in *Gendered Nations: Nationalisms and Gender Order in the Long Nineteenth Century*, ed. Ida Blom, Karen Hagemann and Catherine Hall (Berg, Oxford and New York, 2000), pp. 41–61, here p. 41.

11. Benedict Anderson, *Imagined Communities: Reflections on the Origin and Spread of Nationalism* (Verso, London and New York, 1991), pp. 5–6.

12. On the development and effects of this setting of boundaries between nationals and non-nationals, see especially Gérard Noiriel, *La Tyrannie du national: Le Droit d'asile en Europe 1793–1993* (Calmann-Lévy, Paris, 1991).

13. Nancy F. Cott, 'Marriage and Women's Citizenship in the United States, 1830–1934', *American Historical Review*, 103 (1998), pp. 1440–74, here p. 1461.

14. J. G. A. Pocock, *The Machiavellian Moment: Florentine Political Thought and the Atlantic Republican Tradition* (Princeton University Press, Princeton, NJ, 1975).

15. Helpful on these questions are studies by Manfred Hettling, *Politische Bürgerlichkeit: Der Bürger zwischen Individualität und Vergesellschaftung in Deutschland und der Schweiz von 1860 bis 1918* (Vandenhoeck & Ruprecht, Göttingen, 1999); Thomas Maissen, 'Die Geburt der Republik: Politisches Selbstverständnis und Repräsentation in Zürich und der Eidgenossenschaft während der Frühen Neuzeit', unpublished professorial thesis, University of Zurich, 2000; and Béla Kapossy, 'Introduction: From Republicanism to Welfare Liberalism', *Schweizerische Zeitschrift für Geschichte/Revue suisse d'histoire*, 50 (2000), pp. 275–303.

16. Anderson, *Imagined Communities*, p. 143.

17. Eric Hobsbawm, *Nations and Nationalism since 1780: Programme, Myth, Reality* (Cambridge University Press, Cambridge, 1990).

18. Max Weber, *Economy and Society: An Outline of Interpretive Sociology*, ed. Guenther Roth and Claus Wittich, trans. Ephraim Fischoff et al. (University of California Press, Berkeley, 1978).

19. Field-defining in this respect is the work of Pierre Bourdieu. See, in particular, 'The Force of Law: Toward a Sociology of the Juridical Field', trans. R. Terdiman, *Hastings Law Journal*, 38 (1987), pp. 814–53, and 'Rethinking the State: On the Genesis and Structure of the Bureaucratic Field', trans. L. Wacquant and S. Farage, *Sociological Theory*, 12 (1994), pp. 1–19.

20. See, for example, Michel Foucault, *Discipline and Punish: The Birth of the Prison*, trans. Alan Sheridan (Vintage, New York, 1979), and *The History of Sexuality*, vol. 1, *An Introduction*, trans. Robert Hurley (Vintage, New York, 1985).

21. Also useful here is Krzysztof Pomian, *L'Europe et ses nations* (Gallimard, Paris, 1990), pp. 214–15.

22. This definition is adapted from Ina-Maria Greverus, *Kultur und Alltagswelt: Eine Einführung in die Fragen der Kulturanthropologie* (Beck, Munich, 1978), pp. 344–6.

23. Examples include the following papers by Gérald Arlettaz and Silvia Arlettaz: 'Naturalisation, "assimilation" et nationalité suisse: L'Enjeu des années 1900–1930', in *Devenir suisse: Adhésion et diversité culturelle des étrangers en Suisse*, ed. Pierre Centlivres (Georg Editeur, Geneva, 1990), pp. 47–62; 'Un Défi de l'entre-deux-guerres: Les Etrangers face au processus de nationalisation et de socialisation du peuple suisse', in *Le Goût de l'histoire, des idées et des hommes: Mélanges offerts au professeur Jean-Pierre Aguet*, ed. Alain Clavien and Bertrand Müller (Editions de l'Aire, Lausanne, 1996), pp. 319–46; 'La Politique suisse d'immigration et de refuge: Héritage de guerre et gestion de paix', *Guerres et paix: Mélanges offerts à Jean-Claude Favez*, ed. Michel Porret et al. (Georg, Geneva, 2000), pp. 661–84; and Gérald Arlettaz's 'La Suisse, une terre d'accueil en question: L'Importance de la Première Guerre mondiale', in *L'Emigration politique en Europe aux XIXe et XXe siècles: Actes du colloque organisé par l'Ecole française de Rome* (Collection de l'Ecole française de Rome, Rome and Paris, 1991), pp. 139–59. See also Rudolf Schläpfer, *Die Ausländerfrage in der Schweiz vor dem Ersten Weltkrieg* (Juris Druck, Zurich, 1969).

24. On the concept of '*Überfremdung*', see Gaetano Romano, 'Zeit der Krise – Krise der Zeit: Identität, Überfremdung und verschlüsselte Zeitstrukturen', in *Die neue Schweiz? Eine Gesellschaft zwischen Integration und Polarisierung (1910–1930)*, ed. Andreas Ernst and Erich Wigger (Chronos, Zurich, 1996), pp. 41–77, and Jakob Tanner, 'Nationalmythos und 'Überfremdungsängste': Wie und warum die Immigration zum Problem wird, dargestellt am Beispiel der Schweizer Geschichte des 19. und 20. Jahrhunderts', in *Fremd im Paradies: Migration und Rassismus*, ed. Udo Rauschfleisch (Lenos, Basle, 1994), pp. 11–26.

25. Women's International League for Peace and Freedom, *Extract from the Forthcoming Report of the International Congress of Women held at Zurich, May 12–17, 1919* (no publisher, Zurich, 1919), p. 13.

26. Chrystal Macmillan, *The Nationality of Married Women* (London, 1929), p. 9; Arnold Whittick, *Woman into Citizen* (Athenaeum, London, 1979), p. 75; Leila J. Rupp, *Worlds of Women: The Making of an International Women's Movement* (Princeton University Press, Princeton, 1997), pp. 146–50. On the position of the BSF (association of Swiss women's organisations), see Bund Schweizerischer Frauenvereine (BSF), *17. Jahresbericht*, 1917/18, pp. 32–3, and Annie Leuch-Reineck, 'Die Nationalität der verheirateten Frau und die schweizerische Gesetzgebung', *Schweizer Frauenblatt*, 31 (4 August 1923) and 32 (11 August 1923).

27. On this question, see Elisabeth Frey, *Über das Bürgerrecht der Ehefrau in der Schweiz und ihren Nachbarstaaten* (Ernst Lang, Zurich, 1942), p. 16, and Ladislaus Vidor, *Die Staatsangehörigkeit der Ehefrau nach schweizerischem Recht* (Buchdruckerei J. Weiss, Affoltern am Albis, 1932), p. 92.

28. Michel Foucault uses the notion of 'pastoral power' to indicate the interest of the modern state in each of its citizens individually. See his 'The Subject and Power', in H. Dreyfus and P. Rabinow, *Michel Foucault: Beyond Structuralism and Hermeneutics*, 2nd edition (University of Chicago Press, Chicago, 1983), pp. 208–26.

29. See Marianne Delfosse, *Emilie Kempin-Spyri (1853–1901): Das Wirken der ersten Schweizer Juristin. Unter besonderer Berücksichtigung ihres Einsatzes für die Rechte der Frau im schweizerischen und deutschen Privatrecht* (Schulthess, Zurich, 1994), and Katharina Belser et al. (eds), *Ebenso neu als kühn: 120 Jahre Frauenstudium an der Universität Zürich* (eFeF-Verlag, Zurich, 1988), p. 178.

30. The paragraph reads: 'Through her marriage, the wife acquires citizenship of her husband's municipality of origin'.

31. This, at least, was the argumentation in the parliamentary debate on the new nationality law of 1952.

32. Federal law on the acquisition and renunciation of Swiss citizenship, 25 June 1903. Apart from marital status, the conditions were a domicile in Switzerland and a period of not more than ten years between the change in marital status and the application.

33. Markus Luther, *Die Staatsangehörigkeit der einen Ausländer heiratenden Schweizerin* (Verlag Hans Schellenberg, Winterthur, 1956), pp. 78–9.

34. Georges Sauser-Hall, *La Nationalité de la femme mariée*, published by the Schweizerische Vereinigung für internationales Recht (Druckschrift Nr. 29, Zurich, 1933), p. 10.

35. Decisions of the Swiss federal court (BGE) 36, I, pp. 225–7; Luther, *Die Staatsangehörigkeit*, pp. 104–5, 110–11, 125–7.

36. The legal development is traced in detail in Cott, 'Marriage and Women's Citizenship'.

37. Carmen Naccary, *La Nationalité de la femme mariée dans les principaux pays* (Imprimerie Atar, Geneva, 1925).

38. Internationaler Frauenbund, *Vereinigter 3. und 4. Jahresbericht der siebenten Geschäftsperiode 1922–1924* (International Council of Women, *Combined Third and Fourth Annual Report of the Seventh Quinquennial Period*), p. 32.

39. Sauser-Hall, *La Nationalité*, p. 8; Vidor, *Die Staatsangehörigkeit*, pp. 97–9; Schweizerischer Verband für Frauenstimmrecht (Swiss women's suffrage association, SVF), 'Zum Bürgerrecht der ausheiratenden Schweizerin, von 1915 bis 1952', p. 3; Nitza Berkovitch, *From Motherhood to Citizenship: Women's Rights and International Organizations* (The Johns Hopkins University Press, Baltimore and London, 1999), pp. 80–82.

40. BSF, *22. Jahresbericht*, 1922/23, p. 24.

41. *Jahrbuch der Schweizerfrauen* (Basler Druck- und Verlagsanstalt, Basle, 1923), p. 156.

42. Decision of the federal court, 24 February 1923, in the case of Frl. Dr jur. Roeder, BGE 49, I, pp. 14 ff., cited in Elisabeth Köpfli, *Die öffentlichen Rechte und Pflichten der Frau nach schweizerischem Recht* (Druck J. Weiss, Affoltern am Albis, 1942), p. 42. See also Brigitte Studer, '"Alle Schweizer sind vor dem Gesetze gleich": Verfassung, Staatsbürgerrechte und Geschlecht', in *Herausgeforderte Verfassung: Die Schweiz im globalen Kontext. 16. Kolloquium (1997) der Schweizerischen Akademie der Geisteswissenschaften*, ed. Beat Sitter-Liver (Universitätsverlag, Freiburg, 1999), pp. 63–83.

43. Beatrix Mesmer, 'Pflichten erfüllen heisst Rechte begründen: Die frühe Frauenbewegung und der Staat', *Schweizerische Zeitschrift für Geschichte*, 46 (1996), pp. 332–55, and Elisabeth Joris, 'Geschlechtshierarchische Arbeitsteilung und Integration der Frauen', in *Etappen des Bundesstaates: Die Staats- und Nationsbildung in der Schweiz, 1848–1998*, ed. Brigitte Studer (Chronos, Zurich, 1998), pp. 187–201.

44. Uriel Gast, *Von der Kontrolle zur Abwehr: Die eidgenössische Fremdenpolizei im Spannungsfeld von Politik und Wirtschaft 1915–1933* (Chronos, Zurich, 1997), and Angela Garrido, *Le Début de la politique fédérale à l'égard des étrangers* (Histoire et Société Contemporaines 7, Lausanne, 1987), pp. 57–60.

45. Arlettaz and Arlettaz, 'La Politique suisse d'immigration', p. 675; Frey, *Über das Bürgerrecht der Ehefrau*, p. 71; Gast, *Von der Kontrolle zur Abwehr*, pp. 233–5.

46. There is little research on Delaquis's leading role in the legal codification of Swiss aliens policy. Important points are made in Arlettaz and Arlettaz, 'Un Défi de l'entre-deux-guerres', pp. 332–3.

47. On Delaquis, see Historisches Lexikon der Schweiz, http://www.dhs.ch (as per 30 March 2001).

48. Ernst Delaquis, 'Nationale Niederlassungspolitik: Vortrag, gehalten in der Neuen Helvetischen Gesellschaft, Gruppe Zürich, am 10. April 1924', *Schweizerische Zeitschrift für Volkswirtschaft und Sozialpolitik*, 30 (1924), pp. 225–42, here p. 236.

49. Ernst Delaquis, 'Der gegenwärtige Stand der Massnahmen gegen die politische Überfremdung: Öffentlicher Vortrag', *Schweizerische Zeitschrift für Gemeinnützigkeit*, 60/2 (1921), pp. 41–9, and 60/3 (1921), pp. 57–66. See especially 60/3, pp. 65–6.

50. Ernst Delaquis, 'Im Kampf gegen die Überfremdung: Die Neuorientierung der Niederlassungspolitik. Vortrag, gehalten im Bernischen Juristenverein am 10. Januar 1921',

Zeitschrift des Bernischen Juristenvereins, LVII (1921), pp. 49–69, here p. 66. See also Gast, *Von der Kontrolle zur Abwehr*, pp. 246–58.

51. Delaquis, 'Nationale Niederlassungspolitik', pp. 230–31.

52. Federal law on residence and settlement of aliens, notes on the police department draft (13 June 1921), cited in Arlettaz and Arlettaz, 'Un Défi de l'entre-deux-guerres', p. 333.

53. Ernst Delaquis, *Der neueste Stand der Fremdenfrage* (Stämpfli & Cie, Berne, 1921), p. 10.

54. See especially Delaquis , 'Im Kampf gegen die Überfremdung', and Delaquis, *Der neueste Stand*.

55. Report of the study committee in BSF, *27. Jahresbericht*, 1927/28, p. 25.

56. Communication from Delaquis to the SVF, mentioned in SVF, 'Zum Bürgerrecht der ausheiratenden Schweizerin', p. 2; Biographical notes on Annie Leuch-Reineck, Gosteli-Archiv, Worblaufen, 1934/BSF/3578.

57. Here I follow the argumentation of Kreis and Kury, *Die schweizerischen Einbürgerungsnormen*, pp. 52–3.

58. See the papers by Arlettaz and Arlettaz; also Alain Clavien, *Les Helvétistes: Intellectuels et politique en Suisse romande au début du siècle* (Société d'histoire de la Suisse romande/Editions d'en bas, Lausanne, 1993).

59. Heinrich Rothmund, 'Die berufliche Überfremdung und Vorschläge zu ihrer Abhilfe: Vortrag gehalten an der Jahresversammlung der Schweizerischen Gemeinnützigen Gesellschaft am 30. September 1924 in St. Gallen', *Schweizerische Zeitschrift für Gemeinnützigkeit*, 10 (1924), pp. 339–40.

60. On Rothmund's anti-Semitism, see Heinz Roschewski, 'Heinrich Rothmund in seinen persönlichen Akten: Zur Frage des Antisemitismus in der schweizerischen Flüchtlingspolitik, 1933–1945', *Studien und Quellen*, 22 (1996), pp. 107–36, and *Rothmund und die Juden: Eine historische Fallstudie des Antisemitismus in der schweizerischen Flüchtlingspolitik 1933–1957* (Helbing & Lichtenhahn, Basle, 1998). For the Second World War see also Ladislas Mysyrowicz, 'Le Dr Rothmund et le problème juif (février 1941)', *Schweizerische Zeitschrift für Geschichte*, 2 (1982), pp. 348–55.

61. The Swiss Catholic women's association did not participate (Christa Mutter, '"Die Hl. Religion ist das tragende Fundament der katholischen Frauenbewegung": Zur Entwicklung des Schweizerischen Katholischen Frauenbunds', in *Auf den Spuren weiblicher Vergangenheit (2): Beiträge der 4. Schweizerischen Historikerinnentagung* (Chronos, Zurich, 1988), pp. 183–98).

62. See Brigitte Studer, 'Familienzulagen statt Mutterschaftsversicherung? Die Zuschreibung der Geschlechterkompetenzen im sich formierenden Schweizer Sozialstaat, 1920–1945', *Schweizerische Zeitschrift für Geschichte*, 47 (1997), pp. 151–70; Doris Huber, 'Familienpolitische Kontroversen in der Schweiz zwischen 1930 und 1984', in *Familie in der Schweiz*, ed. Thomas Fleiner-Gerster, Pierre Gilliand and Kurt Lüscher (Universitätsverlag, Freiburg, 1991), pp. 147–66.

63. Hans Fritzsche, *Die Schweizerische Vereinigung für Internationales Recht (1914–1944), Separatdruck aus der Festschrift Max Huber 'Vom Krieg und vom Frieden'* (no date, no publisher), p. 90.

64. Emil Beck, *Die Staatsangehörigkeit der Ehefrau*, published by the Schweizerische Vereinigung für internationales Recht (Druckschrift Nr. 30, Zurich 1933), p. 14; Wilhelm Stauffer, 'Die Staatsangehörigkeit der Ehefrau', *Zeitschrift des bernischen Juristenvereins*, 64 (1928), pp. 325–32, here p. 326; Hortensia Zängerle, *Die öffentlich-rechtliche Stellung der Frau in der Schweiz* (Buchdruckerei A. Meierhans, Freiburg, 1940), p. 27; Jean Meyer, *La Perte de la nationalité suisse par mariage* (Imprimerie St-Paul, Fribourg, 1942), p. 35; Frey, *Über das Bürgerrecht der Ehefrau*, p. 14; Luther, *Die Staatsangehörigkeit*, pp. 100–25.

65. Sauser-Hall, *La Nationalité*, pp. 34–5.

66. Sauser-Hall, *La Nationalité*, p. 13.

67. This was available to the government between 1939 und 1947.

68. Max Ruth, *Das Fremdenpolizeirecht der Schweiz* (Polygraphischer Verlag, Zurich, 1934).

69. SVF, 'Zum Bürgerrecht der ausheiratenden Schweizerin', p. 4, 'Protokoll über die 72. Jahresversammlung des Schweizerischen Juristenvereins, 13. und 14. September 1937 in Sitten', *Zeitschrift für Schweizerisches Recht. Neue Folge*, 56 (1937), pp. 29a–505a.

70. Ruth, 'Das Schweizerbürgerrecht', pp. 127a and 135a.

71. Meyer, *La Perte de la nationalité*, p. 84; Zängerle, *Die öffentlich-rechtliche Stellung der Frau*, p. 25.

72. Ruth, 'Das Schweizerbürgerrecht', p. 127a. My thanks to Brigitte Schnegg for drawing my attention to Ruth's frequent use of the word 'family' when he meant 'marriage'.

73. Ruth, 'Das Schweizerbürgerrecht', pp. 31a, 128a–129a.

74. Ruth, 'Das Schweizerbürgerrecht', p. 133a.

75. Ruth, 'Das Schweizerbürgerrecht', pp. 134a, 32a.

76. Ruth, 'Das Schweizerbürgerrecht', pp. 27a, 133a–134a.

77. Ruth, 'Das Schweizerbürgerrecht', pp. 138a, 134a–135a.

78. Ruth, 'Das Schweizerbürgerrecht', pp. 80a–81a, 149a–156a.

79. Ruth, 'Das Schweizerbürgerrecht', pp. 154a, 56a.

80. Theresa Wobbe, 'Die Grenzen der Gemeinschaft und die Grenzen des Geschlechts', in *Denkachsen: Zur theoretischen und institutionellen Rede vom Geschlecht*, ed. Theresa Wobbe and Gesa Lindemann (Suhrkamp, Frankfurt a. M., 1994), pp. 177–207, here pp. 191–3.

81. Max Ruth, 'Das Bürgerrecht beim Eheschluss einer Schweizerin mit einem Ausländer', *Zeitschrift des bernischen Juristenvereins*, 78 (1942), pp. 1–21, here p. 9.

82. Heinrich Rothmund to Maxime de Stoutz, 28 October 1935, reproduced in *Documents diplomatiques suisses*, vol. 11 (Benteli Verlag, Berne, 1989), pp. 524–6, here p. 526.

83. August Egger, 'Über Scheinehen', in *Festgabe Fritz Fleiner* (Polygraphischer Verlag, Zurich, 1937), pp. 85–114; Charles Knapp, *Le Mariage fictif et la nationalité de la femme mariée* (Roth & Cie, Lausanne, 1940); Alfred Siegwart, *Die zweckwidrige Verwendung von Rechtsinstituten: Freiburger Rektoratsrede* (Paulusdruckerei, Freiburg, 1936). On the question of fictitious divorces by women who had married a German Jew, see *Documents diplomatiques suisses*, vol. 11, p. 541 (4 November 1935).

84. Sitzungsprotokoll der BSF-Gesetzesstudienkommission vom 14. Juni 1937, Gosteli-Archiv, Worblaufen, BSF, Gesetzesstudienkommission.

85. BSF, *36. Jahresbericht*, 1936/37, p. 32.

86. Sitzungsprotokoll der BSF-Gesetzesstudienkommission vom 26. Oktober 1942, Gosteli-Archiv, Worblaufen, BSF, Gesetzesstudienkommission.

87. *Bundesblatt der Schweizerischen Eidgenossenschaft*, 1 (1940), pp. 30–32.

88. Stauffer, 'Die Staatsangehörigkeit der Ehefrau'.

89. Walter Burckhardt, *Kommentar der Schweizerischen Bundesverfassung*, 3rd edition (Stämpfli, Berne, 1931), p. 503; Ruth, 'Das Schweizerbürgerrecht', p. 14a.

90. Alice Weber, *Die Staatsangehörigkeit der Ehefrau nach dem französischen Gesetz vom 10. August 1927* (Buchdruckerei Gutenberg, Lachen, 1930).

91. Luther, *Die Staatsangehörigkeit*, p. 119.

92. EJPD memorandum to the cantonal authorities supervising registry offices, 26 August 1939, *Bundesblatt der Schweizerischen Eidgenossenschaft* (1939) II, p. 282. See also Luther, *Die Staatsangehörigkeit*, pp. 119–20; Stauffer, 'Ehe und Heimat', p. 273.

93. Unpublished decisions Liais contra Municipality of Rance, 9 February 1940, and Kercoff contra Municipality of Cernier, 31 May 1940. See also *Neue Zürcher Zeitung*, 825 (7 June 1940).

94. Luther, *Die Staatsangehörigkeit*, pp. 120–21.

95. Luther, *Die Staatsangehörigkeit*, p. 93.

96. *Bundesblatt der Schweizerischen Eidgenossenschaft* (1941) II, pp. 325–6.

97. 'Botschaft des Bundesrates an die Bundesversammlung zum Entwurf zu einem Bundesgesetz über Erwerb und Verlust des Schweizerbürgerrechts vom 9. August 1951', *Bundesblatt der Schweizerischen Eidgenossenschaft* (1951) II, pp. 669–720, here p. 689.

98. Stauffer, 'Ehe und Heimat', p. 275; SVF, 'Zum Bürgerrecht der ausheiratenden Schweizerin', p. 4.

99. Ruth, 'Das Schweizerbürgerrecht', pp. 14a–15a.
100. Ruth, 'Das Bürgerrecht beim Eheschluss', pp. 1, 10.
101. Max Ruth, Preface to Henri Werner, *Fremdenpolizei in der Schweiz* (Verlag Schweiz. Juristische Kartothek, Geneva, 1942), p. 5.
102. EJPD memorandum, 'Kreisschreiben zum Bundesratsbeschluss vom 11. November 1941 über das Bürgerrecht der Schweizerin, die einen Ausländer heiratet (und dasjenige der Kinder aus einer solchen Ehe)', cited in Schuppisser, *'Denn im Herzen'*, p. 50.
103. On the situation of Swiss women in the Second World War who lost their nationality through marriage to an alien, see especially Schuppisser, *'Denn im Herzen'*; Lasserre et al., *La Politique vaudoise*, pp. 17, 47, 245–6; Nathalie Gardiol, 'Les Suissesses devenues étrangères par mariage et leurs enfants pendant la Deuxième Guerre mondiale: Un sondage dans les archives cantonales vaudoises', *Schweizerische Zeitschrift für Geschichte/ Revue suisse d'histoire*, 51 (2001), pp. 18–45. On the anti-Semitic underpinning of the authorities' policy on 'foreign Jewish women and Jewish Swiss women' during the war, see Jacques Picard, *Die Schweiz und die Juden 1933–1945: Schweizerischer Antisemitismus, jüdische Abwehr und internationale Migrations- und Flüchtlingspolitik* (Chronos, Zurich, 1994), pp. 208–17.
104. EJPD police department, 'Beilage zu den Weisungen der Polizeiabt. vom 12. Juli 1944 über Aufnahme oder Rückweisung ausländischer Flüchtlinge, 12. Juli 1944', cited in Schuppisser, *'Denn im Herzen'*, p. 57.
105. On the numbers of Swiss women regaining nationality, see Schuppisser, *'Denn im Herzen'*, p. 81–91.
106. BSF, *46. Jahresbericht*, 1946/47, pp. 65–6.
107. The new law providing for nationality, including women's, to be independent of marital status, came into force on 1 January 1992 (*Bundesblatt der Schweizerischen Eidgenossenschaft* (1990) I, pp. 1598–607).
108. Meyer, *La Perte de la nationalité*. See also Jean Meyer, 'Die bürgerrechtliche Einheit der Familie in der Rechtslehre und in ihren heutigen Auswirkungen: Quelques observations concernant l'exposé de M. le prof. A. Egger' (12 March 1951), Gosteli-Archiv, Worblaufen, Broschürensammlung 9101/13.
109. SVF, 'Zum Bürgerrecht der ausheiratenden Schweizerin', p. 5; BSF, *46. Jahresbericht*, 1946/47, p. 55.
110. Documentation of the consultation between the canton governments on the draft legislation of 1 December 1949 and 8 January 1951.
111. Tina Peter-Rüetschi, *Der Verlust des Schweizerbürgerrechts durch Heirat: Vorschlag für eine Revision der geltenden Regelung* (Schulthess, Zurich, 1950).
112. SVF, 'Zum Bürgerrecht der ausheiratenden Schweizerin', p. 5; Elisabeth Nägeli, *Das neue Bürgerrechtsgesetz vom 29. September 1952 mit Ergänzungen vom 7. Dezember 1956* (Schriftenreihe des BSF) (Schulthess & Co., Zurich, 1958), p. 17; 'Botschaft des Bundesrates an die Bundesversammlung zum Entwurf zu einem Bundesgesetz über Erwerb und Verlust des Schweizerbürgerrechts vom 9. August 1951', *Bundesblatt der Schweizerischen Eidgenossenschaft* (1951) II, p. 687.
113. *Amtliches Stenographisches Bulletin, Nationalrat*, 1951, pp. 744–83, 801–49, and 1952, pp. 310–23; *Amtliches Stenographisches Bulletin, Ständerat*, 1952, pp. 66–113 and 269–78; 'Bundesgesetz über Erwerb und Verlust des Schweizerbürgerrechts, vom 29. September 1952', *Bundesblatt der Schweizerischen Eidgenossenschaft* (1952) III, pp. 137–51.
114. *Stenographisches Bulletin, Nationalrat*, 1951, p. 847.
115. *Stenographisches Bulletin, Nationalrat*, 1951, p. 769.
116. *Stenographisches Bulletin, Nationalrat*, 1951, p. 771.
117. *Stenographisches Bulletin, Nationalrat*, 1951, p. 774.
118. *Stenographisches Bulletin, Nationalrat*, 1951, p. 746.
119. *Stenographisches Bulletin, Nationalrat*, 1951, p. 771.
120. Ruth, 'Das Schweizerbürgerrecht', p. 134a.

121. Ruth, 'Das Bürgerrecht beim Eheschluss', p. 9.
122. Zaccharia Giacometti, 'Die Verfassungsmässigkeit des Optionsrechtes der ausheiratenden Schweizer Bürgerin', *Schweizerische Juristen-Zeitung*, 48 (1952), pp. 85–92, here p. 91.
123. On the status of experts, see Pierre Bourdieu, 'Social Space and Symbolic Power', trans. L. Wacquant, *Sociological Theory*, 7 (1989), pp. 14–25.
124. The law is published in *Bundesblatt der Schweizerischen Eidgenossenschaft* (1953) III, pp. 137–51. See also Frey, *Über das Bürgerrecht der Ehefrau*, p. 98.
125. Georg Simmel, 'Der Fremde', in *Das individuelle Gesetz* (Suhrkamp, Frankfurt a. M., 1968), pp. 63–70.
126. Käthe Biske, 'Die Schweizer Frau in der Statistik', *Die Schweiz. Ein Nationales Jahrbuch*, 1958, pp. 5–30, here pp. 9–10; Gardiol, 'Les Suissesses devenues étrangères'.
127. BSF, *Jahresbericht*, 1953, p. 8.

NOTES ON CONTRIBUTORS

Elisa Camiscioli is assistant professor of history at the State University of New York at Binghamton. She is writing a manuscript entitled 'Rebuilding the French Race: Immigration, Reproduction, and National Identity in France, 1900–1939', and has begun a project on pop orientalism and the European appropriation of Eastern spiritual practices in India.

Kathleen Canning is associate professor of History and Women's Studies at the University of Michigan. She is the author of *Languages of Labor and Gender: Female Factory Work in Germany 1850–1914* (Cornell University Press, Ithaca, 1996) and of a number of articles on gender and class, the linguistic turn, history of bodies and history of labour. Her new research project is entitled *Embodied Citizenships: Gender and the Crisis of Nation in Weimar Germany.* She has been North American co-editor of *Gender & History* since 1998.

Carol E. Harrison is Associate Professor of History at Kent State University. She received her Doctorate in Philosophy from Oxford University in 1993. Among her publications is *The Bourgeois Citizen in Nineteenth-Century France: Gender, Sociability, and the Uses of Emulation* (Oxford University Press, Oxford, 1999). Her current project is on gender and Catholicism in post-revolutionary France.

Marilyn Lake has held a Personal Chair at Latrobe University in Australia since 1994; from 2001 she will take up a one-year appointment as Chair in Australian Studies at Harvard University in the United States. She has published widely on the history of citizenship, feminism, nationalism and internationalism. Recent work includes, *Getting Equal: The History of Feminism in Australia* (Allen and Unwin, Sydney, 1999); 'The Ambiguities for Feminists of National Belonging: Race and Gender in the Imagined Australian Community', in *Gendered Nations: Nationalisms and Gender Order in the Long Nineteenth Century*, ed. Ida Blom, Karen Hagemann and Catherine Hall (Berg, London, 2000); and *Women's Rights and Human Rights: International Historical Perspectives*, co-edited with Patricia Grimshaw and Katie Holmes (Palgrave, London, 2001).

Laura E. Nym Mayhall is Assistant Professor of History at the Catholic University of America. She is co-editor (with Ian Christopher Fletcher and Philippa Levine) of *Women's Suffrage in the British Empire: Citizenship, Nation, and Race* (2000). She is currently completing a book entitled *Rethinking Suffrage: Gender and Citizenship in Britain, 1860–1930.*

Pamela Beth Radcliff is an Associate Professor of History at the University of California, San Diego. She has published a monograph on political culture and the origins of the civil war in Spain, titled *From Mobilization to Civil War: the Politics of Polarization in the Spanish City of Gijon, 1900–1936* (Cambridge, 1996), as well as several publications about gender and political culture, including 'Elite Women Workers and Collective Action: The Cigarette Makers of Gijon, 1890–1930', *Journal of Social History*, 27:1, and 'Women's Politics: Consumer Riots in Twentieth-Century Spain', published in a collection co-edited by the author and Victoria Enders, entitled *Constructing Spanish Womanhood: Female Identity in Modern Spain* (SUNY, 1999). 'Imagining Female Citizenship' is part of a larger book project to explore the construction of citizenship during the transition to democracy in Spain through an interwoven analysis of women's organisations in civil society, the shifting legal and political framework, and the meaning assigned to these changes and activities.

Sonya O. Rose is Professor of History, Sociology and Women's Studies at the University of Michigan. She is the author of *Limited Livelihoods: Gender and Class in Nineteenth-Century England* (University of California Press, 1992) and co-editor, with Laura L. Frader, of *Gender and Class in Modern Europe* (Cornell University Press, 1996). She has recently completed *Which People's War? National Identity and Citizenship in World War II Britain.*

Tanika Sarkar is Professor of Modern History, Jawaharlal Nehru University, Delhi. Her publications include *Bengal 1928–1934: The Politics of Protest* (Oxford University Press, Delhi, 1987); *Words to Win: A Modern Autobiography* (Kali for Women, Delhi, 1999); and *Hindu Wife, Hindu Nation: Religion, Community, Cultural Nationalism,* (Permanent Black, Delhi and C. Hurst, UK, 2001). She has co-authored and co-edited works on the Hindu Right, and has published a monograph and essays in Bengali.

Brigitte Studer is Professor of History at the University of Berne, Switzerland. She is the author of *Un parti sous influence: Le Parti communiste suisse, une section de l'Internationale, 1931 à 1939* (Editions L'Age d'Homme, Lausanne, 1994) and co-author of *Die 'schutzbedürftige Frau': Zur Konstruktion von Geschlecht durch Mutterschaftsversicherung, Nachtarbeitsverbot und Sonderschutzgesetzgebung* (Chronos Verlag, Zurich, 2001). She is also the author of a number of definitive essays on the history of citizenship, state and gender in Switzerland.

Elizabeth A. Wood teaches in the History Faculty at MIT. She is author of *The Baba and the Comrade: Gender and Politics in Revolutionary Russia* (Indiana University Press, 1997) and of *Performing Justice: Agitation Trials in Early Soviet Russia, 1920–1933* (California University Press, forthcoming).

Index

ABC newspaper 77–8
1975 equality of rights and duties law 84
Aboriginal Tent Embassy 163
Aboriginal-Australian Fellowship (AAF)
142, 146, 149
gender in 150–1, 158
policy assimilation 161
referendum 155–7, 160–1
United Nations 155, 159
Aborigines Protection Board 147
Aborigines Welfare Board 140, 142, 148
Académie des dames 43
Africa
Kabyles 179
Africans
high birthrate 169, 170, 171
migrants 169, 179, 180
white race menaced by fecundity of 172,
173, 176
Allen, David Elliston
Victorian 'tastes and crazes' in natural
history 38
Alliance 188
1920 effect on post-war legislation 177
birthrates: assimilable immigrants 179, 189
depopulation 177
journal: immigrants 176
naturalisation, citizenship 178–9, 189
populationist policies 177
secular Republicans 181
'Yellow Peril' 178
Anderson, Benedict
'imagined political community' 198, 199
Andrews, Shirley
Council for Aboriginal Rights 155, 158;
male domination 159
UNO 155
Asians
Congress Party 172
high birthrate 169–72
migrants 176, 180
white race: menaced by fecundity of
172, 173

Attwood, Bain
*The 1967 Referendum, Or When
Aborigines Didn't Get the Vote* 159
Australia
Aboriginal rights 140–64
citizenship 141–4, 148, 149, 152, 159
'certificate of citizenship' 145
Commonwealth of Australia 147;
government segregation 158
Constitution 142, 156: Section 127
'a dying race' 147;
campaign for reform 158
feminism 141, 142
gender in campaigns rights 143
lands: collective rights 161, 163
policy of assimlation 141, 149, 152, 160
principle of universality 13
racism 149, 160, 164;
segregation 145–6
'recognition struggles', 'wounded
attachments' 143–4
referendum 1967 140–3, 145, 155,
156, 157, 159–62, 164
'special laws' 155–6, 162
Tribal Council 162
University of Sydney 1965 'Freedom
Ride' 142
see also Faith Bandler, Jessie Street,
Pearl Gibbs, Shirley Andrews
Australian Women's Charter Conference
157
Australian Security Intelligence Organisation
(ASIO) 151
Australian Peace Council 146, 152–3

Bamabodhini Patrika (women's journal)
136
Bandler, Faith
Aboriginal rights 144, 149–54, 156
Australian Peace Council: 'slaves' 152–3
Australian Women' Charter Conference
157
Australian Women's Land Army 153

Bi-Centennial: Captain Cooks 'discovery' of Australia 163
FCAATSI 158, 163–4; Aboriginal Tent Embassy 163
gendered political antagonisms 150, 159, 164
indigenous representation; move to exclude from meeting 162
on Jessie Street 152
referendum 157, 160, 164; citizenship 161
Barrot, Odilon
Capacité: electoral law 24
Beaulieu, Leroy
empire: need for western surplus population 172
Beck, Dr Emil
marriage rule 209
Begtrup, Bodil
Draft Declaration of Human Rights 152
Belgium
migrants: shrinking birthrate 179; naturalisation fee 178
marriage rule 203
Bengalee 131
Benhabib, Seyla
woman as a subject 137
ideas of justice 121
Bergman-Carton Janis
'woman of ideas': 1830s French art 31
Berlant, Lauren
'practices of citizenship' 7
Bertillon, Jacques
French depopulation 182
on birthrate in Africa and Asia 171
Beth, M 185
Biagini, Eugenio
on Giuseppe Mazzini 57
Bourdieu, Pierre
citizenship: 'juridical field' 200
Boverat, Fernand
Alliance 177–8, 188, 189
birthrate 172, 185
pronatalist 175, 178, 191
repatriating immigrants 190
Britain 148
working class men 67
Women's Freedom League 56, 57, 58
Women's Social and Political Union (WSPU) 55, 57
political subjectivity 56
The National Union of Women's Suffrage 57
see also A. V. Dicey, Christabel Pankhurst, Emmeline Pethick-Lawrence, Giuseppe Mazzini, John Stuart Mill
Brown, Wendy
'Wounded Attachments: Late Modern Oppositional Political Formations' 143
Brown, Dr Roosevelt
Black Power 163

Brubaker, Rogers 4, 100, 113
BSF 208, 213
Burckhardt, Walter
marriage rule 214
Bustelo, Carlota
'En favor del feminismo' 83
Cambio 16 77–8, 81, 84
rape law reform 85
survey of the state of Spanish womanhood 86
'How to Rape a Magazine' 89
Caplan, Cora
history and subjectivity 143
Carlos, King Juan 74
Carlyle, Thomas
on John Stuart Mill 32
Celnarts, Madame
Complete Manual of Domestic Economy 41
Chesterman, John
policy change: enfranchisement 156
children 85, 125–6, 212, 166–7, 133, 185, 188
Cierva, Ricardo de la
on feminism 88
citizen-scientist 1–15, 18–47, 66
see also France
citizenship
basic rights 78, 79, 86
claim-making 5, 6, 7, 15
communitarian passivity 79–80
definition 200
democratisation 74–5 3–4
First World War 1917–1930s; '*Überfremdung*' ('swamping') 201
gender 28; masculinity 10–11
identities 4–5, 73, 75–6
modern 199
rights 120
self-determination 14
'subjectivity' 6–7, 10, 15
women's rights to 63
Clark Norma
studies of Thomas Carlyle 32
Clements, H. G.
Australian Peace Council 154
Cobbe, Frances Power
politics: 'a branch of ethics' 58
Coit, Stanton 63
West London Ethical Society 56
Collini, Stefan 58, 63
on John Stuart Mill
colonialism 170–3
Anglo-Indian law 123
takeover of culture 133
Communist
anti- 159
Berlin Youth Festival 153
Party 90, 105, 154; women's membership 114

Corbett, Jean
  studies of Thomas Carlyle 32
Cott, Nancy 6, 12, 115
Council for Aboriginal Rights 147, 155
Crow, Thomas
  painting as male heritage 31
CSN 184
  naturalisation, 'assimilable races',
    the Depression 189–90
  stance on foreign fathers 189, 190
Curthoy, Ann
  study of racial politics 142

Dasi, Krishnakamini
  Chittabilashini 128
Daston, Lorraine 21, 22
de Gouges, Olympe 21
Delaquis, Dr Ernst
  head of Swiss federal administration;
    choosing immigrants 205–8, 210
  loyalty to country 207
  nationality: marital status 207
  welfare benefits: *Überfremdung* 206
Democratic Association of Women (ADM)
  91
Despard, Charlotte 57
  Women's Freedom League 57–8
Detti, Eugenio
  The Feminist Lunacy 88
Dicey, A. V.
  on women's suffrage 66
Diosadado, Ana
  Cuplé 80–1
Donaldson, Revd F. Lewis
  citizenship 66–7
du Châtelet, Emilie 21
Dumont, Arsène
  on birthrates 171
  French depopulation 182
  Italian immigrants 174
Duval-Arnould, Louis
  pronatalism 191
  Social Catholic: CSN 180

El País 77–8, 81, 84, 85
  'Women and Transition' 94
Emulation Society of Lons le Saunier
  relief map of the Jura 36
  Paris exposition 1867 36–7
Europe 153, 198
  eastern 80, 82
  declining birthrates 200
  degeneration 178
  degeneration theory 168, 171
  immigrants 173, 180, 182
  model of rights 79, 82
  migrants: male 175; white 176
  populationist 168
  race: 'Yellow Peril' 172
  science: gendered 20

Fast, Howard 164
  Freedom Road 146–7
Fawcett, Millicent Garrett 57
Federal Council for the Advancement of
  Aborigines 142 (FCAA) 142, 158
  assimilationist 160
  issue of Aboriginal authority 163
  People show: alleged Communists in 162
  'Towards Equal Citizenship for
    Aborigines' 157–8
  Turning the Tide 158
feminism 1, 4, 9, 10, 14, 56, 57, 63, 151
  Aboriginal segregation, racism 141;
    citizenship 142
  citizenship and 73, 81–2
  critiques of T. H. Marshall 2, 3
  depopulation and 175
  Feminist Collective and the
    Antipatriarchal Struggle of
    Authoritarian and Revolutionary
    Women (LAMAR) 91
  language of slavery 59–63
  revolutionary 21, 22
  scholars 1, 72, 75
  see also Jessica Street, John Stuart Mill
Ferguson, William 150
  Aborigines' Progressive Association 148
Finn, Margot
  on Giuseppe Mazzini 57, 58
First World War 202, 221
  Africans, Asians immigrated to France
    169
Flaubert, Gustave 19, 25, 28
  A Simple Heart 43
  Bouvard and Pécuchet 18, 33, 34, 35,
    44, 47
  Dictionary of Platitudes 23, 28, 29, 33
  Madame Bovary 35
Foucalt, Michel 6, 200
Fox, Len 149
  Aboriginal-Australian Fellowship 146
Fraisse, Geneviève 20
France 34, 41, 85
  1791 Constitution 22
  1814, 1830 Charter 22
  Bonapartist 23
  capacité: practices of citizenship 23–7,
    34, 46
  citizenship 19, 47; revolution 19–22, 47
  Code Civil 1804 199
  *Commissions Départementales de la
    Natalité* 179, 185
  Conseil Supérieur de la Natalité 170
  CSN 179, 180
  definitions of the citizen 22, 23, 113
  demographic growth 1911–1938 168
  Enlightenment 20–1, 47; Revolution
    170
  female crafts 41
  gender 175; and science 19–47

Great War 168, 169, 175, 181,
    'feminised' colonial workers 180
Les Modes Parisiennes 40
Revolution 10, 19, 65; Paris Commune
    10; women's citizenship 22
see also societies
Franco, Francisco 73, 82, 85
    Catholic Church; women's higher
        education 78
    citizenship 80; basic rights 78
    Civil Code: women's status 78, 84
    controlled press 78
    regime: women's citizenship 76, 78–9,
        80, 81, 83, 93
Fraser, Nancy
    citizenship rights 121–2
    gender in public sphere 75
French immigration
    Alliance National Pour L'Accroissement de
        la Population Française 170
    assimilable 173, 174, 178, 180, 184,
        185–6, 188, 191; French offspring
        167, 169
    children in foreign household 185–6;
        'voluntary sterility' 185
    citizenship 169, 170, 186, 188, 189,
        191; naturalisation 177, 178, 186
    Code de la Famille 1939, Haut Comité de
        188
    'demographic crisis' 167, 168, 170,
        180, 188; birthrate studies 170–1
    Fédération des Associations de Familles
        Nombreuses de France 188
    female reproduction and health 168
    feminism 177: women's fertility decline 175
    gender 175–6,186, 188, 191;
        gender and citizenship 21, 26–7
    La Plus Grande Famille 180
    Malthusian reproductive practices 167,
        170, 183, 184, 185, 186
    marriage rule 203
    nationality legislation, citizenship 214
    opponents of non-white immigration
        171–4, 176, 179
    political rights 22–3
    pronatalism 167
    racially appropriate foreign men
        169–70, 175–6
    repatriation 190
    Revolutionary 26, 170, 186, 191
    Social Catholics 180–1
    Third Republic 46; male citizenship 46
    welfare funds 188
    women's role 186, 188
    see also Ludovic Naudeau
fremdenpolizei 205

Gagnier, Reginia
    'subjectivity' 6
Garibaldi 55

Garrison, William Lloyd
    abolitionism: slavery 65
Gavarni,
    Le Tiroir du diable 29, 30, 45
Gay, Delphine 31
gender 2, 4, 150
    arts 31–2
    blackness 62
    citizen-scientist 27–8, 34
    citizenship and 73, 75–6, 81, 186–8;
        political press 77–8, 81
    critiques of public sphere 75
    educated 134, 136
    'female individualism' 182
    history 142–3
    ideologies 19–20, 72, 94
    marriage 200, 211–12, 220–1
    science 19, 29, 44, 46, 47
    social order 26–7
    structure of public and private 80
Germany
    Jews 216
    Nazi citizenship law 216
    state citizenship 113
Gesellschaft Für Internationales Recht
    (Society for International Law)
    nationality of married women 204
Gibbs, Pearl 155, 147–8, 160
    Aboriginal-Australian Fellowship 146,
        149, 150–1
    Aborigines' Progressive Association:
        League of Nations 148
    all-Aboriginal conference 1965 161
    'Day of Mourning' 1938, 150th
        anniversary of British 'invaders' 148
    New South Wales Land Council 162
    referendum 156–7
Glenn, Evelyn Nakano
    American citizenship 2
Greeks 179
Groves, Bert (AAF) 150–1, 159
    Aboriginal identity 159–60
    paper on assimilation 160
Guitermann, Rosine
    on Jessie Street 157, 160
Guizot, François 29

Habermas, Jürgen 121, 137
Haraway, Donna
    on scientific collectors 43
Harper, Samuel Northrup
    'a kind of super citizenship' 102
    Civic Training in Soviet Russia 101–2
    disenfranchised 102
Haury, Paul
    pronatalism 191
    empire: need for western surplus
        population 172
Havard, Henry
    dictionary of furniture styles 43

L'Art dans la maison 38
Hobsbawm, Eric
  nation-building 200
Holborn, Muir
  Fellowship of Australian Writers 149
Holt, Thomas
  'the problem of freedom' 59
human rights 13, 156
  women's social movements 75
  Universal Declaration of Human Rights 152
  nationality law based on 1–2, 216
  United Nations 152; Commission 154

India 120–38
  cheap print: debates on laws 133–4
  child marriage 125–6, 133; The Age of
    Consent Act 126–7, 133
  Christian missionaries 133; schools 134
  colonialism: men rights 122, 123, 125;
    law 123, 125, 126, 131, 133
  cultural nationalism 126, 131, 133, 134;
    religious communities 122
  customs: constricted women 125, 137
  Hinduism 122, 123–4, 131, 133, 137;
    conjugality, *Manusmriti* 129;
    customs for widows 123, 129;
    rightwing 121
  Manu: ancient lawgiver 126; female
    autonomy 128
  men: lack of high masculinity 123;
    citizenship rights 136
  morals: murder trial 1873 131–2
  reformism initiative 124
  widows: 'The Great Unchastity Case'
    131; immolation 126, 127, 130 133;
    human sacrifice 125; remarriage Act
    1856 127–9; Dayabhaga law 129–31
  women: citizenship rights 120–1, 136–7;
    immunities 122, 130, 132, 133, 137;
    acts of legislation 123–4, 133–4;
    illiteracy 134–6; sexual difference
    134; writings 134–5
International Alliance of Women (IAW)
  202, 204
International Council of Women (ICW)
  202, 204
International Federation of University
  Women (IFUW) 204
Interviu
  feminist attack on 89
Isaac, Auguste 185
  La Plus Grande Famille 172
  French immigration 178
Italy 63, 85,
  migrants 173, 179, 181, 190, 191
  nationalism 55, 64, 65
  pronatalist view of 169, 174, 175

James, Susan
  citizenship and women 76

Jacquette, Jane
  transitions gender reassessment 72, 73
Journal pour rire
  women's arts 41–3

Kidd, Ronald H.
  *For Freedom's Cause: An Appeal to
    Working Men* 67

L'Illustration 181
Landry, Adolphe 188
Landsdowne, Lord
  Age of Consent Bill 133
Le Comte, René
  Italian fecundity; 'Yellow Peril' 174
League of Nations
  women's nationality legislation 204
Lenin, Vladimir 98
  bourgeois democracy 101
  'What Is to Be Done?' 105
  women in politics 100
Leon, Charles
  Aboriginal-Australian Fellowship 151
Leroy-Beaulieu, Paul 182
  studies of birthrate 170–1
  'The masculinisation of women' 175
Leuch, Annie
  Swiss nationality reform 210
'Levantines' 179
Lister, Ruth
  feminist citizenship 81
Louis XVIII
  citizenship 22
Lutz, Bertha
  UN charter on equal rights 152

Mansfield, Nick
  'subjectivity' 6
Markus, Andrew
  *The 1967 Referendum, Or When
    Aborigines Didn't Get the Vote* 159
Married Women's Property Acts 1870, 1882
  59
Marshall, T. H. 2
Martin-Fugier, Ann
  on the dandy in high society 32–3
Mauco Mauco, Georges
  pronatalism 191
  study of immigration to France: children
    186–7
Mauss, Marcel
  ethnologist 198
Mazzini, Giuuseppe
  definition of democracy 58
  role of the family in politics 59, 67
  slavery 56, 67; abolition of in USA 65
  The Duties of Man 67; suffragettes 8, 10,
    55–8, 62–4
  working men and citizenship 66
  see also Ronald H. Kidd

Mehta, Uday 3
men 18–9
  artistic activities 31
  bourgeois 24, 25, 27, 29, 33
  dandy 32–3
  masculinity 26, 27
  'men of letters' 32
  suffrage 22–4, 46, 47
Meyer, Dr jur. Jean
  marriage rule 217
  on Swiss nationality 210
Mill, Harriet Taylor 58
Mill, John Stuart 10,
  analogy of slavery 59–62, 65–6;
    USA 61
  French Revolution 65
  gender implications 62
  role of the family 67: sexual
    subordination of women 59, 68
  The Subjection of Women 8, 59, 63–5;
    suffragist 10, 56–7, 60, 62
Monnier, Henri 33
Murshidabad Patrika 131
Mussing, Faith Ida 144–7
  Aboriginal-Australian Fellowship 146

Napoleon III 25
The National Union of Women's Suffrage
  Societies 57
Naudeau, Ludovic
  fertility of Marriages 184–5
  French women 184; social citizenship
    182, 186–7
  immigration 'integrity of the White race',
    Italians 182–4
  Le Temp, L'Illustration, La France se
    regarde; le problème de la natalité 181
  L'Illustration 170
Nicholls, Pastor Doug 159
  public meeting; first Aboriginal chairman
    156
  National Aboriginal Affair Association 162
Nussbaum, Martha 121

O'Connor, Maura 65
Offen, Karen 175
Ong, Aihwa
  'cultural citizenship' 7

Pankhurst, Christabel
  Women's Social and Political Union
    (WSPU) 55–7
Pateman, Carole
  'civil body politic' 3
Pederson, Susan
  on Alliance's view of depopulation 177
Pérez-Díaz, Victor
  on democratisation in Spain 74–6, 94
Perkins, Charles 162
Pernot, Georges 188

Pethick-Lawrence, Emmeline 57
  The Meaning of the Women's Movement
    58
Pethick-Lawrence, Fredrick 67
Pocock, J. G. A.
  modern citizenship 199
Poland
  migrants 169, 173, 175, 178, 179, 181,
    190, 191
population policy 181, 191, 200, 213
Prudhomme, Joseph 33

Quarterly Review
  'Woman Suffrage' 66
Quinche, Antoinette
  Swiss marriage rule 209

racism 141, 142, 182
  Malthusianism 171
  opponents of non-white immigration
    171–2, 176; 'Yellow Peril' 172
  see also Alliance, Howard Fast
Rawls, John
  conception of justice 121
Read, Peter
  Aboriginal segregation 140
Rendall, Jane
  analysis of Giuseppe Mazzini 63
Reybaud, Louis 44
Robeson, Paul 146
Romania 179
Rosanvallon, Pierre
  l'impossible citoyen capacitaire 24
Rothmund, Heinrich
  Swiss immigration policy 208
Rousseau, Jean-Jacques
  condemnation of salonnières 21
Roy, Rammohun
  widow immolation 127
Ruth, Dr jur. Max
  children 'compulsory naturalisation' 212
  'Das Schweizerbürgerrecht' 196–7,
    'nationality of lineage' 210–12, 219
  marriage rule 212, 214, 215–7, 219;
    social-welfare 211
  new nationality law 1946 216
  staatsvolk (people bound to the state)
    212, 213
  wartime; women belonging to enemy
    state 211–12

Sander, Bob
  People show 162
Sauser-Hall, Georges
  marriage rule 209–10
science 18–9, 25
  citizenship and 23, 24, 34
  field collecting 43
  history and archaeology 33–4, 37
  Linnean classification 21

men's status 19–20, 24, 33–5, 44–6
professionalisation 46
savants 27, 35, 37, 41, 44–6
Victorian natural history 38–41, 43
women 27, 47; exclusion of 19–20,
22, 26
see also societies
Second World War 201
Shanley, Mary Lyndon
marriage as slavery 60
slavery 10, 56, 59
Anti-Slavery Society 154, 155, 160
Smith, Rogers
*Civic Ideals: Conflicting Visions of
Citizenship in U.S. History* 4
Social Democratic party's women's group
209
societies 24–30, 33–5, 44–6, 57
corresponding membership 46
excluding women 32, 37
exclusion of the arts 28–9, 32;
contaminated with femininity 29, 31
Friends of the Arts 28
learned presentations 36–8
Les Modes Parisiennes 35, 40
prix de Rome 32
state recognition 25
see also Gavarni
Somers, Margaret 1
Sontag, Susan 84
Soviet Republic
citizens in training 98–115
citizenship 100–1, 113, 115; courts
102
Constitution 1918 101
gender: equality 100, 104–5, 107
goverment women's emancipation 105
marriage rule 209
mock trials: male characters 104, 106–8,
111–13
Moscow Show Trials 99
nationality and marriage 211
October Revoltion 101, 103
The Trial of the Peasant Woman Delegate
105, 107–11
The Trial of the New Woman 98–9
The Trial of the Old Way of Life 106
*The Trial of the Peasant Medvedev Who
Wrecked the Election of the Women's
Candidate to Village Council* 111–3
women's mock trials 99–100, 102,
103–5, 114 citizens 102–3, 113;
delegates 103–9, 111, 113–5;
in training 99, 107, 113–14
see also Samuel Northrup Harper
Soviet Union marriage rule 203, 204
Spain 169, 173, 175, 178, 179, 181,
189, 190, 191
citizenship 74–5, 78, 83–5;
passive 79–80, 81, 86, 93

Civil Code 79; women's status 78;
Constitution 78, 82: 1978; Articles
(14, 32, 35); rights 79
critics of 'rational choice' model 74
feminism 81–7, 89, 92; extremism
87–90; groups 90–2; *Hite Report*
90; *Vindicación Feminista* 88
gender: *Cuplé* 80–1; in democratic
transition 72–95; equality vs
difference 76–7, 79, 93–4;
the press 77–8, 81–7
'Jornadas de la Dona' (Women Days)
89, 90, 91, 92
new democracy 72–6, 79, 86, 92;
female citizenship 73, 76–7, 80–4,
86, 92, 93, 95
'New Spain' 78, 87, 94
Parents' Association 84
transition 72–5, 82, 84; elites
pact-making 74, 77, 94, 79;
'transitologists' 72
see also Francisco Franco
Spanish Workers' Party 90, 91
Street, Jessie 141, 151, 155,
Anti-Slavery Society 154, 160
Australian Women's Charter 154
FCAATSI: United Nations 159
Feminist Club 151
foundation of United Nations
Organisation, Commission on the
Status of Women (UNO), Declaration
of Human Rights 152
male domination of coalition politics
158–9
referendum 156
'Towards Equal Citizenship for Aborigines'
157
World War Two Sheepskins for Russia
campaign 151–2
Street, Kenneth
Chief Justice of New South Wales 151
Suarez, Adolfo 74
Spain: *ruptura pactada* (negotiated break)
74
Sun newspaper 162
Swanwick, Helena 57
Switzerland 196–221
Association of University Women
208–9
'*Burgerrecht*' dual dimension 196
Cable Act 204
children's nationality 207, 208, 211,
212, 220
'classical', 'traditional' principle 202,
210, 220
community 211, 219; 'community of
destiny' 211–12
constitution 206, 207, 208, 212; 1848,
1874: individual equality of all citizens
202–3

family 211, 212, 218
Heimatgemmeinde (community of origin) 203, 207
immigration policy 203, 208,
   Fredenpolize 1917, policing of foreigners 201; Ministry of Police and Justice (EJPD) 205, 210, 213, 215, 216, 217; fictitious marriage 213–4
jurists 203–4, 205, 210, 213, 214, 219–20 'rights of option' 217
loyalty 211, 213, 219, 220, 221
'marriage rule' 197–8, 201–4, 209–10, 214–17, 220, 221
'modern' principle 199, 202, 204, 217–8
nationality 197 loss of; law 198, 199, 201–3, 207–10, 214–5, 217; government decree 1940 215
naturalisation 199–202
notions of ethnicity 213, 220; organisations of civil society 207–8
Organisation for International Law 209
parliamentary debate 1952; right of option 218–9, 221
principle of *jus sanguinis* (blood line/heredity) 199; *jus soli* (birth/parents) 199, 206, 207, 208, 212
   of universality; nationality 197; 'gender technologies' 198
Überfremdung 201, 206, 208–9, 212 'war culture' 201, 210, 211, 215, 218, 220, 221; stateless women 197, 202, 215–6, 218
   Vollmachtenrecht, special mandate law 210
women's lack of political rights 204–5
women's organisations 203, 204, 208, 209, 213, 216–9;
Swiss women's suffrage association (SVF) 202, 204, 207, 208
see also Dr Ernst Delaquis, Dr Max Ruth, Heinrich, Rothmund

Taylor, Charles
'politics of recognition' 3, 143
citizenship; threat to minority cultures 121
Troullier, Albert
selecting immigrants 175, 177, 178
Turner, Bryan
typology of citizenship 79–8

Umbral, Francisco
Spain: marginalisation groups 88
United Nations Organisation 155
Charter 141
Commission on the Status of Women 152

Conference on Women 82
Convention on the Nationality of Married Women 197
Human Rights Commission of the Economic and Social Council 154
Protection and Prevention of Discrimination against Minorities 160
Universal Declaration of Human Rights; Article 2 152
United Associations of Women (UA) 141, 151, 152
United States 179
anti-communism 154
codified nationality 1855 199
marriage rule 203; Cable Act 204
nationality 'community of settlement' 211
slavery 59, 61, 146
see also Howard Fast
Universal Exposition 38–9
University of Sydney 151
University of Chicago 102

Vanneufville, Gaston Monsignor
Social Catholic: Asian and African immigrants 180
Venturi, Emilie Ashurst 57
Vidyasagar, Ishwarchandra,
Indian: Act on Widow remarriage 128, 129
Vigée-Lebrun, Elisabeth
Royal Academy of Painting 20
Von Steiger, Eduard
head of EJPD 217
Votes for Women 55

Walker, Kath 161
Aboriginal poet: campaign for constitutional reform 158
Committee for Aboriginal Unity 1970 162
men's manhood and their authority: Tribal Council 162–3, 164
Weber, Max
state: bureaucratic administration 200
Werbner, Pnina 4
West London Ethical Society 56, 57
Wobbe, Theresa
women's 'vulnerability' construction of community 212
women
artists 28, 29, 31
Cartesian dictum 21
citizenship 67–8, 75, 78; *Votes for Women* 55
crafts 43
El País 'Women and the Transition' 94
Enlightenment 47
illiteracy 134–6
International League for Peace and freedom (WILPF) 202, 204, 208

international organisations   202, 204;
  Versailles Conference 1919 on married
  women's nationality   202
Married Women's Property Acts 1870,
  1882   59
politics   61–2, 81, 93, 100, 103, 114
scientific   19, 20–2, 27; denied
  citizenship   26
suffrage   8, 10, 55–68, 78, 84, 202;
  anti-suffragist writings   57
'Tribunal of Crimes against Women'   89
UN Commission on the Status of Women
  152; UN conference   82

Women's Freedom League   56,
  58
Women's Social and Political Union
  (WSPU)   55, 57
Woodcock, Lucy
  New South Wales Teachers' Federation
  149
  United Associations of Women   149

Yuval-Davis, Nira   4

Zerilli, Linda
  definition of politics   56

CPSIA information can be obtained
at www.ICGtesting.com
Printed in the USA
FSOW03n1435231116
27588FS